THE
BRANDED
GENTRY

THE
BRANDED
GENTRY

HOW A NEW ERA OF ENTREPRENEURS
MADE THEIR NAMES

CHARLES VALLANCE & DAVID HOPPER

Photographic credits:

Author photos reproduced by permission of Dan Burn-Forti; Lord Bell, courtesy of *Campaign/ Haymarket Media Group*; Emma Bridgewater, by Ari Ashley, reproduced by permission of company; Jackie Cooper reproduced by permission of company; Sir James Dyson reproduced by permission of company; Sir John Hegarty reproduced by permission of company; Robert Hiscox reproduced by permission of the subject; David Linley reproduced by permission of company; Tony Laithwaite, by Yves Gellie, reproduced by permission of company; Julian Richer reproduced by permission of the subject; Lord Sainsbury reproduced by permission of the subject; Sir Paul Smith reproduced by permission of company; Jonathan Warburton reproduced by permission of company.

First published 2013 by Elliott and Thompson Limited
27 John Street, London WC1N 2BX
www.eandtbooks.com

ISBN: 978-1-908739-78-0

Text © David Hopper and Charles Vallance 2013

9 8 7 6 5 4 3 2 1

A CIP catalogue record for this book is available from the British Library.

Printed and bound in the UK by T. J. International Ltd., Padstow
Typeset by Grade Design and Marie Doherty

To our families
Irina, Miky, and Evgenya
Karen, Louise, and Will

CONTENTS

Introduction   1

Prologue: Eponymous beginnings   3

1. LORD BELL OF BELGRAVIA   19

2. JOHNNIE BODEN   43

3. EMMA BRIDGEWATER   61

4. JACKIE COOPER   85

5. SIR JAMES DYSON   111

6. SIR JOHN HEGARTY   131

7. ROBERT HISCOX   147

8. TONY LAITHWAITE   169

9. DAVID ARMSTRONG-JONES, VISCOUNT LINLEY   191

10. JULIAN RICHER   211

11. LORD SAINSBURY OF PRESTON CANDOVER, KG   237

12. SIR PAUL SMITH   255

13. JONATHAN WARBURTON   273

Epilogue: What's in a name?   293

Acknowledgements   309

Index   311

INTRODUCTION

Every era, every society has its gentry and ruling elite. Wealth, authority, and power are seldom static for long. Dynasties come and go, political systems rise and fall. Money changes hands in new ways.

In the eighteenth and nineteenth centuries, heavily whiskered industrialists challenged the landed gentry for social ascendancy. Financial mobility had arrived and was accelerating.

Later in the nineteenth century and through the course of the twentieth century, the advent of consumer markets saw commerce evolve further. A new era of entrepreneurs put their name to a new model of wealth creation. And they did so literally. This was the era of Mr Cadbury, Mr Sainsbury, Mr Marks, Mr Spencer, Mr Lewis, Mr Boots, Mr Walker, Mr Sharwood, Mr Warburton, Mr Lipton, and Mr Tetley.

This is a book about men and women such as these who have succeeded in becoming an eponymous aristocracy. Who aren't known by the name of the land they own, but by the name of the brand they have become. Who have made their name by making their name into a brand.

This is a book about the Branded Gentry.

———

'I've never lived in a building without my name on it.'

IVANKA TRUMP

———

PROLOGUE

Eponymous beginnings

DAVID HOPPER: I grew up facing a line of eponymous brands. The front windows of our terraced house looked out across a busy road onto a row of shops called 'Moore's' (the butcher), 'Gray's' (the baker), and 'Gallon's Grocery' (the grocer, obviously, but he probably did have some candles somewhere). The effect was spoiled by the bookends: on one side, a fish and chip shop calling itself 'Fish & Chips'; and on the other, a similarly imaginative chemist ('Chemist'), but at least there was symmetry.

Not that I knew what *eponymous* meant. And a *brand* was something that the black-and-white television cowboys burned into their grey cattle. It never occurred to me that there was actually a real person called Moore, Gray or Gallon, let alone a real removal man called Pickford, or a pair of shoemaking brothers called Clark, or that somewhere on earth there was actually a real engineer named Frank Hornby living the dream, making model train sets.

The proud Yorkshire city in which I grew up was not in thrall to retail science as are the identikit shopper-villages of today. Then, you either took it or you left it, and people then were happy to take it, clag-black buildings and lard-grease cafes and all. Early sixties existence, like the television of the day, was pre-colour and enjoyed plenty of time not being open for business. No one suspected that the retail future – and life itself – would end up at the other extreme of digital, 24-7 uniformity. West End marketing gurus, talking of attention spans and brand modelling, were twenty years away at least. In those slower days, shop-window crypts would stay sealed up and airless from one month to the next, and many of the signs and logos above the shops and factories had been in place for decades.

Many of these signs were the hallmarks of their eponymous owners, with toil and history in the lettering. Proud, unselfconscious names, with tough, stocky vowels reflecting the dispositions of their founders, and thick-boned consonants supporting each other like the girders of railway bridges: Hammond's, Harrison's, Hepworth's, Warburton's, Whittaker's, Ramsbottom's, Booth's, Leadbetter's, Crawshaw's, Collinson's, Redfern's, Shaw's, Duckworth's, Duckham's, Looker's, Crofts, Jowett, Seebrook's (a fortuitous spelling error by the crisp company's clerk, who should have written the more insipid 'C. Brook's'), Arnold Laver's, Wallace Arnold, Samuel Ledgard...

Behind these names were the gentry of the industrial era, who were part of an historical transition of wealth going back centuries – from men who represented God to men who exploited the land, to men who used motive power, and which would soon be on the move again to men and women who knew how to communicate ideas.

But the question for now was this one: Who were the men (and they would almost always be men) who had got to the point where their very names now graced the buildings and shopfronts between which lesser people walked? I'd never actually asked that question, yet one summer I got to find out its answer.

During the long school recess of 1973, I blagged a labouring job at a garage called L. G. Mason (Bradford) Ltd, working on the forecourt, serving petrol (3 gallons for £1), checking tyres and oil, and washing the used cars on sale. Once a week, Mr Mason himself (in those days, important people and teachers did not have Christian names) would arrive in his Rolls Royce, and hand over the keys for us to valet the car.

This was my first interaction with a member of the entrepreneurial class of that era. Here was a West Riding business magnate who spent a lot of his day at mellow-voiced meetings with his kind, where he would drink fine brown liquids, suck on his brown pipe, and talk of his two-itemed garage empire. It was the first time I'd come across an actual (as opposed to television) owner of a Rolls Royce; albeit a fading vehicle that had, by then, given over most of its molecular structure to Virginia Flake Cut tobacco. The floor mats and carpets were originals, curling at the edges and tinged with, and smelling warmly of, rust and grit and more tobacco (with some comforting lower notes of wet dog in there as well). Here then was a member of the Yorkshire industrial elite with a business named after him: that name (plus a reference to the beloved home city, there in brackets) appeared in large letters above the forecourt and on the stickers in the back windows of the pre-rusted, every-car-a-Friday-car vehicles that we sold.

My next student holiday job, in 1976, took me to another eponymous brand. But this time, it was owned by a different kind of founding family who would eventually take their name way beyond the streets of a hilly Yorkshire town. Wm Morrison was as Bradford a firm as you could get, having set up a stall in Rawson Market before the turn of the twentieth century, and always preserving a native empathy with the locals who regarded Leeds, a mere 9 miles away, as trumped-up (so you can imagine what they thought of the south). But in 1961, Morrison had opened up something new, called a supermarket – a shop where you picked up the goods yourself, put them in a basket, and paid for the whole lot all at once before exiting.

Mr Mason had been a Rolls Royce man, who lived within the status quo of the Northern industrial aristocracy; but the Morrison family, despite all their authentic Bradfordian provenance, were pioneers, with an altogether more radical perspective of the world – and *they* ran German Mercs.

My dad had seen an ad in the *Telegraph & Argus* asking for someone to clean the management cars at the Thornton Road headquarters. I had, shall we say, the relevant credentials and they gave me the job. There were about twenty motley cars in the fleet – Marinas, Hunters, Cortinas, Dolomites – because by that time the reps were travelling all over West Yorkshire and beyond. Ken Morrison had a large Mercedes 280SE, with its own private plate, and I knew something unconventional was going on here because the ashtrays were unused.

My cleaning den ran alongside the supermarket, with the managers' offices next door in Hilmore House (another eponym, based on Ken's wife Hilda), giving me plenty of time to witness the forward-looking nature of this burgeoning retail enterprise. The store paraphernalia would change not every decade but every week. Signs were made not of steel and wood but of paper and plastic. Speed of service, stock management, and volume of footfall were the new indicators of success. Moore's Butcher, Gray's Baker or Gallon's Grocer, this was not. Nor was it Mr Mason and his brace of garages. No, this was something of greater scale.

Wm Morrison was a retail brand that had its sights set on a future of fmcg (fast-moving consumer goods) transience. Richard Branson's Virgin Records had already upset the music industry apple cart, and Freddie Laker's planes were offering cheap flights to the US. The next phase of wealth creation was replacing the last. Out with the old; in with the new. By 1978, my old employer, L. G. Mason (Bradford) Ltd, would have closed down, but by 2011, Morrisons (the name having taken on the plural) would have 455 UK stores.

There was a tailwind for this change. In London, a small woman with a (to the Northern working-class ear) ridiculously supercilious voice (she had not been gravel-effect voice-coached at that stage) was on the move into Downing Street. Jim Callaghan had been slapping her down in the Commons, but as prime minister, Margaret Thatcher would over time neuter the trade union politbureau – Scargill, Jones, Scanlon, Feather, et al – and thereby indirectly recraft the ground rules on which new businesses, big and small, could be launched. In the next decade, the face of industrial relations, the economy, and, of course, advertising and marketing, would change beyond recognition.

Eventually, with help from the internet revolution, these new trading conditions would open up opportunities for anyone, at least in theory, to launch their own brand, using their own name if they were minded to. Britain would, in due course, become pre-eminent in brand engineering and self-starter entrepreneurship, due in part to the shrill, newbie Conservative PM and daughter of Alfred Roberts, owner of an eponymous Grantham grocery brand.

The position of Thatcher's PR advisor would be taken by Tim Bell, in later years heading the Bell Pottinger agency. As part of the newly empowered entrepreneurial class, there was emerging a whole new support industry based on the 'gatekeepers': eponymous companies in their own right, none more famous than Saatchi & Saatchi, comprising brand Merlins who knew the alchemy needed to turn a word or name into fame and money. A whole new tier of wealth was coming into being (much of it located in the erstwhile porno-land of Soho in London). The owners of these communications agencies (BBH, DMB&B, CDP, BMP, DDB, TBWA – companies that used their initials like bullets) would themselves become branded gentry; kingmakers becoming kings (and queens, of course). It is appropriate, then, that a proportion of this book be given over to these pioneers; these gatekeeper-wizards, such as Bell, Hegarty, and Cooper.

There are numerous books that examine what it takes to make a successful brand, and, indeed, how success can be defined. But what, we ask, is the importance of having one's name over the shop or on the side of the truck or in the hands of the millions who are buying your goods? Does proprietorial nomenclature define the brand, or does the brand maketh the proprietor?

We thought that, by interviewing a selection of the brand-owning gentry of this country, we might get to understand more about what this means and duly reach some useful conclusions about the nature of success in the eponymous brand universe.

Of course, things used to change over hundreds of years and now they change in real time or in no time at all. Looking around, it's possible to wonder if eponyms have already had their day, to be superseded by brands that are named after fruits and baby noises. Are they set to go the way of Mr L. G. Mason of Bradford? Whatever the case, the extraordinary people of our book might, we thought, have some extraordinary lessons for us, in terms of their creativity, enterprise, endeavour, imagination, and guile.

Media and commerce have made the world smaller, and these people have contributed to the shrinkage. It seems to shrink as we get older too, as time connects things up. Things have a habit of coming full circle, so that one minute you're cleaning their cars, and in the next forty-year-blink of an eye, you're writing a book about them. In the spirit of such ruminations, here is one last anecdote from my Bradford childhood, from I guess around 1963. I am with my mother buying a round-pin plug and some fuse wire from the main town-centre electrical store on Market Street. It is a biggish store, with cotton-bagged Hoovers and hardwood valve-driven television sets, and has a large sign over a sixties techno-modernist window display. It is another eponymous brand, and it is called Vallances. And half a century later, one son of that named family business – an eponymous ad agency gatekeeper himself – has co-authored this book.

C HARLES VALLANCE: Unlike David's, my father wasn't a miner. He and my uncle had taken over the family business from my grandfather in the sixties and proved to be a formidable team. My Uncle Martin fronted the TV ads and my dad quietly terrified everyone behind the scenes, nailing down costs with a ferocity that only a Yorkshireman (or, I concede, a Scotsman) can muster. Over a twenty-year span, the Vallance brothers built an empire of shops that bestrode the Yorkshire Ridings like an electrical retailing colossus. From the spa town of Harrogate in the north to the steel town of Sheffield in the south, from Ilkley's western moors to the eastern shores of Hull and most towns in between, you'd find a Vallances. With hindsight, being part of a family of moderately successful north-eastern electrical retailers might not sound too grand, but it felt quite grand at the time.

This was perhaps one of the reasons my bedroom window didn't look out over the local butcher and baker. Instead it looked out on to the leafy undulations of Gledhow Wood, with the view extending to a tree-tipped horizon where the distant backsides of the houses on Potternewton Lane were visible in winter. (Even my home was eponymous: The Homestead, 136 Gledhow Wood Road, Leeds 8.) From this vantage point there were no shops to be seen. The nearest parade involved a brisk five-minute walk along our road and then left onto Thorn Lane. I remember the journey vividly, right down to where the greatest risk of treading on a dog turd lay. (By the gatehouse to Gledhow Wood, if you're wondering. I'm afraid our dog Hughie was a frequent contributor.)

I remember it so vividly because this was the route to Rainer's, the local sweet shop and newsagent. Every Saturday morning, my sister, brother, and I would make our pilgrimage there, collectively enriching Mr Rainer to the tune of about 30p. Mind you, 10p each went a long way then. Three foamy prawns cost 1p; a sherbet dip was 2½p (as was a second-class stamp, as it happens). Fruit salads and Black Jacks came in at four to a penny, and 5p bought an almost infinite supply of Parma violets. Loose pineapple chunks also represented tremendous value if you were looking to bulk out your purchase.

Until I started moving up to the pricier world of Marathons, Topics, and Picnics, I never really encountered anything that might be described as a brand in the advertising sense of the word. What Kate, James, and I had bought, clutched tightly in our hands in a white paper bag, were more of a sugared commodity which, we assumed, had always been around and would always be around. Like sugar, only more interesting. Mr Rainer sold his sweet shop to a chain of bookmakers when I was ten.

At home, the brandscape was rather different. Being of electrical retailing stock, a constant stream of new devices and contraptions washed in over the threshold, some of them British, some of them European. But all the really cool ones were Japanese. In particular, I remember an extraordinary Sony music centre, which was so sleek, silvery, and futuristic, it looked as if it couldn't have been invented yet. In an era when television sets were still frequently concealed behind faux mahogany, it flagrantly broke every rule of front-room decorum; a massive, mildly menacing slab of techno-ostentation. With a smoked-glass top and a cassette tray that eased gracefully forward out of nowhere, it sat there like an alien spacecraft looming superciliously over a lesser civilisation. Not that I am disparaging any of my mum's décor.

In time, I was old enough to have holiday jobs in my dad's shops. I should also say my uncle's shops, but at the time I gave my dad all the credit, despite Uncle Martin looming out of the pages of the *Yorkshire Post* or interrupting Richard Whiteley in YTV's ad breaks. Sorry, Uncle

Martin. What a lot of branded kit there was. From the humble Pye and ITT, to the mid-market Philips, Hitachi, and Ferguson, to the upper echelons of Toshiba, Panasonic (Quintrix), and the peerless Sony (Trinitron), not to mention the faintly regal Dynatron which the old ladies loved and wouldn't hear a word against. Nor would I, much to the ridicule of Keith, assistant manager of our Corn Exchange shop on Briggate, one of the less salubrious streets on the Leeds shopping scene. It was two doors down from a nightclub called Jacomelli's, and those two doors were boarded up. I'm trying to be romantic about life as a trainee electrical retailer in the wrong part of Leeds in the seventies. But the truth be known, it wasn't entirely glamorous (barring the odd trip to Cecil Gee's).

As one spell of holiday work gave way to another, it has to be said that the tide seemed to be turning against Vallances. Specialist shops like HMV made us give up on record sales, while a new kind of discount retailer leveraging greater economies of scale made life difficult for a salesman trying to sell the same Sony for £5 more, even though at Vallances it came with a plug (I know, because I screwed most of them on) and more knowledgeable staff (by which I mean Keith, not me, because I was screwing the plugs on in the storeroom).

Customer service was a byword at Vallances, summed up in the magnificently terse mission statement: 'Our aim is to give 100% customer satisfaction, not dividends to shareholders or jobs to employees.' Motivational stuff, but I'm afraid not motivational enough. In 1987, the brothers bowed to the inevitable and sold out to Thorn EMI. The shops were absorbed into the Rumbelows chain, which shut down soon afterwards, but not before dad and Martin had made their fortune. These days, EMI is not doing too well either; nor is HMV. Sometimes you have to know when to get out. Especially in the electrical retail game.

In addition to making dad and Martin a tidy sum, the sale of Vallances had another obvious consequence. It closed the door to any of the children following in their father's footsteps (on the arguable assumption that any of us would have been invited to do so).

So Vallances ended after two generations and never needed the services of the founder's grandchildren. In the course of writing this book, we've been lucky enough to interview representatives from brand dynasties that go back one generation in the case of James Dyson, and considerably further back to a great-great-grandfather in the case of Jonathan Warburton. I won't pre-empt their chapters by saying too much about what we learnt from them as individuals, but one piece of combined learning is very clear: contrary to what you might expect, those who inherit a brand legacy can be just as fanatical as those who start one. They too have something to prove and to live up to, and perhaps even more of an ethos to uphold.

I was studying English at Nottingham University when Vallances was sold. It's fair to say that this was not an obvious degree choice if I was looking to join the family business, and I certainly had no imminent intention of asking for a job. That said, the sale did come out of the blue, and I do remember the vague feeling of a distant door shutting on my future employment options (not to mention my plug-screwing prowess).

The mid-to-late eighties was a time of relative prosperity and high employment. Unlike today, students didn't think much about what they would be doing after university. Or, at least, this one didn't. There was an assumption that something would come up. Probably in London. And so it was, shortly after my finals, that I found myself writing letters to advertising agencies asking if I could have an interview. I even went so far as to buy myself a shirt at Paul Smith's fantastically cool shop on Byard Lane, about which we will have plenty to say in that particular chapter. I may have got the shirt right, but I had got the timing horribly wrong, having missed the 'milk round' which had happened a full nine months earlier. Quite a few of the agencies to whom I wrote were quick to point this out. Nonetheless I ploughed on, buying the odd copy of *Campaign* to keep me informed about what was happening in adland.

I managed to get an interview at BMP (Boase Massimi Pollitt), Zetland Advertising, and Saatchi & Saatchi. At this last agency, the man who interviewed me (and whose name I have shamefully forgotten) obviously thought I had potential as an account *planner*, but not as an account *manager* (which is the role I was convinced I was cut out for – I was wearing a Paul Smith shirt after all). He was utterly right and I was utterly wrong. Despite him organising an interview with their planning director, I declined the invitation. I even went so far as to write him a letter describing his refusal to take me on as an account man as 'the worst mistake you've ever made in my life'. No wonder I was struggling to get a job.

After a brief stint at Colman RSCG, I found my first proper agency home at Burkitt Weinreich Bryant, where I spent three glorious years, learning roughly half of what I know about advertising in that duration. I then selfishly left to further my career, having received an offer that, back in the eighties, you couldn't refuse. The offer was to work for an agency called Bartle Bogle Hegarty.

Normally in advertising, four or five agencies are in the ascendancy at any one time. For most of the eighties there was only one. BBH was, quite simply, the best at everything. With the best accounts, the best people, the best ads and, frankly, the prettiest girls. My time at BBH, therefore, completed the other half of my advertising apprenticeship. Although John Hegarty has become by some margin the most famous of the three founders, I learnt equally from John (Bartle), Nigel (Bogle), and John (Hegarty) when I was there.

After BBH, I went to an agency called WCRS where I would probably still be working but for a few ups and downs to do with succession management. As it was, I decided to look around and, in the process, was presented with an opportunity to start my own agency with three marvellous individuals called Rooney Carruthers, Adrian Coleman, and Ian Priest. So it was that I became (albeit only a quarter) eponymous in a company called Vallance, Carruthers, Coleman, Priest which, for obvious reasons, is generally shortened to VCCP. Our founding client was and is O2, to whom we remain eternally grateful and which launched on 02.02.02, about a month after the agency started. It was a busy January. But not for me, because I was on gardening leave.

Ten years later, I have had the pleasure of working on a number of different accounts. In the strange overlapping way of things, three of those accounts were Dyson, Hiscox, and Laithwaite's – so I had got to know a little about three more of our interviewees before I asked them to participate in this book.

Which brings me to the topic in hand. Wherever you go in Britain, you will be near the birthplace of an eponymous brand. Some of them made it big, some of them didn't, some of them never wanted to. Some of them survive and some of them don't. From brewers to shopkeepers, chemists to confectioners, the names are part of our tradition. But it may be a tradition that is dying out. The new generations of brand builders favour a different approach, keeping their name one stage removed from the businesses they create. Pret a Manger, Virgin, Innocent, Carphone Warehouse (not to mention Google, Apple, Facebook, and Microsoft) are shining examples of the new paradigm. While these founders may be synonymous with their brands, they are not eponymous.

Just in case they had some wisdom to impart, we thought we'd talk to some of the eponyms while they're still around.

O**UR APPROACH: Think what it was like to be in their shoes. Being invited to an interview where you will be** asked about the magic ingredients of your personal success is at best a mixed blessing, only made worse if the interviewers have a fascination with your name.

Being in the public eye is not quite the dream it's cracked up to be. You may have the money to spend, but the fun fades if the media are likely to turn up in your dustbin sifting through to check what you've spent it on. No nation envies success quite so much as the British, nor takes such a coprophagous pleasure in its reversal. In these circumstances, it is not surprising if paranoia or lack of trust eats away at the very optimism and determination that were factors in your success in the first place. You may increasingly feel that anyone new you meet has to be vetted (at least in your mind; perhaps by your professional handlers) for motives and intentions best not taken at face value. It's a slightly sad process that can leave some in the public eye forever untrusting and emotionally desensitised. Indeed, as an interviewer, one can spot straight away the vacant PR-prepped gaze and bulletproof cataracts grown from years of hurt from prurient journalists, unhinged web-gossip, and honeytrap assassins.

So you have to admire those who manage to preserve their inner humanity, and especially our willing subjects here. Most of them can still walk out of their front door without being recognised or having to sidestep the paparazzi. But they are still in the public eye, and it was refreshing the way they gave of themselves here.

Our original ('ideal') list of participants was not so different from the one that appears in the following pages. Inevitably, there were those who refused our requests, for a variety of reasons – some understandable, some less so. In one or two cases, we were unable to penetrate a one-mile-thick protective polystyrene doughnut. But such cases were few, and that's football for you.

In most of the cases where people agreed, there wasn't much in the way of neurosis from PR and PA intermediaries, and in fact we were more often buoyed by the interest and enthusiasm shown by the subjects in the project. Most welcomed the opportunity to pass on their life experiences and insights. And whether their motive was to encourage others, to have some fun, to generate some publicity, to indulge an ego, or just to enjoy a moment of therapy – or all of these – we didn't mind, because their tales were so worth telling. If, for their part of the bargain, it involved a leap of faith (over our abilities and our motives as the writers), our final subjects presumably felt that this was a good moment to make it, and we were grateful to them for doing so.

Which begs the question of why we chose these particular people in the first place. Coming up with a provisional list that we thought might bring the idea to life in an interesting and compelling way was actually quite easy. Our aim was to get a variety of characters and industries and hope that, within these, there would emerge other varieties, such as in personalities and routes to success. Some people were obviously import-ant to such a subject matter; others were at a stage in their journeys that made them especially interesting.

From the start, we felt the book should be based on a 'live' interviewing process – and on what we hoped would be the unique insights that come directly from conversations – rather than on desk research, which would, we feared, be going over ground already well covered by other material.

In the chapters that follow, large portions of text are direct quotations (edited as sensitively as possible to take out interruptions, ruminative pauses and digressions, coughing fits, and excessive blasphemy), which, we felt, would make for the most representative and most interesting approach. Most of our interviewees are well-publicised individuals (to varying degrees), and in most cases, it is straightforward to find articles about them through a few minutes on Google. But we wanted to depict the true colour and texture of entrepreneurial success – in a way that could only be achieved by our actually meeting the-people-with-the-names. To shake their hands and look into their eyes, as it were.

Here, then, is what we found.

—

'Politics is supposed to be the second-oldest
profession. I have come to realize that it bears a very
close resemblance to the first.'

RONALD REAGAN

—

LORD BELL
OF BELGRAVIA

(Bell Pottinger)

INTERVIEWED 21 DECEMBER 2011

C urzon Street, Mayfair: home to peers, embassies, oil oligarchs, expensive escort girls; houses with high drawing-room ceilings behind wide black doors; high-end stationery boutiques, Victorian pubs, government offices, and British secret services, where Eton-educated spies once used to offer each other cigarettes during gentlemanly *Tinker Tailor* interrogation interviews.

At number 14, Lord Bell is chain-smoking. He does it in the uninhibited 1950s *Mad Men* way that you don't see anymore, and which deserves proper cigarettes with woodpeckers and sailors on the pack, not the low-nicotine-bandwidth Benson & Hedges Golds piled on his table. The man we are about to interview is rueful about the 'improvements' brought by the post-internet era – to the point of having only recently replaced his fifteen-year-old Scotch-taped Nokia.

Lord Bell – Timothy John Leigh Bell, Baron Bell of Belgravia ('call me Tim') – is the eponymous co-founder of Bell Pottinger, one of the most famous of global public relations companies, recently the subject of a management buyout (from the parent company, Chime) reported to be in the order of £20 million. The industry's growth has been driven, in part, by the expanding pressures of a media that individuals and companies cannot possibly handle on their own, and by a corporate perception that 'managed publicity' can sometimes offer better value than conventional advertising. Company, country, or rock chick – it seems everyone in the media eye now needs a PR agent.

The image of the PR man can be unflattering, be it one of sitcom buffoonery or 'spin doctors' disguising political malfeasance as benevolence. It's a job that has evolved with the Westminster landscape, from the bulldog Bernard Ingham (one-time Chief Press Secretary to Margaret Thatcher) to the terrier Alastair Campbell (Tony Blair's Director of Communications and Strategy, who became known as 'the real deputy prime minister'). And somewhere in between these two differing styles is where we find Tim Bell – a man who never actually had a formal role as a government 'press secretary', but who was widely seen as the brains behind Margaret Thatcher's victory in 1979 – and many of her successes after that. He is regarded (to his chagrin, whether it is true or not) as being responsible for coaching her voice down an octave and pulling the plug on the electric-shock perm.

Bell Pottinger shares its foyer with an entrance to Benugo cafe bar – a not-quite-comfortable concession to the practicalities of the modern era, whereby, if you say you want a coffee when you arrive, the receptionists totter next door and buy you one, corrugated cup-holder and all. Bell's office is five floors up, and when we meet him, he has been occupied for several days marshalling the company's own PR firefight, following a newspaper sting operation. The company has broken the first rule of public relations consultants, which is never to become the story, and Bell himself has been drawing flak and facing the vitriol of one newspaper in particular.

It is hard not to begin the interview by coming straight to this issue, and it is obvious that he is irritated – not so much by what they're saying about him (which he sees as going with the territory), more about what he feels is another example of the political media losing its 'reasonableness'.

To illustrate the point, he shows a picture of an internet-inspired mob, holding banners on which names of arbitrarily chosen public hate figures have been scrawled in blood-red paint; barely known figures who have been unfortunate enough to momentarily transgress political correctness and now have a demented street mob demanding their heads be put on poles. 'We've lost balance... common sense...' he muses. 'Mad ideas are now able to move far quicker than steady judgement. It's mad.' He feels that the press, rather than calm the waters, like to shark-feed on this kind of thing. Whatever happens after the Leveson Inquiry, there is, he feels, no self-motivated check on press hypocrisy any more; only a relentless Glenda Slagg chutzpah, condemning something one minute, while exploiting it in the very next column.

Bell does, however, have his own version of inconsistency, and gauging his mood can be treacherous. He's the pessimist one minute, the optimist the next. At one point, he tries to resolve his indecision in front of us, concluding, after a slightly magnificent pause (during which it's hard to tell whether he is unable to decide or is just being Shakespearean), that his optimistic side shall today be the more persuasive.

Actually, I have taken the trouble to try and deal with the pessimism. I have a mantra which I've developed in the last few years, which is to take care of yourself, mentally, emotionally, in health and in spirituality.

Give or take the occasional sprint relay of cigarette smoking, of course. It suggests that the man is not so much a wavering optimist as a walking paradox – it being a miracle that this particular paradox is still walking at all.

I've had a cancer operation on my colon, the top layer of my left lung removed because of latent tuberculosis, and my gall bladder taken out. That was a direct result of all the chemotherapy and radiotherapy after the cancer operation. I've also had a triple heart bypass. The majority of what happened to me physically is my own fault because I lived a certain lifestyle and was careless. I'm aware of every piece of information about smoking because one of the first clients Saatchi & Saatchi had was the Health Education Council with the anti-smoking campaign, so I've studied all that stuff and, if I'm honest, I prefer to think it happens to other people, not me. That's the normal human attitude, but it can oddly be quite helpful, because it means you're prepared to put yourself in harm's way, and by doing that you become stronger. You take risks. You stare it in the face.

Then a quick mood-swing to penitence:

But every now and then, the world kicks me and when the world kicks me, fuck it hurts. And I sit down and I think, 'You fucking asked for it. Serves you right.'

His reputation for recklessness certainly precedes him. In his early days at Saatchi & Saatchi, he had ordered a Ferrari before most directors had got desks, but he justified this by saying he needed to show clients, if they ever rejected the agency's work, that the company still had the upper hand. 'They have their Vauxhalls; I have my Ferrari.'

Then there is the story that one time, after having had major surgery, he discharged himself from hospital against all sensible medical advice, just so he could attend dinner with the Sultan of Brunei. Which is either insane or inspired, depending on your view of risk. He says he can't remember if this tale is true or not: in his time, he's had a lot of surgery, and more dinners with plutocratic sultans than most people have had with their TVs.

What is not open to much doubt is that Bell can play the polemicist: he reacts strongly to many a thing, be it a new Middle Eastern war or an ad for cocoa, without mucking about too long with the messy business of equivocation. Which is probably why he has garnered wealth and criticism in equal proportion. Indeed, despite this polemicism, you get the feeling that his is a life where opposites have always co-existed, like forces in an atom; a life where the ups and downs and lefts and rights and goods and bads seem to travel in pairs. His is the story of relentless contrasts, one of which is his journey from humble to grand. Bell now has access to substantial wealth, but it didn't start like this, and for all the elegance of the life he now enjoys, his origins offer the contrast:

I was born in 1941 and brought up in a middle-class, north London, semi-detached house. My Irish father left home when I was five, and my mother was subsidised by my grandfather and worked at a laundry at night to supplement her income. We went to state schools; myself and the two sisters; one emigrated at 18 to live in America, and the other one eventually married an architect and lives in Brookmans Park and makes her own chutney.

Theirs was an upper-middle-class existence without the associated comforts, and it goes a long way to explaining the genesis of his political convictions:

There was much more division than people ever realise, and subdivisions within each class: there was an upper class and a middle class and a lower class, with subdivisions within all of those, and within the middle class were the nouveau riche, which we weren't. Upper middle class, which we were, meant that you observed etiquette and manners and protocol rather more than other people did. You were embedded. You had got a generational history of being the middle class. My grandfather's job was the classic sort of upper-class managerial role. But there was no money in the family.

I couldn't go to university, because it would have been another four years of contributing nothing and living off my mother, who was already working and nearly killing herself. I understood that I had to get a job. I'd been to a grammar school and that was the ethic: you went to school to be educated to get a job. You didn't have career development programmes run by Richard Branson and people like that. You had schoolmasters and an education system, the point of which was to qualify you to get a job. We were, to paraphrase J. K. Galbraith, as functionaries without capital: Canute-like we stood against the rising tide of proletarianisation, and that's what's happened to my life.

From an early age, Bell had a moral certainty that would define his world view. And from that early age, he wanted to get into politics. The main reason being that it seemed the quickest route to a shag:

At home, my stepfather was very aware of politics and talked about politics, through him being a City alderman and a mayor. We lived in a constituency of very high profile politicians: Reg Maudling on one side, Cecil Parkinson to the north, and, as it turned out, Thatcher to the other side. I joined the Young Conservatives because that's what you did if you wanted to be connected and meet people. You joined the church, you joined the Boy Scouts, you joined the community structures; all of them were unquestionably conservative with a small c, and most of them were Conservative with a capital C. That's how you mixed.

I went out with the Conservative agent's daughter. Everybody did actually. You joined the Young Conservatives because that gave you access to her: it was as simple and obvious as that. We all tried to shag her.

As it happened, the lady in question wasn't having any of that kind of thing, so, alas, she must now disappear from our tale as quickly as she arrived, leaving us with the wisdom that politics can be a frustrating business.

Perhaps opinionated at times, Bell is not an overconfident person: more often charming than angry; more Humphrey Appleby than Malcolm Tucker. He is very aware and proud of his successes, yet only too well aware of his failings.

I am naturally good at certain things, but I can never be bothered to practise to make myself excellent at them. It's been the story of my life. I was good at cricket, but not great. I was a fanatical modern-jazz fan and I played the trumpet, but my trumpet-playing days have now gone – it's the lips. I have a natural ability to play the piano, but I don't practise, so I don't play it as well as I could do.

I never made any secret of the fact that I wanted to be somebody, not just be a piece of cannon fodder. And I think I measured success by visibility. I recognised that nobody would know who the hell you were if you didn't do something that they could see. For a period, I played in bands. You'd get £10 for playing at the London Palladium, £20 for going to Manchester, but that would cost you £30 on the train to get to play in Tommy McQuater's Pick Up Band. Or play at The Marquee Club, which you had to do for nothing. But then I would think, will I be good enough or should I do something more serious?

At the point where he could quite easily have carried on as a musician, Bell took another route. And he was rewarded with some good luck, reinforcing his view that just because you are doing well at one thing, you should not pass over the opportunity of doing something different.

When I was 18, my mother said it was time to go and get a job and it didn't occur to me to question it. It was like telling me to put some trousers on. She sent me to an employment agency called The Stella Fisher Agency, in Fleet Street, who got me three interviews: one with an insurance company for post-boy, one with a publishing company for post-boy, and one with ABC Television as post-boy. All three offered me the job.

The one with the television company turned out to be wonderful because on the first day I walked through the door at Vogue House in Hanover Square and held it open for a young, thin girl called Jean Shrimpton and a long-haired kid called David Bailey. They were promoting Sammy Davis, Jr on Sunday Night at the London Palladium, *hosting the press conference in the reception at Vogue House, so I walked in, and there he was. He was going out with a Swedish girl called May Britt at the time, and there was Sammy. I mean, it felt like I was entering showbiz.*

Right place, right time. One man's good luck is another man's smart management and the line where one stops and the other starts is moot. There are many such instances that pepper his life story, and none is better known than Margaret Thatcher's election victory in 1979: a moment that transformed Britain, although whether for better or worse is an argument that has been raging ever since. By the late seventies, Bell had made his way from ABC post-boy to advertising executive, working for Geers Gross and then Saatchi & Saatchi, where he became media director in 1970, moving on to become managing director and then CEO. Another day; another phone call; another lucky break.

A man called Gordon Reece rang up Saatchi & Saatchi and asked to speak to Maurice Saatchi who was on holiday. So they put the call through to me. He asked me if we wanted to handle the Conservative Party account, and I told him that I would be happy to do it, but I'd have to consult with my colleagues because I didn't think they voted Conservative. I rang Maurice and said to him, 'Do you want to do this?' and he said 'Ring Charles', so I rang Charles and he said, 'OK. As long as you do it, all right?'

By the close of the decade, Britain was filling up with uncollected bins and unburied bodies. Sunny Jim Callaghan had hung on too long and an enormous poll lead had chilled into a winter of discontent and a government in denial, prompting *The Sun* headline, 'Crisis. What crisis?' After a Parliamentary Motion of No Confidence, the General Election was called; it would see the iconic Saatchi poster 'Labour isn't working'.

I was asked by Gordon Reece to go to the Leader of the Opposition's room in the House of Commons, to meet with Airey Neave and then to meet Margaret Thatcher. In those days there were no police. You just drove in past the Parliament gatehouse and parked in the St Stephen's entrance, where nowadays you have to go through about fourteen different metal detectors. We walked up an incredibly complicated spiral of staircases, to meet this rather shambolic figure in a raincoat in the corridor, Airey Neave, who spoke with a pronounced Irish accent. I didn't really understand a word he said...

I was shown a door which said it was the Leader of the Opposition's office and there was an anteroom with two girls sitting at old-fashioned typewriters and one of them looked up and said, 'Who are you?' and I said 'I'm here to see the Leader... I'm from Saatchi & Saatchi'. She said, 'Oh, Starsky and Hutch! Sit there!' So I did what I was told until Gordon eventually appeared and we walked in to see Margaret Thatcher herself.

There was a brown velvet armchair and a brown velvet sofa. She was sitting at her desk. She just said, 'Sit down'. But instead of sitting in the chair, I sat in the middle of the sofa like a fucking idiot where you've got no arm support and you just float. I sat there like a complete prat.

She said, 'What's your favourite poem?' and I said 'If'. She looked at me very suspiciously, fumbled in her handbag, took out a copy of that same poem and said 'Who told you?' I said, 'Nobody told me. It's my favourite poem.' Then she said, 'What's your favourite speech?' and I said 'Abraham Lincoln'. She said, 'I fail to see how making the rich poor makes the poor rich. Who told you?' I said, 'Absolutely nobody. They are my favourites.'

So then she just said, 'We're going to get on. But I want you to understand three things. Firstly, politicians have very, very large toes and very large fingers, and it is very easy to tread on them. But I have neither. You will always tell me the truth.' 'Yes, Leader,' I said like a good boy. She said, 'Secondly, if you've got some trick that will get me elected, please don't use it, because if the people don't want me, it won't work.'

Now, I think that is probably about the purest definition of democracy that I've ever heard. Then, she said, 'Third. You will get a lot of abuse for working for me. I hope you're a big boy.' I said, 'I hope so.' She said, 'Right. Well, we'll get on then. Take him out, Gordon.' And, at that, I was escorted from the room.

Bell makes no secret of his veneration of Lady Thatcher. She was at his side when he was introduced into the Lords in 1998, and he even calls her his 'heroine'. The fact that some members of the British public still regard her as the Devil incarnate only serves to confirm to him that she had the right idea and that the enemies she made – from within and from without – were exactly the enemies she should have made.

There was just this sort of aura that surrounded her. And I did always tell her the truth, without hesitation. She didn't always accept it. She didn't always see it as the truth as I saw it. But she was just fantastic. She changed me completely. She made me 100% politically aware of everything. Everything I now do or think, I think about from a political point of view and that came directly from her.

She had absolutely no small talk and you didn't do small talk with her. I was brought up in a well-mannered society, so I would always compliment her on the way she looked or, if she'd got a new dress on, I'd say it was a nice dress. But she didn't have any reaction to such comments.

We became known as 'courtiers' from the cynics and the faceless, insecure men who hadn't got the courage to speak in front of her, which was about 80% of the Shadow Cabinet at that time, because they were unbelievably uncomfortable with her. They couldn't come to terms with what had happened. It was as if their wife had come into the office and had turned overnight into their boss. They simply couldn't understand it. How could it have happened? How could it be that this woman was in charge?

'This woman' looks at us as we do the interview. There is a large portrait of her in Bell's office, propped up on the floor. The eyes follow you around the room, sternly, disapprovingly, whatever the angle, whatever you're doing.

The great privilege of my life was working with Margaret Thatcher and Ronald Reagan, who were both people of great vision. But neither was in the least bit interested in what the personal rewards were from the achievement. They weren't interested in power because of the title or because of the robes or because of the grand cars. They had a vision about their society, their community, or their country.

I met Reagan in Washington. Bill Brock [chairman of the Republican National Committee] had asked for someone to present to the nominees for the Republican candidature in 1980. I'd just done Thatcher's election, and there were some commonalities with inflation and unemployment, and they thought there was something to learn, so I trotted across to Washington. Unbeknownst to Maurice and Charles Saatchi: I never told them because I knew if I did say anything, Maurice would say he'd go, and as he hadn't done nearly as much as me in handling the election campaign I was fucked if he was going to get any of the glory.

I gave the presentation to five people sitting behind a desk: Gerald Ford, Ronald Reagan, Howard Baker, John Connally, who was the

Governor of Texas, and John Anderson, who in the end stood as an independent candidate. My presentation was really embarrassing because I wasted 20 minutes of it trying to explain the difference in the electoral systems which, of course, they had not the slightest interest in. Then Reagan gave me a jelly bean. He had a big jar of jelly beans on the table in front of him.

One is reminded at this juncture of Reagan's famous comment, 'You can tell a lot about a fellow's character by his way of eating jelly beans.' Presumably, Bell ate them in an approved way, because Reagan took a liking to the English guy in front of him, embarrassing presentation or not.

Ford was there because he was the sitting president, and he was unbelievably charming and polite and courteous. Then there was John Connally. If you'd asked me which one would you expect to be the president, I'd have picked Connally, because he was dark-eyed and seemed extremely smart. [During the JFK assassination in Dallas, Connally had been travelling in the presidential car and was seriously wounded.] Howard Baker was like a secretariat; a minister of questions. I would never have picked Reagan to win, because the image of him as the cowboy Hollywood buffoon had permeated everything. But he came across as very charming, very well mannered, and was a very, very big man. I felt like he was like my grandfather. He was physically big and big in presence.

In the end, I spent quite a lot of time with Reagan, most of which I'll never tell anybody about because it's entirely private. He wasn't like Thatcher in the sense of understanding detail. He didn't do detail. But he understood a very simple thing: that there is no reason for America not to be the greatest country in the world, and his one job as president was to achieve that.

Thatcher's philosophy was very similar. She said, 'I will make Britain great again and I will do so by making British people think they're great.' The overwhelming feeling that you got from her was that anything was possible. That she would lead you and take all the bullets and all the bloodshed and all the shit, just to get there. She didn't care at all for herself.

Bell must be a man who has a coffee-table-sized address book and still needs a supplement. The phones ring throughout the interview, and he answers them, but not so as you feel he's being impolite to us, his inter-viewers. Sometimes, it is the kids wanting money; other times, it is a foreign dignitary or an American movie star; sometimes it is from a floor below; sometimes, from a distant embassy. In his time, Bell has worked with governments across the world, some more wholesome than others; some he is proud to have been involved with, such as de Klerk in South Africa (which was controversial, but which he feels did a lot of good); others he feels in retrospect should have been avoided.

The calls are all answered in the same way, same voice, same tone, same mannerisms, regardless of the caller being kings or kids, not at all inhibited by our awkward presence there in the room. 'Sorry. Won't be a minute.' 'Sorry about that.' His phone is a modest one, and he eschews smartphones because of the 'acres of spam' that he doesn't want to look at, and the fact that he can't work them anyway. 'E-mail is a monologue and I prefer telephone dialogue,' he says.

Bell left the Saatchis in 1985 and went to work with the advertising guru Frank Lowe. 'I adored Frank, and didn't know what to do next, so I went to work with him.' But it didn't work out. It's another example of a life with as many downs as ups. Even his peerage was not a straightfor-ward matter, generating bitter controversy at the time.

I got a knighthood in 1990 in Mrs Thatcher's Resignation Honours List, which anybody will tell you is the only list to be on. Then I got the peerage at the recommendation of William Hague to Tony Blair in 1998. It gets me very good tables in restaurants. It makes my driver call me 'my lord', which I laugh at, but he's a Gurkha and he likes calling me it. I don't take it seriously. I don't think it puts me in some different part of life than anybody else.

Bell claims that he is 'well off' rather than 'rich', which is the kind of thing that will annoy the Polly Toynbees of the world. In what he sees as a significant contrast with Champagne Socialist hypocrisy, he is proud of his wealth and sees no reason to hide it. Money has played a role in his ambitions from a young age.

I'd always had this feeling that I should carry a higher price ticket on my head than anybody else. I was competitive because that made me feel better, and partly because my stepfather always had the view that the best things were the most expensive things, and he inculcated me with this idea.

What does all the money bring? Comfort is the answer. I get up in the morning in a big house. I have a rack of clothes to choose from. I get in a chauffeur-driven car to go to the office. I can go to any restaurant. But in the past, I've had an irresponsible disregard for the value of money. I got money, I spent it. I made £9 million when I sold my shares in Saatchi & Saatchi, but wrote a cheque for £6 million to the Inland Revenue because, like an idiot, I sold the shares three months before Margaret reduced capital gains tax to 40% and I even knew she was going to do that. I'm just careless like that. The rest I spent on indulging myself and buying a house. One third of it was put into a very good investment, and the rest was frittered, but it gave me a lot of experience. I had fun. I enjoyed myself...

And I've never wished to leave some lasting edifice. I'm not interested in having Bell Pottinger preserved for a thousand years – though I believe you should run a business as though it were going to be there for a thousand years because that makes you make the right moral and ethical decisions about the way you run it and to some extent the right commercial decisions. I don't give a damn about material possessions. I don't care if my house disappears, once I've gone. I suppose I'd want to write a really trite epithet for my gravestone: 'He made a difference'... I find the status quo frustrating and annoying and full of anomalies and bad things: if only I could feel I'd helped remedy that. I'm not a pioneer, but I like pioneers and I like working with them.

Bell often mentions the idea of risk. He has an understanding of it, and an interpretation of how it should be managed. *Money, ambition, risk* – he makes them sound like the three gifts brought by the kings to the stable in Bethlehem.

I take risks. It comes from my father who was an alcoholic. Also, from the brothers Saatchi who had an enormous influence on my life, and Charles [Saatchi] is an inveterate risk-taker. But I also try to be reasonable. To the extent that I have a correct analysis of myself, I think I am an intensely reasonable person and I think that's why I have been a fairly successful entrepreneur: because I take reasonable risk and not unreasonable risk.

But I believe that what is wrong with our society is that the negativity of risk is overwhelming the positivity of risk, so that it is the unreasonable risk, not the reasonable, that wins out. As we saw in the financial crisis. What happened to this country in particular but, actually, to most of the Western empire, is that the degree of risk was taken beyond the reasonable.

After the decline of religion, we've lost our moral compass, and there is no sense of what is reasonable. We are taking more and more unreasonable risks – such as with our own energy [supplies] – and we're now in a self-destruct mode. Because of the various governments we've had, and because of the political persuasions, and mainly because of the information superhighway now, the percentage of negativity in a risk is growing and growing, and the positivity is shrinking and shrinking...

Look at the internet: nobody is controlling the upside to exploit it fully and make sure that it works, but everybody is exploiting the downside.

He also talks a lot about responsibility. His mantra is that it starts and ends with the willingness of the individual (and certainly not the state) to take charge.

One of the things I've been trying to learn is to avoid being co-dependent; to stop imagining that other people's behaviour determines your life.

You have to stop trying to control other people's behaviour, which you can't do. You can only control your own behaviour. And as I've had various crises in my private life, I've had to go to some trouble to make myself handle it properly.

You've got to work to keep your optimism. You've got to get up in the morning, and look out, and count your blessings. Everyone's got something good in their lives. And if you do try to be an optimist, then the chances are you will radiate some kind of positivity, and that positivity is contagiously engaging and it makes other people more positive. And, ironically enough, it reduces the amount of negativity that gets passed to you.

It's one of the reasons why I'm successful in this business. Because people come to me with problems and I immediately start from the position that these can be turned into an opportunity.

Bell lights another cigarette, and checks his e-mail which has just pinged. The computer is not a new model, and the battered landline phone looks like it pre-dated Bakelite. His office is not what you expect from the head of a PR firm. No swish decor; no fancy tubular-chrome chairs. On the walls are some old map prints; in the corner, a modest wooden bookcase, with all the day's newspapers on the rack. The television is on, but muted, looping the news ticker, with a female presenter miming to images of men in bandanas and soccer tops carrying RPGs past fire-damaged tenements. Could be Mogadishu; might be Tottenham. In front of him, Bell has a few documents, a copy of the Christmas edition of *Private Eye*, a bottle of Evian, and a corrugated take-out coffee from five floors down. It's neither tidy nor chaotic. You get the impression that he can turn off the screens and walk away.

I read far less than I should do, and pay far less attention to detail than I should do. I read a huge volume of information, but I don't have a great edit facility in deciding that which actually is going to have an impact and that which isn't. I make the mistake of watching 24-hour news, even though I know that most of the bulletins are not being watched by everybody. But I love news. My escape route is cops-and-robbers. I watch Criminal Minds, *I watch* Law & Order, *and I watch all those American crime dramas.*

But I am a real Englishman. I speak no foreign languages. I like American drama, but I do not understand Americans at all. I've no idea what they're saying. It takes me half an hour to understand what the fuck they're talking about. And you know, every time they say 'Eye-raq' I want to vomit.

Bell is, without doubt, a man of power and wealth, who advises others of power and wealth about how to grow their power and wealth. Because of this, there are people out there who despise him.

I'm confronted by people who say in the court of public opinion that I'm a very bad person. Maybe they don't know the half of it. But if they want to be balanced, maybe they need to accept that it might equally be a good half instead. But they don't know one way or the other until they've had the conversation with me. Then they have a right to judge.

People ask me why I do work for terrible people. Look, I'm so bored with saying this and I think it's made me sound so self-righteous, but I try to take a completely non-judgemental view of my business life. My job is to earn money for the company, manage it at the lowest cost-base, produce the best return to the shareholders and oversee a relevant payout of the proceeds among the shareholders and the staff, the other stakeholders in the business and so on. I do not think it's my job to decide that so-and-so has no right to speak for himself or should not put across his message. I genuinely do believe that this company is a force for good; that we are agents of change. Not in everything that we do, but in a lot of the things that we do.

Various people claim they want to live in a fair society. Fat chance. And I think it has got worse, not better. I think that this government should apologise for some of its behaviour, but I think the Blair-Brown government should actually wear a crown of thorns and tear itself to pieces in public for what it did. The Thatcher government should rise up in pride for the good that it did, because it came at a moment in the slow decline of Britain. The tragedy was that there was nobody to follow.

What is happening now, which is what really frightens me, is that we're losing our stability. This wouldn't matter if it just meant that people's living standards were a bit lower. But what's happening now is of a different order. Things are happening that you can do nothing about.

Anyway, all of this makes me sound very pessimistic. My abiding philosophy is that you are responsible for your own behaviour, so if I choose to be pessimistic, I'm going to be fucking good at it. But in the end I choose to be optimistic. It's particularly hard to maintain when you open some papers; hard not to be self-righteous and cross, and arrogant at the lies and nonsense that get printed.

Some journalists hate me because I won't answer their questions. That's because I know they're going to manipulate the answer; they're not interested in telling the truth. They're interested in selling newspapers; in scoring points against their competition, and claiming an exclusive. They have a deluded idea about what the Fourth Estate is there for. The worst thing is the manipulation of public opinion, which you may think seems strange coming from someone like me. But lies are a tragedy of our society. And the worst people at it are the politicians because some tell lies deliberately.

They never used to. Sometimes lies are sort of justifiable, like when Callaghan said he wasn't devaluing. Of course, if he'd have told the truth, the markets would have been in turmoil. But now the politicians lie all day long and then rail against the fact that public opinion doesn't understand the truth. And I get accused of contributing to that process. I get written up as the original spin doctor, or the first political advisor, or Thatcher's spin doctor or whatever. But it is completely and totally without merit that criticism about me lying. I would liken myself to Larry Speakes, who was Ronald Reagan's spokesman. Larry Speakes told the truth to the press. And if he couldn't tell the truth, he just didn't go to the press conference; he didn't turn up. I actually think you do

*have a responsibility to turn up, but if you can't tell the truth, then say
you can't answer that question, or you don't want to. Just tell it as it is.
But for God's sake, don't go and lie.*

This is why it makes sense to regard Bell as a man of principle. His encapsulation of that, whether you agree with it or not, is what he sees as being a keeper of the Thatcherite flame of absolutism, unwavering patriotism, focus on the individual, belief in market forces, and an uncompromising approach to one political vision. Bell feels that the only effect of compromise is to allow the cynicism of leftist ambition ('opportunistic cynicism' is exactly what he sees it as being) to triumph.

*I believe that people of the right, whatever that means, are people
who believe in individual responsibility, self-reliance, and a lack of
dependency on the state. They basically think people are good and will
come to the right decisions, because they are making the decisions
themselves, and it's in their self-interest to get them right. The people
may be wrong sometimes, but they should know what is in their best
interest better than anybody else does.*

*In contrast, people on the left believe in collectivism. They do
not believe in individual responsibility; they believe in collective
responsibility. So, by definition, they believe that most people are
incapable of making the right decision but have to be led to doing
what's right.*

*And I think what's happened is that left-wing thinking has become
the prevalent thinking – in the whole world, but particularly in Britain
where they've infiltrated the media to such an extent that you no longer
get balance. Maybe I'm wrong. Maybe we people on the right who believe
that basically people are good and that good will out, are wrong. Maybe
we're the deluded ones. But isn't it better to have that delusion than
adopt the cynicism of the left?*

*Take the BBC. The great thing about the private sector is it is called
to task every single time it wants to sell its product. The consumer
has to part with some money so they have to make a decision. You*

don't make any decision to watch the BBC; you have no choice. You get sent a formal notice to buy a television licence otherwise you can't watch any other television station. It's the only hypothecated tax in Britain, because it is recognised that the power of communication is so important that it should have its own tax to fund it. And as part of this, the BBC is supposed to be balanced. But I don't believe that it is. And that's what's gone wrong.

Bell is as critical of the centre as he is of the left. Yet he stridently defends the idea of avoiding early judgements on company clients. Some might see this as commercial expediency (or selective hearing), but Bell makes a convincing case for not taking anything at face value. He sees this as an element of right-wing, free-market thinking, not of the liberal centre-ground.

In this business, the moment you meet a client, the very first thing you should do is challenge every assumption. That's what I do for a living. One of those assumptions might be that country X is a bad country run by a bad person, but I don't accept that just on its face value. I meet the person and I ask him questions. Perhaps I arrogantly imagine that my assessment of his answers has some relevance – well, actually, I don't, because I usually check them out on Google. But we have the debate in this office all the time – whether we should work for this person or that person. It's never occurred to me to sit in hasty judgement of anybody. I don't. People say that, based on this standard, I'd have accepted a job working for Hitler? Well, clearly I wouldn't, because it would have been difficult for me to miss the rather obvious fact that he'd just annexed Poland and Hungary and been murdering the Jews.

Bell's explanation is that his political stance supports his professional one. That the right is far more attuned to freedom of expression (and all it entails) than is the left. His frustration, however, is that the freedom he so cherishes can come back and bite.

It's that freedom to communicate that enables us to develop and make good choices. This does not mean to say that media people won't from time to time cheat, behave badly, and do the wrong thing, but I actually absolutely agree with freedom to communicate.

Yet I hate the internet. Because, unlike advertising, it has no governance. People say to me that this disproves my whole theory, because the balance of the democratic decision taken on the internet by the people is a free one. Well, I agree with that too. And if I were a weaker soul, I'd cry and hang myself.

The process by which the internet allows anyone to say anything and get an audience (in tens or billions) means that PR companies like Bell Pottinger have less control over, or have to work a lot harder to control, the news agenda. Bell doesn't think much of the wisdom of crowds, nor how those crowds harness the instruments of progress in the cause of anarchy – as seen in the London riots, where attacks were organised over smartphones. His detractors will argue that Bell is worried about this because of its effect on his own power, rather than a genuine concern over the way society is heading. But whatever those detractors believe about his motives, Bell sees the problem in the crumbling edge that divides the safety of freedom from the drop into anarchy. He is convinced that what he and his company do in 'managing' communication pushes us back from that precipice.

Bell has been eager to talk and enjoyable to listen to, belying the view in some newspaper articles that he is a difficult subject for interview. His diction embraces both erudition and blasphemy. One minute, he seems a confident, self-assured man, with little to prove at this stage of his life; a minute later, the humility and self-doubt are there as well.

Fame makes you lose your sense of proportion. Vast amounts of money make you lose it; your sense of proportion. I'm indulgent, but because I'm so self-indulgent, I worry about being unreasonable. Of course, I can be unreasonable like the rest, but when I am, I hate it. I mean, I really do go home and cry about it. I wake up at night worrying about what I've done, you know, when people have sent me something and I've rejected them or said 'no'. They think I've just written 'no' without a thought and carried on with the next thing, but I haven't done that. I don't. I sit there and worry that I've said 'no'. I wake up at night and think, 'Fuck, should I have said "no"?'

When we meet, *The Iron Lady* is ready to open at the Curzon cinema across the street, with Meryl Streep as Thatcher, and with several scenes about the PR makeover. He hasn't seen it, although the *Evening Standard* has quoted him as saying he dislikes it. For about half a second, he refuses to say one way or another, then states he doesn't want to see it. It just feels wrong. He regrets that his children, 'who, as babies, Thatcher bounced up and down on her knee', will now only remember the Hollywood caricature and think that it was Meryl Streep who did the bouncing. He's seen the trailer and picks on the scene in which Thatcher wears a hat at the dispatch box.

It's absurd. One of the fundamental rules of the House of Commons is that no one, man or woman, is allowed to wear a hat. Why have they allowed that? I'll tell you why. We work in advertising. We know why. It's because some idiot in Hollywood stamped their foot and said, 'I want her to wear a hat,' and no one had the gumption or knowledge to say, 'No, that's wrong.'

Maybe, maybe not. After we did the interview, the 'hat question' temporarily became a discussion point for political nerds (she certainly wore one for State Openings and some parliamentarians of the period claim to remember her in a hat on other occasions at the dispatch box). Yet hats aside, what Bell fears, sight unseen, is that the American film will be too 'casual with detail'; that the faith will be broken; that the Thatcher story will be made less consequential by a sentimental, but perhaps factually imprecise, biopic.

A few blocks away in Belgravia, the real person herself is battling dementia and is in sad decline. Despite Bell's seventy-odd years and what seems like the same number of cigarettes each day, her ex-PR man appears full of energy and confidence. It allows him to go on *Newsnight* and give as good as he gets from Paxman: 'People can publish all sorts of claptrap on [the internet], and they frequently do, about you and me: *your* Wikipedia entry [Jeremy] is not so great either, any more than mine is.'

Bell is a man of firm resolution, who despises the equivocation and intellectual tardiness that characterised the post-Thatcher eras, be it with Major, Blair, Brown, perhaps even Cameron. 'You've heard me say this a thousand times: the centre ground is not in the middle between left and right; it's in the middle between right and wrong. And I prefer to choose what's right.'

Those could have been his heroine's very words, delivered without a hat. Even today, she would have approved of this man, in a way that she never approved of her prime-ministerial successors. That's fine by Bell. Whether others like it – or him – or not.

———

'Life is sometimes sad and often dull, but there are
currants in the cake, and here is one of them.'

NANCY MITFORD

———

JOHNNIE BODEN

(Boden)

INTERVIEWED 30 APRIL 2012

British summers can be as capricious as the country's politics. In 2010, David Cameron took over as prime minister: at ease going into number 10, at ease in his own skin (in a way his predecessor perhaps wasn't), and easy on Middle England sensibilities – the Sunday-supplement family guy, at one time photographed on holiday on the south coast, wearing beach gear from the Boden home-shopping catalogue.

It couldn't last. The British sunshine runs out of charge very quickly – just like the economic climate. With recession hurting and political upheaval in the air, someone needs to be blamed, and the mob has decided that beneath the Boden T-shirt and floral shorts lies an Eton toff and Bullingdon bounder. The air of 2012 is heavy with blog-raging envy, and anyone who enunciates their consonants is in mortal danger of being outed as a posh boy. As if there is some kind of spiritual connection between the UK premier and the source of his beach trunks, some sections of the press have been having a go at the latter as well as the former. 'The Boden backlash' reads one headline, claiming that Britain is falling out of love with the middle-class favourite that is Boden, and, by implication, its Eton-and-Oxford-educated founder.

Boden: a stellar British success story, and representative of all that British entrepreneurial acumen can achieve when it puts its mind to it; the home-shopping brand of choice for yummy-mummies and *Daily Mail* readers and many others besides; for over twenty years, supplying Middle England (and a lot of the sides as well) with bright, colourful, good quality clothing. Each year, tens of millions of Boden catalogues find their way into British households, with over one million repeat customers in the UK (and many more worldwide), regularly generating annual double-digit growth. Turnover in 2011 reached an impressive £232 million, with pre-tax profits of £32.5 million. Boden ranges have become as ubiquitous as M&S socks and knickers; the name as familiar in the kitchen coffee-morning chatter as Kellogg's or Nescafé.

But in Britain, nothing is unconditional, and no matter what the success, the headlines can be ready to make mischief. One of the first things that Johnnie Boden asks us, almost immediately after the introductions, is why this is so. He takes it in his stride, but there's a frustration at being misunderstood, especially where he feels it a function of his country's preoccupation with class.

The middle class association was completely accidental. You might argue that it was something that I encouraged, because, in my first press releases, it said I went to Eton and Oxford, so I can't complain that they won't stop talking about it. But people are obsessed with it in this country. The way we shot our catalogues was meant to be uplifting, not to make some social class point. I think customers respond better to images of people looking happy in pleasant surroundings; simple as that. For journalists to interpret this as some sort of middle-class strategy to alienate other people is just nonsense. Sure, there is envy, there are all sorts of things, it's a story, and in today's climate, it's inevitable. However, we've had the benefit of a lot of good press as well, so you have to be philosophical about the things they will eventually say about you.

The last sentence is pure Boden. He is not David Cameron and he self-deprecates in a way that a politician never would. Any time Boden starts to talk about his own achievements, he catches himself, and selects reverse, as though someone is about to accuse him of inflated self-importance. Of which there is no danger.

Nor is there much danger of people falling out of love with the Boden ranges. The mums and daughters of Middle England may want their revenge on the bankers and politicians – but they'll still take it wearing their chic Portofino summer-print dresses and bow espadrilles. Boden may be the aspirational motif of sunnier days in Middle England, but this is not a transient brand.

As it turns out, the Boden headquarters do not conform to any known middle-class stereotype. The architectural cues of the concrete-rich buildings in North Acton feel more North Korean than Etonian. The scene in NW10 is one of anodyne grey neutrality with interludes of rusty matt brickwork. A few dark clouds coming over and the changing of the traffic lights will probably be the peak of the day's action. At the Boden offices, someone has a sense of humour: the sign on the rectangular column outside says, 'Ugly building. Nice clothes'.

The inside of the building is better than the outside. The reception area could still be mistaken for that of a tractor manufacturer in Pyongyang, but, as you go further into the place, the tone changes. People are friendly and enthusiastic and more colour seeps from the walls; young staff are dashing about with small bits of cloth that seem extremely important.

Round a corner is Johnnie Boden's large-ish office: an ill-defined composite of artistic creativity and box-files. His welcome is warm and open, with a pastoral scattiness reminiscent of characters on a *Wind in the Willows* boat trip. Asked for his earliest recollection, his short surreal tale is worthy of Mr Toad:

My first memory is of a teddy bear. I remember waking up with it in my cot with the morning sun. I was probably kept in that cot with the teddy rather longer than I should have been. Then the house burnt down and teddy with it.

Boden is no stranger to the interviewing process, and is a frequent contributor at events and conventions. He is a well-built, tallish man (which doesn't quite come over in photographs) who cuts a presence in a room – helped by a head of tawny-auburn hair. He is an immediately accessible, friendly type, with one of those faces that always looks like it's smiling, even if he has the back of his head to you.

Of course, part of this is the well-trained, well-mannered bonhomie that can come from a certain kind of public-school upbringing – which can turn you into either a really nice guy or a really obnoxious one. Boden unquestionably took the first route, but there is something behind the sunshine. Perhaps shyness or worry or self-doubt. At certain moments, Boden averts his eyes and drifts into a kind of rueful reflection, suggestive of admonishment from a tough boarding school regime. He closes his eyes completely from time to time, making it difficult to tell if he is mentally exhausted or is anticipating a jolly good slap across his face for underachievement. For a person who makes everyone else feel so good about themselves, Boden is an anxious individual – wanting to be helpful while hoping not to disappoint. He would probably say 'sorry' spontaneously to someone who elbowed him in the ribs.

And being permanently self-critical, he has, it seems, done some hard self-analysis.

I had a lovely half-sister who married and left when I was in my early teens, so I was in many ways like an only child. My mother was very popular, but, like me, rather neurotic, wanting everyone to like her. I was the same: slightly detached, determined, but with feelings of inadequacy. My father was quite old at 45 when I was born; a strong, successful soldier, old-fashioned, but a complicated man, who hadn't had a normal upbringing himself and he was very hard on me. He had such high expectations, so I always felt I was never good enough. My parents were not big on praise. So I always wanted to do better. If I got 7 out of 10, I just was cross with myself. A lot of people are very comfortable in their own skin, but I wasn't.

Boden speaks a lot about the slim margin between success and failure. Indeed, he puts a figure on it: '51% is successful, but 49% is awful.' It's this awareness of the fragility of it all that marks him out.

My parents' social world was quite narrow, so even though I had a creative gene, it was not really exploited. I never came across anyone from advertising or business. My father's world was all soldiers, landowners, diplomats; very conservative, and they'd been left behind by the modern world.

Self-knowledge wasn't a big part of my upbringing. It was all about duty; you had to have very good manners, work hard, and get a respectable job. There was no sense of what was most suited to you. So whenever I felt success, such as when I made the first XI cricket team at school or I got into Oxford, my parents were still very hard on me, giving no praise, and telling me not to get too big for my boots. I'd had an interest in fashion by the time I was 16, and I got recruited to edit the menswear section of the Harpers & Queen *Teenage Edition of 1977. When I came back from it, I was really excited. But, I'll never forget, my father was so dismissive. He called it a 'bloody stupid job'.*

Crestfallen from the Lieutenant Colonel's displeasure at his son's dalliance with unmanly fashion-land, Boden returned to a more orthodox career path, via Oriel, Oxford, into stockbroking with Barclays Merchant Banking – which 'seemed reasonable'. He talks politely about the happiness of his childhood, but underneath, his story reveals some bruising. He is the child of circumstances that show how a privileged upper-middle-class upbringing may not always be quite the advantage it's cracked up to be. Boden's adolescent years tell of much unrecognised success and wasted opportunity; the prelude to even more disappointments, before things would get better.

The City was my first job, to which I was thoroughly ill-suited – really bad at it. I had no feel for the product and I didn't really respect the people. Every share I recommended went down. The frustration became a sense of failure. I noticed my friends were doing things they really enjoyed and were good at, but I felt a failure.

Then I received an extraordinary inheritance from a childless uncle. It wasn't enough money to retire, but enough to escape. I was able to buy a flat, and I left the City job. At first, I ran a couple of pubs, but I didn't enjoy that very much: I didn't have the experience.

I'd never enjoyed the pub-culture thing anyway. At Eton, there was a thing called Tap: a sort of pub for boys which allowed us to drink alcohol in school. But I hated it; don't know why; not out of affectation. I was a member of all the hooray drinking clubs and I could do it, but it was all a bit of an act. I was good at playing sport and I've always got on well with people, but I think I'm just a bit girlie. I don't like talking about football or cars. I just don't like that clubby, laddish thing.

Running a pub certainly wasn't his thing, and so Boden turned to teaching, which he says he enjoyed, apart from the poor salary. Like so many of our interviewees in this book, Boden treats each disappointment as a springboard for another renewed attempt at success. You simply can't keep this kind of person down for very long.

Despite his father's displeasure, what *was* Boden's thing was fashion. Ten years of wrong turns and a banking secondment to New York gave him the impetus. While on Wall Street, he was struck by the effectiveness of the US mail-order system, with its ambitiously successful brands like J. Crew and L. L. Bean, and by the apparent gap in the market: it seemed busy executives needed quick and easy access to good-quality casual clothing. Boden hadn't quite kicked the fashion habit after all, and his light-bulb moment was about to annoy his parents all over again.

When I was a schoolboy, I would visit Portobello Market and buy old overcoats, and American check jackets from Flip in Covent Garden. I always had this fashion interest. Then, when I went to America as part of the stockbroker job, I saw all these mail-order businesses. It stayed at the back of my mind. I could see how businesses like Land's End were successfully selling clothes directly, and remember thinking it was a good idea because busy people are always pushed for time.

I've always been an admirer of America. The brashness is slightly annoying, but I really love their positive attitude. I love their great service; I love their openness; there are many things I like about America. We have quite a big business there now, and there's so much I admire. But it's quite a tough place to do business in.

In 1991, working from his flat in west London, Boden launched the eponymous catalogue, not knowing that within a decade, millions of these booklets would be essential reading matter alongside *Tatler* and *Hello!* in living-rooms and loos across Britain. The pictures were hand-drawn by one of his pals, and there were fewer than a dozen menswear items for sale. The style – so familiar now – was a kind of softened, slightly Sloaney look: cords, checked shirts, cheery boxer shorts... And although Boden never took on professional designers until much later, he did a good line in cajoling old friends and relatives into various jobs, from manning the call-centre phones (as did his wife) to, in due course, actually pulling on the items and strutting in front of a camera as real-life models. Even in the first few years, there was a political connection: his early modelling guinea pigs included some Tory MPs and Boden even tried to enlist Peter Mandelson ('I wanted a good-looking socialist').

I actually asked Hugh Grant to model for us. He'd been at university with me – a year above me. He agreed, but then, on the day, he had a hangover and didn't do it. He's very funny and he's had his moments, but he's incredibly entertaining.

The early nineties were not the best of times to be launching a fashion company, but within three years Boden had his successful womenswear range in place, with Mini Boden following in 1996. It all chimed perfectly with the optimistic pseudo-rural fantasies of Middle England, where everyone arriving down late for Sunday brunch still looks lovely without even trying.

Before long, Boden clothing was the relaxed lifestyle choice of the modestly comfortable, gym- and gastropub-going professional classes, from Dawlish to Durham. Unaggressively stylish liberation was the philosophy. Boden's skill was in spotting that women were no longer willing to dress their age or be trussed up in uncomfortable clothing; they wanted to work and play with equal importance and be able to live to tell the tale. The world was pre-9/11, Britannia was still Blairite and cool, and Boden summed up the days of sunshine and gentle prosperity. According to *The Spectator*, 'The Tories would only succeed when they started to exemplify life in a Boden catalogue.' Boden and Britain were inseparable. He was building a retailing giant.

However, behind the scenes, he was expending both energy and capital.

I did lots of things really badly. We completely ran out of money; my inheritance disappeared within three years; that was one thing. Then I hired a guy who I thought I could trust, who turned out to be dishonest. Then we had a major burglary. Then I had a really tricky investor. It was at least ten years before things became financially stable. I had to put the house on the line, which was pretty stressful for the family. Even in 2000, we were still having to find money. Having been there, I don't want to be there again. It's never a nice position to be in.

Boden has a near-pathological dislike of debt and borrowing. He respects money in a way that is often characteristic of wealthy people who were once in dire straits. There but for the grace of God…

I think if you had access to a limitless supply of money, you would definitely cock things up. Stresses and disciplines are useful really. I had to learn lots of hard things, but what really helped was that I knew how to ask somebody something and say 'please' and 'thank you'. That was the best thing my parents gave to me. It was the importance of good manners.

The door bursts off its hinges and Sophie (Mrs Boden) and Sprout (the dog) enter the office at speed. Actually, it's less an entry and more an arrested carrier-landing. Sprout is yanked to a halt just before flying across the room and out of the upper-floor window into the Acton sky. Mrs Boden, attached to the other end of the dog's lead, is checking the room for inefficiency. She is a nuclear-powered life-management unit, and having met her for only two minutes, you feel like you really ought to go away and shape up. In seconds, this sibilant pair, Sophie and Sprout, have filled the room with enough energy to power a small American state.

Sophie has been wonderful... as I said, my upbringing was quite formal: I wouldn't have dreamt of teasing my father or being familiar. But Sophie's family were extraordinarily frank with each other. I couldn't believe it: the swearing was indescribable and they even called their father by his Christian name. My parents were good at socialising, but not so good at being intimate. Sophie's family were quite the opposite; they were very, very close to their parents, but just didn't see the point of socialising. Sophie would call her father by his Christian name, swear at him, and there were no elephants in the room. With my parents, there were herds of elephants in the room, several in each corner. They had issues about their own childhoods, about my father's career; there were all sorts of things that were completely no-go areas. It didn't make for huge amounts of happiness actually.

When I met Sophie and I saw all their happiness, I thought how much better a way to do things. And, even now, if I ever behave in a pompous way, she makes it known to me – as do the children. When I met Sophie, she said to me, 'You know, you're a bloody failure. You've had the most amazing start in life, but you're squandering it. You keep swapping and changing. What the hell do you want to do?' I got rather crestfallen at that, but accepted that she was fundamentally right. So I told her I had this idea for a mail-order clothing business and she said, 'Well, let's just do it! You're in the last chance saloon. Get on with it!' So that's why and how it started.

Sprout also gets on with things, in a manner of speaking. Mrs Boden was originally unsure as to the wisdom of a pet, and its implications for household sanity. However, the children felt more ready to embrace risk, hatched up an acquisition strategy, and brought Sprout home on Christmas Day 2009. Small, round, cute; like a hand grenade.

The Boden family are a close-knit unit. They have been through things together and it shows in the strength of their bonds.

Sophie was incredibly supportive and strong and believed in me. I needed that, because I can get pretty low. It's incredibly annoying to admit it, but it does hurt when the press write incorrect things. It's very frustrating and quite hurtful. On the whole, I'm quite a positive person, but I do try to be honest with myself. If the telephone stops ringing, it's because I've done something stupid.

The thing about retail is that you are only as good as your last range and you can never rest on your laurels. In fact, if you ever feel you're doing something right, you're probably about to make a terrible mistake – so it's not a bad thing in this business to be neurotic and self-doubting. We've had some recent hiccups and sometimes we get products wrong; we can get service wrong; we can get marketing things wrong. If you become satisfied with your success, you become boring and complacent and that is fatal. I'm constantly thinking how I might do things better and that's what makes it exciting actually. It's a sense of incompletion, if that noun exists, that drives you forward.

The press, of course, like to emphasise the links between Boden clothing and the political classes; something that Boden himself knows is inevitable, given his background. He knows both Boris Johnson and David Cameron, but 'not very well'. And he admits to being casually interested in the political village (his degree was in Politics, Philosophy, and Economics), but its fierceness and fickle nature are not for him. Although he once did give it a try:

I don't know why I got involved, but I went to see our local MP called Dudley Fishburn at his surgery. His secretary was an amazing woman called Charlotte Blacker, and she asked why didn't I stand for North Kensington as a local Conservative councillor, a completely unwinnable ward. They couldn't find anybody to do it, so I stood and duly got the lowest vote. It was hysterical, walking round these really rough housing estates with great big dogs trying to attack me. But I quite enjoyed it. I've got quite a few friends who are MPs although I'd never do it myself. I quite like elements of politics, but I would hate the cabals of Westminster. It's not my type of thing at all.

Boden's thing is fashion, and his brand is the love of his life, second only – by a very healthy margin, it seems – to his beloved wife and family. There is a symbiosis between man and brand; Boden takes everything personally, be it the hurt when things go wrong, or, of course, the praise when times are good. There is no real separation between the different elements of his world.

Sophie is quite punchy. When I'm under the weather or getting cross with the children, like you do when you're a bit low, she'll ask me why I don't sell the business. But this is a vehicle for my talents, such as they are, and I enjoy it. I know people who have done it – sold out – and they've regretted it. They get bored. I don't want to do nothing at all, and I don't want to go back into the early stages of another business because it's bloody hard. And if I were under her feet at home all the time, actually I would drive her bonkers.

Boden says, using a rather odd expression, that he 'enjoys people's emotions'. He remembers how the guiding principle of the early catalogues was that the images should be shot in exactly the same way as photographs in a family album – something that, he feels, was revolutionary when he first started, though it is a fairly standard approach these days. First, get the product right, then the imagery; the aim being to establish that brand and people are on the same page, literally and figuratively. He takes his commitment home with him.

If Sophie buys the children something awful-looking, even if it's something really basic like a cagoule, I get really upset. I want them to wear nice things, even around the house. I do think design is very important and I think it affects your mood. It's infectious, so although this is a shitty office – and it's important that we don't waste too much money on it – we try to make things a little bit nice around ourselves. We've got a rather funky canteen down the back there, and we built a rather lovely roof garden for everybody.

It's a very crowded marketplace. So you need as many things as you can to make your business stand out and actually putting my name behind it gives the customers some sort of extra reassurance; a guarantee over quality, design, service. It upsets a lot of people who think I'm a pompous arse, but I think there is still the sense of a person behind it who is on the customer's side; who is ensuring that, if you put your name to something, it'd better be good. It's like putting your house on the line; if you're not willing to do it, your business doesn't deserve to succeed. If you don't believe in your name, how can you expect other people to give you money? It leads to some problems, but it makes you bloody determined to sort them out because it hurts you personally if you get something wrong.

Boden rather self-effacingly describes how, at a board meeting in 1998, he forecast that retail use of the internet would never take off. Only around one-fifth of the business is now based on the catalogue, but he acknowledges that it remains a very important channel – for 'as long as people have lavatories' on which to sit and read it.

It is odd – or maybe it's just a personality trait – that Boden concentrates so much on where he has gone wrong, when so much of what he has done has plainly gone right. Had he not defied the wrath of the Lieutenant Colonel, one of the greatest British brand names would have been one of the worst City stockbrokers.

There's that wonderful story of Ted Turner when he broke the billion-dollar barrier of profits or something, and he got up to the podium, looked up to the sky, and said, 'Is that good enough, Dad?' Although I'm not thinking quite so directly in those terms, I do think a bit like that. Jim Collins, the business writer, has a very famous Venn diagram. If you're good at a job, and have a passion, and then have an economic interest: if you can find the job that's in the bull's eye, you're lucky. That's where I am. If you find something you enjoy and you're relatively good at it, you're pretty foolish to stop doing it. I think that, put simply, is why I'm still doing it.

He talks about his original ambition, which was to make the business single-mindedly personal, so that people felt they were talking to him, writing to him – and, indeed, for many years, they often were. At first, Boden answered all his own mail until the task became physically impossible. He is an honest man wanting to be honest; wanting to do something that reflects a high benchmark to which people can aspire. (He claims that the business was one of the very first to make it easy for customers to opt out of future mailings.) Maybe the liberation suggested by his catalogues is an expression of something that was not available to him in his early upbringing.

I really like people. My mother was very like this. She loved people. She didn't like stuffy people and she loved mixing around. Although we had the regimental background, she was a very open, warm person and I tried to learn from that and be approachable. I try and have that culture in this office; not to be too stuffy.

In the street, I do sometimes get recognised and that's fine by me. It's my choice and people will come up and talk to me about clothes. Occasionally, it can be awkward, but usually people are nice. It's funny, I was in the airport when we came back from holiday a couple of months ago and I went up to this woman who was wearing one of our things. I just wanted to say that it was a lovely shirt she had on. I thought she'd be really pleased – a nice thing to do – but she was just so embarrassed. People sometimes do get quite embarrassed actually seeing you; it's not necessarily a nice experience for them.

It comes down to this: the man likes people. One of Boden's most obvious strengths is his empathy. Along the company corridors, this translates into a belief in upholding good levels of staff morale. He explains how, when things are going badly, he tries to be the first to take responsibility: a kind of fault-owning from the front. He says he hates blame culture and defensive behaviours. Hence, he likes upward appraisals, where junior staff give feedback on seniors. It's all about people being aware of both their skills and their shortcomings, and dealing with each in a way that benefits everyone.

When Julian Granville – now my fantastic MD – came in as finance director, I realised very quickly that he was a much better manager than I was. Entrepreneurs like me make for terrible managers. So I stepped down. I've got many faults. But from having a demanding father, I think I developed a lack of arrogance. I suppose I'm arrogant in certain ways, but in many ways, I'm not. So if somebody tells me I'm not very good at something, on the whole I listen. I think that does slightly set me apart. I think a lot of entrepreneurs fail because they have too strong a self-belief, which means that they don't listen.

The Boden operation is growing worldwide these days, and there are plans for more expansion in the US (which accounts for around one-third of revenue), Germany, Austria, and France, where the enthusiasm of UK customers has been mirrored. He is aware of the pitfalls, such as overstretching. And, of course, there is the dreaded 'Boden fatigue' phenomenon, whereby women don't react too well when they turn up for a garden barbeque wearing the same print as the host. There is even a story, apocryphal or not, that Holkham in Norfolk was once rechristened Boden-on-Sea.

You can't be too confident, because you need to be sympathetic to what your customers want. The biggest mistake you can make is to stop listening to your customers. That's my sort of wanting-to-please gene. I sometimes overhear people saying, 'Oh, that's not very Boden.' Even if I'm in the room. Some people know the brand better than I do.

The 2012 *Sunday Times* Rich List puts Boden at number 255 of the UK's richest estates, valued at £320 million. Yet still he is 'terrified of losing money and having to borrow, because of what I've been through.' It's all relative, though, and, for Boden, money is the by-product (if a very handy one in practical terms) of his driving business ambition, which is his consuming motivation in life after his family.

Obviously, I am affluent and I'm extremely grateful for that, but I've worked hard for it. Now, I want for nothing financially, which is great, although in retail, one is only as good as one's last range. Anything could happen. There are upsides to wealth, but there are downsides as well. If you're neurotic like me, you worry all the time. Once, I used to worry about the credit cards bouncing and all that kind of stuff. That's now been replaced by loads of other worries that crop up. I slept quite well last night actually, but I'd say three nights a week I wake up at about four o'clock and worry. You worry that you're not being a very good father because you're so bloody worried about work all the time; you worry about your children growing up; there's still loads of worries but they just become different sorts of worries.

As the session concludes, Boden worries over whether he has given enough information during the interview, and will probably stay awake all night fretting about it. He is cursed by self-doubt, but gifted with an entrepreneurial skill that uncomprehending parents and a lot of bad luck could not stifle. His business acumen may be a consequence of those circumstances – but it shows, perhaps, that the good guys can win in the long run. Outside the sun is shining; recession or no recession, Acton or North Korea, an hour or so with Boden makes the world seem all right. That's why people love the brand. Because it bears the name and spirit and set of values of a truly likeable character.

Sprout, meanwhile, has taken Mrs Boden home.

———

'A work-room should be like an old shoe; no matter how shabby, it's better than a new one.'

WILLA CATHER

———

EMMA BRIDGEWATER

(Emma Bridgewater)

INTERVIEWED 20 JULY 2012

The taxi drops you in Lichfield Street, outside the factory: an ascetic Victorian building, with thick Trent brickwork, that has escaped the humiliation of being converted into unoccupied apartments. Instead, it remains occupied by those who belong there, who can be seen through the windows making something that is real and physical. This Stoke-on-Trent factory is now a tinderbox for revitalised UK pottery manufacture, where a British economic recovery – founded on industrial expertise rather than on services – might just get rekindled.

The cluster of pottery factories that remain here have history and ghosts – from a time around the eighteenth century when stern-looking Staffordshire beadles, usually called Josiah, were building a local economy from clay. Stoke-on-Trent had the right earth and water for making pottery, along with plenty of miners nearby digging coal. And it had the right attitude. Its entrepreneurs, if they required a canal, just dug one, losing a few lives or peasant cottages as necessity demanded. With such determination did the area build its global reputation for celebrated ceramics brands like Wedgwood, Spode, Minton, Royal Worcester, and Royal Doulton.

Alas, by the end of the twentieth century, ever more production had been sucked into the cheaper Asian markets, and the pottery industry in Stoke had all but collapsed. The exceptions were a handful of British ceramics brands – Dudson, Steelite International, Churchill, Johnson Tiles, and Portmeirion (owners of Spode and Royal Worcester) – who refused to quit their spiritual homeland. And in the middle of it all, not a Josiah, but an Emma.

Emma Bridgewater, in fact. A relatively late arrival to the industry, this company has become one of the largest, and arguably most high profile, of the fully-UK-based ceramics operations. From a turnover of £30,000 in its first year of trading in 1985, the figure reached £15 million in 2011. There are now 265 staff, turning out about 25,000 hand-decorated items every single week, using techniques that would not have seemed unusual a couple of centuries ago. It's all allied to an enthusiastic publicity machine, equipped to deal with public tours and entertainment, and an energetic retailing facility on site as well. A polka-dotted sign on the gable end says, 'You've just spotted Emma Bridgewater.' Not quite yet we haven't. In fact, we can't even find the office, of which there is literally no sign at all.

Instead, the factory shop has to be the place to start looking for the figure leading this minor renaissance: the person who has been getting her hands dirty with real old clay, rather than ephemeral City money. Private equity and pension fund managers would frown at what is going on here, because they don't like anything that defies easy analysis, and probably can't pigeonhole indomitable females like this one, who know what they want and how to get it.

Recently, Bridgewater and her husband, Matthew Rice, were awarded honorary degrees from Keele, just up the road, for what was described as their 'enormous contribution to the ceramic industry of North Staffordshire and the local community'. At the ceremony, Rice said, 'When you join a family, you get involved with what they love, whatever that might be, and what I got was Stoke-on-Trent.' That, as they say, is the territory that comes with this particular woman.

Progress back in the shop is leisurely. Satisfied that we don't want to buy a plate or paint our own polka-dot pattern onto a mug, the friendly lady at the counter gives a convoluted series of directions, which we follow to reach a reception area. Another friendly lady (who looks so identical to the first friendly lady that she probably *is* the first friendly lady) arrives, taking over the mantle of guide, as we step into a catacomb of corridors, doors, stairs down, stairs back up, then across shop floors, and back up more stairs, more corridors, and through more doors. You would not be surprised to find a few World War Two soldiers unaware that the war has ended. After further travel we arrive at something called the 'Studio', and here we finally find our Emma Bridgewater.

Born in 1962, Bridgewater used to talk about reaching 40 as her low point. Now that she's put another decade on that figure, she's become more philosophical.

I don't think I'm unusual in that most women don't like those big landmark birthdays at all. Once you're there, you can't think what the fuss was all about, but most people have a midlife crisis, don't they? I think that somewhere in your forties, you wonder who you really are. You've been carrying a lot of different versions of what you're going to be – a rock star, a novelist, a literary agent, and all the other things – and then somewhere north of 40, you have to let go of all that and accept your one life. I've got a lot of parallel lives unlived, but you suddenly realise it's probably not going to happen. It's the inherent sadness of ageing…

In fact, nowadays, she feels that she has less time than ever to be side-tracked by something as trivial as mortality.

When we meet, she is sitting in the corner of the large, busy studio, which she shares with some of her executives and an unidentifiable clutter that fills a good proportion of the physical space. Creative disorder is a comforting thing for Bridgewater, and it makes her feel at home. Getting up from what could pass as a kitchen table, she does a circuit of the room to deal with a handful of administrative issues, and then sits back down, applying lipstick without a mirror and while still speaking – a trick she completes in one impressively accurate, linear action.

Gypsy-dark-haired, with unusual, deep, smiley brown eyes, her accent is a peripatetic's curry of stretched *Made in Chelsea* vowels seasoned with North Norfolk, East Midlands, and what sounds a bit like media-trained royalty. All in all, she cuts a rather feisty, elegant-without-trying presence, moving and speaking in a brisk, no-nonsense fashion. Interviewing her is a fun, but slightly formidable venture; it feels that any momentary lapse in intellectual rigour may incur a rap across your knuckles with a ruler.

A capable spokesperson, Bridgewater has made numerous media appearances, including on *Newsnight* opposite Paxman. In that situation, you would bet on her ability to fend off any mean opening delivery, but she actually downplays it all.

We were on for the easy bit at the end, so we didn't get a roasting. Paxman is such a pro and he's in total control. Watching your telly at home, you might think you could have a pop at him, but it would be a huge mistake. On the night, he was very nice, but he had just given some poor girl an absolute grilling, so you knew that by our turn, he was easing off. I was talking about Stoke-on-Trent, so it wasn't going to be difficult for me. My only difficulty was that I was on with Ed Vaizey and Tristram Hunt and, frankly, if anyone can get a word in edgeways between those two, they're doing well.

One of eight siblings (from three different marriages), Bridgewater spent the majority of her childhood in Oxford, sitting, for what appears to have been hours on end, around a buzzy, crumb-scattered kitchen table where no item of crockery matched any other. With the nearby academic spires making their influence felt, she became a prematurely well-read child, in a way that would qualify her as a nerd in today's progressively ill-read society. By the time she was eight, and with her parents divorcing, books seemed like the safest place in which to hide rather than risk exposure to the kitchen angst.

I was the oldest and an observant, watching kind of child. I don't remotely feel scarred by what happened in the divorce, but I learned early on that if I was reading, then I got more leeway. So I got a book, and hid in airing cupboards and behind curtains and read and read. I developed a huge fiction habit and I reckon it saved my life. I'm sure that it is a major trait of the eldest children during a divorce. We're just quite good at finding ways to disappear.

Before the divorce, we'd lived in Bassingbourn in Hertfordshire near where my grandfather was the vicar. I've got an enormous family, and there are lots of cousins all over the place. After the split, we went with Mum to live in Oxford. She always said she was very sad to stop being Charlotte Bridgewater after the divorce, but I still felt like a Jane Austen heroine. We were Emma, Sophie, Tom, Eleanor, and Clover – she went a bit off-piste with the younger one.

Here in the studio, Bridgewater sits talking in front of a dresser stacked with mugs and plates and other crockery, and were there a few more empty breakfast plates on the table and the smell of grilled bacon in the air, it could easily pass for her own domestic kitchen (or that of her mother, 40 years ago). Most of her own publicity shots feature her in front of a plate-stacked pine dresser, suggesting that the furniture is dragged along behind her wherever she goes, caught in her handbag. It's an obvious way of showcasing her wares, but is also a sign of the emotive link between the woman and her business.

Indeed, there is something eccentrically personal about this company and the environment. Without ego, the place nonetheless feels *hers*. Her domain; her thing; her name on the bottom of the mug. *Emma* Bridgewater. It's what people – staff, customers, and the residents of Stoke-on-Trent – love about the company: the fact that she has given of herself.

When the brand became just Bridgewater, *it became less to do with me – and I felt it became a sort of blander brand. So when I stepped back in to restructure the company, it felt really important, to make it absolutely clear, that it was* Emma *Bridgewater and that it* is *me. I love the fact that people assume, largely because we're in a Victorian factory, that this is a very old family business, but, of course, that ain't the case.*

But it is still an emotional thing. Very. I get emotional about the closing factories and people being made redundant without there being any engaging in it. When a company stops being run as if it were a family business and as an impersonal, ever bigger conglomeration, decisions are made about redundancies and outsourcing in a very heartless way and I hate that.

It helps if you have a name that invites respect (and you can see why she has held on to her maiden name): hers is so replete with solid consonants and inbuilt metaphor that, in one of her parallel lives, it might have been provided with a definite article and put on the bows of a transatlantic steamliner. For this life, a Staffordshire factory will have to suffice as a home for her name. In fact, Bridgewater is as proud of the grimy edifice as she would be if it *were* her own home.

She mentions that she has been thinking about her life recently, and has been trying to put things into a perspective of sorts. She doesn't say whether she has always done this, or if it's a new pastime, but Bridgewater is a deep-thinking and erudite individual. Like many aspects of her life, her relationship with literature is notable for its personal element, and she talks of famous literary figures as though they were a current gang of libidinous Bloomsbury bedfellows.

I fell very badly in love with Shakespeare at about 13 or 14 and then came along Thomas Hardy. Then Charles Dickens – I just had one massive, massive crush on him. Then I did American literature: Steinbeck, Faulkner; I hate Hemingway, but now I absolutely love Cormac McCarthy. A lot of my life is spent with my head in books. Somewhere in my second year at university, I really got the point of what I was doing. I read a lot of Middle English – completely thrilling stuff. I'd got quite serious about my work and I loved the business of knowing that you can do something well. It's left me with a passionate conviction that education should not be vocational, but broad and humanities-based. I think it's a big asset to bring a liberal education to industry. If this business works, it's in no small part because I didn't train as an economist or a lawyer but as someone who read Anglo-Saxon literature with passion and pleasure.

She missed getting a University of London 'first' from Bedford College, but reckons that she might have done so had she got herself into gear a bit quicker (self-evidently so, but we all say the same thing). Nonetheless, literature is, in no small part, a strong influence, and much of her character seems less likely to have come from kitchen table chat than from the heroines of Shakespearean and Victorian literature who have been squatting in the study-cubicles of her consciousness since she was hiding behind the curtains at the age of eight. She argues that, even in today's net-savvy world, traditional and classical literature combined remains one of the most effective of ways of inspiring people.

No surprise, then, that after university, with her graduation gown still tepid, she went off to join the London literati. The advice she got there foreshadowed much of her thinking today.

I thought I'd be a literary agent and went to talk with Felicity Bryan, the great doyenne of agents. She said it was a really lovely career and thought I should try for it, but then she asked me why I didn't write a novel, because that would be even nicer than being an agent. And if it wasn't published, it wouldn't matter because that makes you a much better agent. I loved that logic. It was hugely influential advice. She made it look as if life can be a win-win. Just roll your sleeves up and get on with it whatever. Whereas my mum would say things like, 'But darling, you're not really qualified to design plates, are you?' I felt much more in tune with Felicity's philosophy, which was to just have a go, and, if you don't succeed, you'll know more about briefing a person who can.

But instead of becoming a literary agent or novelist or playwright or other metropolitan *bon vivant*, Bridgewater took a job at a knitting company. Not much difference there then. It was her first and only full-time salaried position, and looking back, she still regards her experience at the rather implausibly titled (for a knitting company) Muir & Osborne as seminal.

After my finals, my dad said that he would pay me an allowance until the September, but after that I'd be under my own steam. That summer,

I was living with a photographer in Brixton. September came and I still didn't have a job and he was starting to panic about me. But then there was a friend of his whose small knitwear business was having a surge and they needed an extra pair of hands.

They were hilariously funny, good, clever, girls with no formal training but a great enthusiasm for what they were making. It was a great experience of the kind that people leaving university should have. If you're interested in a creative career, go and work in a small, creative company and ask a million questions. They drew a veil over some of their finances, but by the time I left I understood most of the strengths and weaknesses of their set-up. I'd sewn on a million labels and buttons and even walked the dogs. It's really important that you understand that you're not good for much when you come out of university, but if your brain's working then you can learn. But to do that, you've got to be willing to pitch up at nine in the morning and stay there until ten at night. Over time, I got to do the trade fairs in America, recruited hundreds of home-knitters, and packed up a million knitting kits to cope with their demand. There were so many interesting challenges.

What I learned from them meshed with what I'd seen in my father's more businesslike, suited-and-booted kind of set-up... so I thought, 'Well, that's great. Now I know everything there is to know about running a business. I've got £350 in the bank and so I'm going to start my own business.' It's marvellous what ignorance can do at a time when you've nothing to lose. My deal with myself was to cast around and find a project, a service, a product or something.

As a student, I'd been hugely overdrawn at times. I progressed from working for my father in the holidays to working as a waitress in Covent Garden, which was far more lucrative. So, each holiday, I could earn loads of quick money and pay off my debts. The bank saw me as the perfect customer; they could make lots of money out of me, but then I always came back into balance. Now, I was prepared to get to a certain level of indebtedness, and trade out of my current account, which is pretty much what I did.

Bridgewater sees her 'ambition' (as she phrases it) as coming from her father, who ran his own publishing business. She claims that she saw what he did and wanted to do better: 'I always thought I would build and sell and beat Dad, and be quicker at making money than him.'

However, the genesis of her own business occurred in a china shop in Cirencester when she was looking for a gift for her mum. Over and above the paternal entrepreneurial genes, the reason why this business began was Bridgewater's love of her mum's kitchen. No matter where you are in this story, that single meeting place in the house in Oxford is never far from the narrative. Perhaps that is what she means when she says that a business should be founded in reality.

I was standing in a shop wondering what I could get Mum for her birthday. I wanted to buy her some cups and saucers, because kitchen life was central to her and how I think of her: in her house, the kitchen was a very, sort of, convivial place where everybody wanted to be. I stood in that china shop and thought that nobody sensible would want to buy any of it, compared to the feel of the china in our kitchen at home, which was a complete mixture. There were some nice things available, such as from Habitat, but there was very little available that acknowledged the fact of real life lived around the kitchen table. I had a picture in my mind of exactly what it ought to look like.

I'd loved art at school, but if you were capable of it, they wanted you to do academic subjects, not art. However, I still had a built-up reservoir of creativity and could picture how these things needed to look: the cup and saucer that I wished I were giving Mum... I was talking about this to a graphic-designer friend, older than me, who was very businesslike and successful in London. He knew a model-maker in Stoke-on-Trent... in the Potteries, and so I made an appointment.

I set to work with him, using my imprecise drawings, and then went back a few days later after he'd turned them up in plaster and we played around some more: I wanted it fatter here and thinner there, then he turned another one and we played with flat paper profiles of the spout, the handle. The dish, the jug, and the mug are still in production and the original bowl has been through quite a few versions since. It was thrilling. I was designing, to my mind, a quintessential English earthenware look, which is what I like best. He then slip-cast some for me and biscuit-fired them, and I rattled back to London in my Mini Metro and experimented with the decoration.

It wasn't long before she had bought her own kiln and stuck it in the bathroom of her rented flat in London. Dragging something the weight of a Steinway Concert Grand compressed into the dimensions of a fridge up a few flights of stairs must have made for an interesting morning. Before long, Bridgewater was not only designing her own mugs, jugs, and dishes, but actually firing them as well.

The story of my life is to walk out to the end of the plank. When I got on the train at Euston, I'd no idea what lay ahead. And when I got off at Stoke [to visit the model-maker], I was absolutely blown away by it; astonished by the extraordinary decrepitation of a city with such amazing traditions. That was in '84, when there were many more factories than now. Even then, as you walked through the city, you could see cobwebby windows with piles and piles and piles of all this pottery. It just felt so completely gripping. There was something going on: they were making stuff. In Oxford, where I grew up, they'd been making brains and, now I'd come here, I saw how they were making pots.

I'd always had a real feeling for ruins, clambering over the walls as a teenager in Norfolk. I like a ruined church or a ruined castle even more than the compete version. So when I got off that train and saw Stoke, I thought that this was one ruin that I really could love and would really like to see thriving. In my mind, I could see a big Victorian factory making my things.

By 1985, Bridgewater had her own business up and running, and she did not think too long about putting her full name on it. This seems of huge importance to her, as though it acts as a guarantee of emotional as well as financial investment. To this day, each person at the factory who hand-paints a cup or plate adds his or her own initials. 'A business doesn't work unless you throw yourself at it,' she adds.

Yet, although the company is a one-person eponym, her husband, Matthew Rice, has, almost since day one, been an intrinsic part of its operation and its success. Born in the same year as Bridgewater, Rice is well-known in his own right, as a painter, designer, and author. Having trained as a theatre designer, he developed a bespoke furniture, desk accessories and stationery business with David Linley (the son of Princess Margaret, and his old school friend from Bedales, who features in a later chapter), based out of a seriously trendy shop on the New King's Road.

My drawing skills are nothing like my husband's. When I saw his work and some of the ceramics designs he was doing with David Linley, I thought, I really don't want to be competing with him. I really loved what he was doing and I could see it was going to be good. So, if you can't beat 'em...

I was manning a stand at a little trade fair called Top Drawer, which still exists, and which is very good for start-up creative companies. I didn't know anything about trade fairs and so I treated it more like a party. I'd get several cases of wine and buy armfuls of daffs and put them in tin buckets. Matthew went past and I saw him and David return a couple of times, staring, and I was a bit shocked when he came over and started asking a lot of questions. But I said, 'Look, come on, you can see I'm on my own here. I'm really busy. I know where your shop is. If you want to buy some stuff, why don't we talk about it after the show?' I was a bit sharp. Anyway, we did and one thing led to another. Luckily, my secretary (who's still a very good friend, actually) spotted very quickly what a very unusual and marvellous person Matthew is, and accepted on my behalf that I'd have lunch with him.

Reader, she married him. In 1987. From the start, their partnership was seamless, with no clear distinction between life inside and outside of the business. Nowadays, they are often to be seen promoting the company together, and harmonising their complementary talents. However you look at it, for this pair, it's all personal.

As they got into the rhythm of a shared journey, with the nineties approaching, the way ceramics were viewed on the high street was starting to change. In trendy parts of west London, boutiques were selling mugs with stripes and dots and dogs' names on them, alongside the daft chrome juicers and acid-yellow Italian corkscrews. In the cinemas, Demi Moore and Patrick Swayze would soon be spicing up matters pottery-style by mutually onanising a clay vase. Bridgewater had been ahead of the game, but now other companies were thinking the same thing as she had been doing in the Cirencester china shop. Pottery really could be colourful and trendy, it seemed.

Bridgewater was on a roll, when, in 1992, her suppliers went bust – yet another legacy of the bad management and outdated practices that had been crippling Midlands industry since the seventies – leaving a small workforce about to be wiped out. True to character, she simply bought the factory and took over the payroll of the 35 staff. When, after another five years, Bridgewater had outgrown those premises, the company relocated again into the Meakin building in Hanley, overlooking the canal – the current site.

Most people in our position would have eventually diluted their shareholding, taken on investment, and hooked up with a lot of VCs, which would have led us away from manufacturing in Stoke-on-Trent. But Matthew and I wanted to hang on to our majority shareholder position and all that went with that. We are obsessed with remaining here in Stoke within the tradition of British industrial ceramics. So many rats have left the sinking ship, when actually, it's not sinking at all; it's perfectly sound as it happens. In fact, it's a fantastic place to manufacture. But if people only think profit, they make dreadful decisions: there is more to life than a profit margin, and companies should, where possible, audit themselves on more than the bottom line.

Over the last 50 years, the effect of closing factories in the Midlands has been catastrophic. It happened without a plan for what was going to happen to the people that were left behind. These great cities were written out of the national narrative and just dumped. There was that magnificent moment when Gordon Brown turned round, with the City collapsing in ruins around his ears, and said, 'but of course, our marvellous British industry can save us.' There was a loud noise of ministers going, 'Oh my God, what's industry? Where is it? Brief me, brief me.'

At which juncture we come back to Bridgewater's mother, Char Stroud – not to discuss further merits of her eclectic kitchen, but to splice the narrative with a tragedy. It occurred over 20 years ago, but its effects are not of the kind that can be easily resolved, or, for that matter, put into any kind of rational perspective. At the age of 53, out horse-riding, she was thrown to the ground and left severely brain-damaged. She is still alive, in care, but has literally no idea of her environment, let alone what her children have done with their careers.

The business was fairly established and I was married with two small children when it happened. Nothing prepares you for it. It was a very traumatic time. I suppose what it did was precipitate us out of London. After it happened, my stepfather sensibly waited two years before making the decision to sell the house, by which time he had realised that she would need to be looked after by someone else. She had some time in intensive care in a coma and then a bit more in recovery, but physically she was back to normal fairly quickly; so they soon discharged her from hospital. But she was impossible for us to look after. We tried doing it as a family for two years, but then my stepfather took the sensible view that whatever benefit we were giving her by being at home, it was being outweighed by the enormous disbenefit to all of us of trying to do what was just far too difficult.

I think a tragedy like this fires you up. I don't exactly understand why, but in some strange, probably quite simple way, what you're doing in your career, you're doing it for her. It's often unfocused and there can be anger, but there's a real longing to put it right – even though you can't really.

One of my sisters has a circus, a travelling circus, which is about as difficult a life as you could possibly imagine, such is the hardship and pressure she puts on herself. Yet the result of what she does is incredibly beautiful. I always think when I go see her that maybe she is doing it as a tribute to Mum. Maybe I'm doing that too; trying to put misery right. And, you know what? It's actually the last thing Mum would have wanted. She was a marvellously restful, peaceful, gorgeous person, and the thought that the accident has inspired Nell and me to have such restless lives... she'd be really amazed and not especially pleased. So it's not as though it's all a well-thought tribute; it's just how we've been fired up; the coping mechanism, maybe.

As we've already said, Bridgewater belonged to a large family and she and Rice have followed the pattern with their four children (from grown-up Elizabeth to a young teenage Michael, with Kitty and Margaret in between), who have become accustomed to a disorganised kitchen being the most important room in the house. The dresser that appears in every company picture is also there at home, full of her own designs and antique china handed down from mother and grandmother – treasured stuff that she's known all of her life.

Bridgewater says that this kind of thing is how she stays 'connected to my roots, which is incredibly important'. Nowadays, thankfully, her home life has settled down somewhat from the traumatic years – an experience that she does not downplay. 'Those times were a nightmare... Horrible,' she says, without bothering to choose her words too carefully.

The years after the accident were incredibly hard. I rented a friend's room in London, and stayed in cheap B&Bs in the Midlands. I was trying to be frugal and did everything myself. As anyone knows who has his or her own business, there was no end to the working day. Just at a time when the children were needing me as well. We were living in Norfolk and I would come here, and it was an absolutely awful, four-hour drive, over the Fens and Leicestershire Wolds a million times, down to London, back to Norfolk.

I've spent so much of my life at the wheel of a car, although at least it's meant lots and lots of contemplation time. I've still got a filthy Volkswagen Golf, 08 reg. Apart from a brief time with a people-mover, I've been brand loyal, so if you could get me a sponsored top-of-the-range Golf, that would be absolutely marvellous. Actually I don't care, because I like the one I've got. When you find something that works, you can absolve yourself from decision-making. I'm keen on not having to make decisions all the time.

After the accident, around that time, I was running up an absolutely huge mileage before even starting on schools and shopping and going to hockey matches or whatever. So it was just mad. But it was also lovely living in Norfolk with Matthew's wonderful parents nearby, and the schools were working for the children and Matthew had made a lovely garden, so there were so many reasons not to move as well. So I thought I could cope with the strain for a bit.

She couldn't. Bridgewater refuses to elevate it to the status of a breakdown, but she reached a point where she simply could not carry on, physically and mentally, with the task of running a company and a family, both of these in the formative stages of their development. She says that she was made of sterner stuff than to visit the doctor, but she also stresses that she eventually had the self-understanding to see that the problem needed a solution, or else it would have crushed her and everyone and everything around.

I think it was the driving, more than anything. That, and building a business. Whatever it was, I was exhausted. And I started finding the work pretty ghastly... and lonely. But then you think that it's very selfish on the other people who are struggling to be failing on not one, but two counts: the business wasn't growing and I was personally finding it exhausting as well. You feel there must be something very badly wrong with you personally. You've got to be ready to admit that things have to give. It's a little bit like making your house look impeccable for a magazine, which I've always been very careful not to do. You can make yourself extremely miserable trying to do everything perfectly. No one is perfect, but women get forced into thinking they have to be.

The trouble with then being an entrepreneur is that you never think you've finished. You're always thinking of things you haven't done. We employ over two hundred people here and I wish it was two thousand, and at two thousand I'd be wishing for five thousand. I never feel satisfied. I can only ever see the bits still to do. I never say to myself, 'Well done.'

I got rheumatoid arthritis and was quite incapacitated by it, but I still pushed myself on. Then I got a message from a friend of my dad who said, 'Tell Emma that she won't sort out the rheumatoid arthritis unless she takes the stress out of her life.' I had been pushing myself on and on and I suddenly realised that I had to do something: I couldn't carry on. It was at that point that Matthew got engaged in the administration. I think he'd seen how tough it had been for me, but it turned out that he could do it just as well as me; better in fact. I'd tripled the size of the business and then he more than doubled it.

I've built a switch-off mechanism, otherwise I'm not sure I'd have survived. I can remember the horror of sleepless nights I've had. Sometimes, you have to sort of use an escape like fiction; theatre is very good; cinema is brilliant; cinema and alcohol are very, very effective. I can remember going to see Gosford Park, *at a very hard time, sitting in the front row having had two large vodkas, feeling absolutely no pain at all.*

Bridgewater's narrative can, at times, be as unstructured as her dresser, but that's part of the appeal and probably a clue to her success. One minute, she'll be talking about Georgette Heyer's Regency romances (she loves her romances but hates her crime novels), then she's moved on to remedies for backache, while switching mid-sentence to mentioning what the government should be doing over its latest energy and VAT policies. Few people would be able to make such pertinent connections between things like macro-economic policy and domestic gardening.

There are many people like me who have pedalled against the tide of complete political ignorance over what industry needs. Such as energy policies after energy policies that are so ridiculously nonsensical, and the way that government has implemented the VAT changes. It indicates that no minister has ever gone anywhere near a retail operation.

At last, we're now getting friends in government, which is marvellous. Having not seen them for decades, you can't move for ministers these days, and suddenly we're flavour of the month. I've been made an industry champion, which means they just wheel me out to go on a panel with Vince Cable. Even so, it's really important that we try and get across the message that making real things is important, and that children leaving school and university might contemplate an industrial career from the start. I often talk to undergraduates in Oxford about this, but it's hard for them to resist the blandishments of the banks and law firms who roll out the red carpet into the good universities. In this country, we're still not training enough engineers or investing enough in design and we're being overlapped by the rest of the world. If I had my way, I'd like all children to go round factories while still at primary school. We do bring quite a few in here, but not enough.

The West has really got to think very hard about what's going to power us through the next century. Unless we make things, we're doomed. It always felt crazy to me the idea that you could push money around and make money: it was going to end in tears and it did. We make things, and I feel that everyone else should. On a basic level, you should cook from scratch, you should garden, and you should, wherever you possibly can, touch real life and claim your own life for yourself.

The company recently reached its 25th anniversary, celebrated by the Potteries Museum, but Bridgewater eschews self-congratulation or self-indulgence. She has the dismissive humility that is often evident in the strong, who know only too well that strength is a relative asset, and can be one of the most transient too. She feels that her job is not yet done, and indeed stresses that all visions she has of the future of the company are based around her commitment and involvement.

You know how it is: be careful what you dream of, because you might just get it. Actually, it feels like what I dreamed has come to be. But you don't realise how difficult it is to let go of the inherent things that you still haven't got quite right. Matthew and I get quite wrapped up in all we do. We love the designing and we love the making here, but it takes up an enormous amount of one's time and energy. We probably don't spend enough time outside the business, but that's our choice.

I don't get frightened easily. I've taken us to the brink, but my view was that we simply had to pull it off, rather than worry over what might happen if we failed. For me, the principal driver isn't money. It's the brand; the business; achieving what I envisaged when I first came to Stoke, which is what's so exciting to me and what I steer by.

Although my parents and stepfather were always generous, I think I inherited a bit of angst about money from my grandparents: not having quite enough, living tight, feeling worried. Maybe I did too much earwigging of distant adult conversations – there's a lesson there – and combined it with an overactive imagination and too many Edwardian children's novels. However, once you start to make what once might have seemed a lot of money, it brings its own new set of hideous complications and responsibilities. In Matthew and me, you just couldn't find a couple who have less desire to stay in fancy resorts or hotels or drive fast cars. For him, money means land to do something beautiful with; to me, it's about trying to make some lovely things happen here. And do funny things: like, I have a sister with learning difficulties and it's her birthday next week, so I'm hiring a pink stretch limo to collect her and take her to the circus. I just like to do stupid things like that. It only cost a few hundred quid, but it's what Mum couldn't have done because she was always careful with money.

We've bought the site of Bampton Castle, but all that's left is a shard and ruins. It's a beautiful place in a lovely, funny, mad village, obsessed with morris dancing. I've increasingly realised, when you lift the carpet of metropolitan silliness, even in the soft south of England, that there's still lots of real life going on in Britain, and this is an example; another really strange and interesting connection we've been able to make with a very rural community.

Rice has been busy planting hundreds of trees in the castle grounds. It's the kind of thing that the pair love to do in their spare time, seeking to add extra layers of meaning to their lives – in between their enthusiasm for inviting large numbers of people to their home practically every other weekend. She explains that Rice and she have skills well suited to pottery, but that there are many other strings to their bow as well.

Bridgewater says that some of the tasks she has set herself in life have not turned out as intended. 'It's all too easy to set yourself goals, and work tremendously hard, but when you get there, it isn't always what you thought it would be like,' she says. She warns against seeing challenges as too linear, and says that age and wisdom have taught her instead that life is more like a complex trip along numerous intersecting routes.

I like being in the eye of the storm; I'm not trying to get in from the rain. I seek out stories of strong women – fictional or real. I come from a line of very self-determining women: Elizabeth Garrett Anderson, the first woman surgeon, was my great-great-aunt or something and Elizabeth Fry [the prison reformer] was my five-greats-aunt. Educated, pioneering women who assumed that they were going to get things done. The notion of pioneering is hugely resonant for me. I was inspired by a book by a woman called Willa Cather – My Ántonia. It's about the Bohemian settlers in Nebraska and the women pioneers. In fact, there's a whole wonderful world of literature on the building of America, which I totally love.

That's why I'm gripped by the bits of America, such as across the Midwest, that nobody ever visits. Some of our best holidays have been there. It fills me with an enormous sense of a life unlived: the vastness of America; the opportunity and the stimulation of it; of an unfulfilled area of possibility. Maybe one day I'll go and live there. But I doubt it.

Stoke will, and Britain should, be relieved to hear it. Bridgewater's own story is the kind that the country needs to hear now more than ever. At its peak in the nineteenth century, the Potteries had more than two thousand kilns on full output, making millions of products each year. By 1970, about two hundred factories were left. Between 1998 and 2008, around twenty thousand jobs were lost. And by 2012, with Britain in the grip of a fierce economic slump, there were only around thirty factories left, the success of one of which is resting on the shoulders of this determined woman who draws inspiration from talking about her mum's old kitchen.

But 2012 was also the year when the Olympics returned to Britain, and Stoke-on-Trent took its place in the unique street phenomenon that the torch relay became in British hands. As it passed the Potteries Museum nearby, tens of thousands of locals braved predictably dull weather, as they had done in just about every other town in the land, to wave in secular rapture at the small figure in white with a stick of gold. A global concept, literally embraced by, and interpreted through the lens of, British enthusiasm. The mood for the Queen's Diamond Jubilee was the same, allowing people a channel for patriotism, optimism, and felicity – at a time when a good deal of the media narrative is of either breathtaking grimness or whingeing curmudgeonliness.

The uplift in mood, at times like these, is Bridgewater's told-you-so moment. She is a fan and vociferous advocate of her country, and it was hardly surprising when the company went big with its unashamedly jolly Diamond Jubilee line, much of which was specially designed by Rice. It was, of course, an outstanding success. But this kind of optimism does not please everybody. The era of austerity has given an excuse to those disparaging anything that hints at middle-class aspiration.

A large majority of people love what she does, just as they loved celebrating the Olympics and the Diamond Jubilee. They love the optimism and the dedication. And that is really what Bridgewater is advocating. 'Britons can be all sorts of things which are hard to understand... but great things happen when they are allowed to express themselves in the way that comes naturally to them,' says Bridgewater. And, in many ways, she has been an inspirational catalyst for that.

Bridgewater never stops banging the drum about the potential in her country. 'After 25 years in business, I don't understand why more people are not doing something more about it.' Signally, Bridgewater *is* doing that something more: with her factory here in Stoke and shops in London, Bicester, and Edinburgh selling ceramics, but also expanding into stationery, gift-wrapping, and even bedding. The Royals have been here (twice) to recognise the fact.

It's so hard to be objective about your own life – your own career – isn't it? You're just in it. I feel very, very focused, but Matthew calls it obsessive: I don't let things drop. But as long as you don't set yourself up, then it's fine, isn't it? Sometimes, you find yourself pretending it's been easy. It hasn't; and it isn't. At some point, no matter who you are, you have to tread on faces and you'll need to have that in you if you're successful. For women, more so than men, it's quite hard to come to terms with that.

At the same time, I think that the brand is very informal and I think that, luckily, I am as well. I think it's what my mum was. Mum's influence is very pervasive; strangely, probably more in the business than in my family life. I feel that I'm trying to capture the spirit of what she made my home life like as a child; what was unusual and special about it. And then turn that into a business. It's a strange thing to want to do really, isn't it?

Mum is still alive, so I can't mourn her because she's alive, but I want to explain *her. I sort of feel that when we get this business right – in any aspect of the business – it's explaining her and what she stood for. And that feels very necessary – strangely.*

It is hard to define what exactly Bridgewater is battling *against*: government inertia, economic ineptitude, industrial decline, loss of local investment, uncaring fate, lack of room for another plate on the dresser. It could be any or all of these. But, in a way, it doesn't matter. Because she is battling *for* something: and that something is easy to understand. It is the country she loves, and what she is convinced is its reservoir of creative skill and artisan traditions; a belief that when people here put their minds to it, they can generate manufactured goods the envy of the world. 'These people have great skills. It's absolutely daft to fly halfway around the world when what you need is all here... it makes me hot with rage,' she says.

Central to her belief is Stoke-on-Trent, a place that 'really hit me between the eyes': a messy kitchen of a city for this southern bookworm to have adopted back in 1984 straight off the Euston train. Now she will have no bad word spoken against it and its people; she loves it as though she had been born and bred in the place and fights for it most days of her life. She is, of course, an equally odd child for it to adopt, but the city has surely taken her to its heart as she has it to hers. Neither would be what each is without the other. It may be North Staffordshire rather than Red Flag, Nebraska, and the early part of a different century from that of her heroine, but the woman sitting in a warm studio rather than on an arid American plain can, without hyperbole, call herself a pioneer. Not least because she is the type of modern SME entrepreneur on whom Britain's future economic prosperity now rests.

The people for Bridgewater's next appointment have arrived, and it's time to end the interview and leave. She is running behind schedule now, and excuses herself from acting as guide back to reception. 'Forgive me,' she says, 'but I'm sure you know the way back out.' It is the only moment in the entire interview when Bridgewater's faith seems misguided.

'The truly important things in life – love, beauty, and one's own uniqueness – are constantly being overlooked.'

PABLO CASALS

JACKIE COOPER

(JCPR Edelman)

INTERVIEWED 27 SEPTEMBER 2012

After our earlier discussions with the political guru Tim Bell, we now return to the world of PR, but this time venturing to a different part of the industry, a very different style of company, and a very different style of entrepreneur; to the London offices of JCPR, which stands for Jackie Cooper Public Relations. The eponymous co-founder is our next interviewee.

Since launch, well over two decades ago, JCPR has handled a range of iconic brand 'properties': from Wembley Stadium to the Concorde airliner; from Levi's to MTV; Mars, Microsoft, O2, Wonderbra, Covent Garden, Mary-Kate & Ashley Olsen... Today's client list is a roll call of pre-eminent and familiar household names in both established and emergent markets alike. In 2004, the company was acquired by Edelman – the world's biggest and arguably most successful independently owned PR company – which led to our interviewee, Jackie Cooper, initially becoming creative director of the London business, then global vice-chair of brand properties for the combined international entity.

Here in London, Cooper's name is still over the door. We have come to a tall, shiny building in Victoria Street, which bristles with brisk business and decent suits. We wait in the reception area, perched on large black Alcantara sofas, so deep, you sit with your feet not reaching past the cushion; like Stuart Little, lost among the hectares of opulent fabric. This is PR land, easily (and sometimes unfairly) caricatured as a world of imagery and gloss. In reality, it's not Perfect Curve or *Ab Fab* – but it's not quite not, either.

connected to any culture at all until I was about 15. I was an only child, and you end up in a bubble-like unit with your mum and your dad and you...

The interesting part of this experience was that I would read a lot and have always loved being lost in the power of a wonderful story. My imagination was vivid and that remains to this day. I love being inspired by the imagination and not allowing myself to be restricted in thought – or letting account teams or clients be restricted in theirs.

Cooper married a fellow only-child, whom she mentions spontaneously ('a funny, upbeat, brave, generous, and pragmatic soul, who has supported me through thick and thin'). It's as though both she and her spouse share a common insight into the solitary state of being the sole child in the family.

My mum, who's still with us, is a New Yorker. My dad was terribly British, in a sort of David Niven-esque way. He was in marketing all of his life – a brilliant entrepreneur. So the culture that I grew up with was very mixed. I was so very aware of my American heritage – which I'm very proud of to this day. It makes what I do here much easier, because I'm very comfortable with either side of the pond. Plus, there was my dad's business entrepreneurial influence. And that was my world: the three of us; a tight sort of unit. But at the same time, I was painfully shy.

A fair proportion of Cooper's narrative is about *being different*. This woman who has built her business from making people and brands stand out was, during her early years, impeded by her own acute sense of difference. Maybe she is exactly the right person to know how to create difference *and* how to deal with it.

What's the point of doing any of this work unless you make a difference? This career has enabled me to make the most of this trait. And be rewarded for it. If everyone is going to the left, take a look at the right.

What is clear, as soon as we enter her office, is that the lady who co-founded this operation does not conform to the slick, Prada-bagged stereotype. There are makeshift photo-collages of gorgeous pouting models (and that's just the men) around the place, but, equally, there is the detritus of office normality too, be it cardboard boxes, stationery, scattered files or IT hardware. In the corner of the room is an enormous globe, so big it probably generates its own weather system.

Jackie Cooper is one of the most sought-after agents in the world. Yet the chances are that you will not have heard of her. Search for her on Google, and you'll find yourself looking at an amiable-looking American actor chap with an Oscar. Check out her YouTube videos, and you might just catch a glimpse of her in the background of an award ceremony. In print, there is a brief chapter about her in a book on *Inspiring Women* (by Michelle Rosenberg). But don't expect much more. Because this lodestar of the publicity world does not show up on the charts; she is the Polaris of self-promotion that does not do self-promotion; someone who wants to make the story, not be it. If you have not heard of Jackie Cooper, it is largely because that's the way she prefers it to be. Which makes this interview an exception to that rule.

I've been quite private outside of my own colleagues and clients. I did rent my first office as Jackie Cooper PR, and the name stayed, but I'm not a fame-junkie, because it's the work that I want to be famous, not me. In fact, it's very unusual for me to do this kind of interview. It was just that with our 25th anniversary party tonight, it seemed kismet, and I thought it was a nice moment to try it.

She takes up position on the black sofa next to the half-size replica of the earth. We perch at right angles to her, on luridly green leather chairs whose Pantone reference does not occur in nature. Her accent is barely modified north London, the voice soft-spoken and easy, and her demeanour has a kind of appealing straightforwardness, all of which serve to draw your attention to her. At the start, she seems more interested in what we are doing than in talking about what she is doing.

It may be politeness or humility, but there is no danger of this being a self-centred diatribe.

Yet when she does get started on her own narrative, it doesn't take long before it is simmering with tales and reflections and thoughts and ideas. Our questioning soon becomes superfluous, because her own questions to herself are better. She abandons anecdotes mid-flow, as she remembers new things to mention; new stuff that happened to her. Maybe it's because she hasn't done many interviews like this before, but her off-the-cuff instant autobiography is unstructured, unplanned, and natural. More likely, it's because artificial parameters and deadlines concern Cooper far less than things that she's interested in and passionate about.

And therein lies a clue to Cooper's success. Everyone says that Cooper is an exceptional listener, able to absorb complex information and subtle cues alike, and cut through to what is pertinent to the matter at hand. Then – as well – there is Cooper's ability to generate ideas and inspire them in others. And it is this unusual combination of attributes – an inspirational person who actually listens – that has made her such an in-demand strategist.

Cooper's earliest memory is of moving into the house where she spent most of her childhood, in Pinner in Middlesex. A touch of the profound is there from the start:

I'm six, and standing outside my house watching the removal lorry. It's that moment when you realise your entire life is in a truck. It didn't seem like it was anything to do with me at all. Our entire lives – Mum's, Dad's, mine – were being moved into this strange house and this was to be our new existence. It's neither a bad nor good memory. But at the time, it was an enormous thought for my child's brain to comprehend.

I grew up in that house. It was on the bend of a road and I could see the garden opposite from my window. As I got older, that garden was sold off and a really ugly new house was built there with its own curved wall. On one occasion, soon after I'd learnt to drive, I reversed out of our driveway, to take the cat to the vet. I had this routine of opening the

sunroof at the same time as reversing the car with the choke out. This time, as I opened the sunroof, a huge spider fell down onto my lap. So I just jumped out of the car, which of course then shot backwards on the choke, with the cat having a complete fit in the front seat, and the driverless car rammed its way through that horrible ugly front-garden wall and ended up embedded in the doorway.

Cooper has plenty of these kinds of stories – of the slightly chaotic young adult years. Yet you know that now, many years later, she doesn't make many slip-ups. At her level in this cut-throat business, she can unquestionably handle herself in a media street-fight. She says, 'I always want to win and mostly I do,' managing to get these words out with no more aggression than if she were talking about picking bluebells. It's the combination thing again.

I do try and do the fighting with grace and courtesy before being tough or shitty. I'm a fighter. I believe you keep going until you get to where you need to. But this is not about aggression – because aggression is not strength. It's about being resolute and smart and decent to get to where you need to. And knowing how to read the situation or read the people you're dealing with. So that you make it easier for everyone t achieve what is needed.

Cooper's success comes not from the kind of hypocrisy and combati ness for which the media industry has a reputation. Rather, it comes f the opposite set of behaviours: empathy, interest, sensitivity. At ti her look could be mistaken for vulnerability, and you can imagine you'd hate yourself if you ever upset her. And if you were a po client, possibly that creates a predisposition in her favour. Th effectiveness of her style.

I was born in 1962: a child of the big era when everything But I don't feel like I was in it at all. I feel like I was disc from what happened during my childhood and that time.

Revel in the unusual. I think that's why our campaigns here work. I love the maverick, the brave, the counter-intuitive...

I didn't fit in at school at all. It was a dreadful education. My mind still doesn't work the way others' minds work. School-life was miserable, and I hated it. I couldn't understand anything. I felt like I was lost in a fog. Like everyone else was programmed to know what they were doing while I was different and didn't. The others all came to school with the same sandwiches, but I had American thick sandwiches; they came to school with two pieces of Sunblest bread and one piece of ham, but I had all sorts of weird vegetables in my sandwich. This kind of thing was so embarrassing at that young age. I was in a culture where being different was not a good thing. I longed to be the same as everybody else, but I didn't feel that I could be while I was still in my own skin.

It is a familiar description of adolescent angst, but it seems as though Cooper can still feel what those moments were like.

It was like that until I got to 15, when socially things started to change, and I got my first boyfriend. Friendships changed, going out became more important, and I started to have a life of my own. I loved dancing and used to go to nightclubs. That was liberating. For the first time, I realised that I could be confident at being me.

Cooper had been slowly coming to the realisation that difference can actually be beautiful, and that she had a gift not a handicap. Her questionable attention to detail may have hampered her early academic attainment, but it is balanced by patience and understanding, and by a sixth sense that has made her so valuable.

My head never worked the way other people's heads worked – still doesn't. I'm utterly driven by instinct. I have very sensitive antennae. At school, I had to learn very quickly how to avoid getting beaten up – which had been happening to me at first. I learned how to anticipate things and how to work people out. So to this day, I can go in and read a room.

Having those over-instinctive antennae is brilliant, but it's also fairly exhausting because it means you're quite vulnerable to everything that's going on around you. I've had to learn how to manage that.

Given the nationalities of her parents, the American parent company, her two passports, and the air miles she generates flying between Heathrow and JFK, we suggest that she can fairly be described as a transatlantic spirit. She scoffs at the idea, then demonstrates its validity.

From the age of three, every Easter, my mum would take me back to New York. My grandfather lived there, and my aunt and cousins still live there. I don't have any family here. I always feel like a piece of my heart is in America – especially New York, but I'm comfortable on both East and West Coasts – while still being a London girl. My dad was a Londoner in all the best ways. I was born and brought up in London, and all the big milestones in my life happened in London.

Cooper often mentions the role that her father played in her career. Indeed, he was the first person to moot a future for her in PR, after she had spent years struggling academically.

He was a massive influence on my life. He was my dad, who I loved with all my heart, and a brilliantly wise man. And very entrepreneurial. But that brought times of great success and times of not great success. There were some really challenging periods for us all because of it. One time, his company went bust and we had no money at all and were on social security for some months. I remember one time my dad being utterly flummoxed when his business partner had got involved in some dodgy dealing and embezzled all the money and gone off. Everything was fine one day and everything wasn't fine the next. I remember our world stopping. That's happened a few times in my life.

Then at other times, the company would do well and we'd have a Rolls Royce and go on holiday to the South of France. But during all of that time my dad never bought a washing machine, and he'd take the

laundry in the Rolls Royce to the local launderette. I look back at some
of those moments and I think how peculiar it was.

Cooper never went to university. She says that it was simply because she
never wanted to. She did, however, spend time at a sixth-form college
in Stanmore where, for the first time in her life, she found herself in an
educational environment that liked her and that she could like back: 'an
environment that was vaguely structured and that I could get on with'.

I was now doing stuff with amateur dramatics. I ended up playing
Elvira in Blithe Spirit, *which did a lot for my confidence. And then I*
decided that I wanted to go to drama school – which my parents weren't
that thrilled about. My mum had been an actress in the States and she
thought I'd be on a hiding to nothing.

At that point, my dad had a friend who ran a small PR agency in
Great Portland Street, and I got a job there, on one of those doll's-eye
switchboards where I sat and electrocuted myself for the six weeks.
I stayed in that agency for four years. I loved it. I felt I'd finally got
somewhere. It was a tiny company, called Co-ordinated Marketing
Services, run by a wonderful guy called Wilf Altman. He'd been an
editor on the FT – *a little, short, fat, old-school journalist with a fat*
cigar. He would write out all the stories on the typewriter and then later
on just shout from the office, 'Jackie, what's happened to that story?' It
was great training. I learned as much about what not *to do.*

My instinctive ability to read things was the important thing.
I remember one guy had a go at me and he said, 'You think you're
so much better than us, don't you?' And for the first time in my life,
because I'd never had any confidence about anything, I thought to
myself, 'Yeah, I do! And you *meanwhile are* missing *all the signals.'*
Some people are so into themselves. You have to realise that it's not
about you; it's about others. You need to be attuned to that.

In an industry that is, in some respects, all about being into itself, Cooper
is the very last person who could be characterised as being into *herself.*

Her early years put paid to that. And even after she had shaken off the angst of secondary school, she would not be free from adversity.

My father was 21 years older than my mother. He was born in 1915, and was the same age as many of my friends' grandfathers. He was ageless in his way, and I was never aware of the fact that my father was older, because he never acted older. He was just my dad, who was always sage and funny. But then he had a heart attack and this completely threw me. It was yet another day when my life changed on a pivot.

I was in the office, on my first job and I got a call from my dad saying, 'Don't panic, but I'm in the hospital. It appears that I've had a slight heart attack. The hospital are saying you could come and see me.' So I had to get on the Metropolitan Line to Northwick Park Hospital. I remember that journey, with the train just not going fast enough, and my world in suspended animation. From that day on, the panic attacks came.

It is perhaps a shame that Cooper is not more widely known. She ought to be an inspiration to more than just entrepreneurs and marketers in her industry; for the many who suffer panic attacks, her story is a source of hope.

Panic attacks are often because of a surprise event that you can't control. Then you have another panic attack and then you feel wobbly because you don't understand why you've had another one, and the fear of the attack becomes bigger than the first event itself.

I stopped being able to go to theatres unless I was on the end of a row, which was awkward as we were a big theatre-going family. I told my dad I thought it was leukemia, at which point he thought that I was nuts. So he took me to his local GP, who was the most practical, acerbic, non-right-on doctor you could possibly imagine: an old school, hardcore doctor who just said, 'Well, when did this leukemia start?' Then he asked me about five more questions and told me that it wasn't leukemia. I just started crying and he said, 'Right. Come back next

Monday, and we'll get this sorted out.' You'd never get a doctor to do that today. And he basically gave me a list of things to do, including making me sit in the middle of a row in the theatre. And in the end, I came through.

I still have them to this day, although I can control them now... these days, I'll recognise the first signs. It doesn't leave you. It's your default state – so you get round it by stopping that default. People think they know me and they assume I'm invincible. But that idea is ridiculous. I'm not like that.

The thing about PR people in the earlier era was that it just wasn't the done thing to show vulnerability. Many were quite ego-driven names above the door. So one of the reasons why I wanted to set up on my own was that I wanted to be the antithesis to that. I have always been quite open about my vulnerabilities. It's funny, but I don't think I could have built the business if I didn't have that.

Cooper makes the obvious but telling point that many of the personalities with whom she has worked are equally vulnerable – or weak, or flawed – and that her role, or perhaps her great skill, has been in knowing how to manage this. She says that she is fascinated by different ways of 'helping people through'; driven by her own experiences, of course.

How can you fix anything if you've never felt like that yourself? You learn what it's like. You have loyalty to the people who've helped you get over it, and you try and give loyalty back. And you end up with people around you – colleagues, clients, friends – beyond the norm. You give – and get a great gift back.

After she left her first PR job, Cooper moved to a sister agency working on industrial PR. She describes working in a small agency, ending up doing everything, as being the perfect early training for her. She was put in an office with two female colleagues. One day, they were all sent to do an article with *Campaign* (the advertising industry trade-magazine), about successful women in their particular kind of PR, because, in her boss's words, 'it's not glamorous PR, but you're glamorous women.' Cooper tells how the three women were worried that the slant of the article would be an inevitably patronising one about sex-and-selling – and it was.

I have the article to this day. Campaign *did its archetypal picture on the fire escape with the three of us – it was the eighties so you should see the hairdo – and the headline was 'Sex and PR Persuaders'. I quit.*

To be honest, I did already have somewhere to go, because I'd been headhunted with an offer of ridiculous money. I was still only 23 or 24. But I ignored my instinct, which was telling me not to go there. But I did. And I ended up hating everything about it. Never ignore your inner voices.

There was one day when they told me to go and pitch for the Sanrizz hairdressing salon business and to do it, they gave me the previous presentation to use as a template. They had no sense of going to see what it was the client was needing. They said to me, 'No, no, no. We have our template. Use it.' I had to present a creative brief for a highly trend-focused business, and use the same template as they'd used for the British Woodworking Federation! I just sat there and thought how awful it all was.

I tried to quit, but had stupidly signed a contract with a notice period of six months or something. They obviously wanted to make sure people didn't keep going off. The finance director found me literally slumped over my desk, just feeling completely trapped. I said, 'I need to get out. I can't do this. It's killing me...' So he took my hand and he led me to his office and he just shredded my contract. To this day, I don't know why he did it. He just said to me, 'Go!'

Cooper's next move seems to have even surprised herself. This time, *Campaign* was the trigger for finding a new job, not quitting an existing one. The magazine had written an article about Greenpeace, the international environmental movement, who, in those days, were far less well known than they are today. As a way of raising awareness and their media profile, the group had just employed Yellowhammer as their ad agency. At the time, it was a bold, unprecedented move, and Cooper fancied a piece of that action.

In those days, you expected charities and pressure groups to be dressed in dodgy sweaters and Jesus sandals, but here was a group who were trying to get their issues across by employing what was then one of the slickest, most contemporary, ad agencies of the time, headed up by a real rising star, Sammy Harari. All that seemed remarkable.

On a whim, I just rang up the guy from Greenpeace and said, 'You've employed Yellowhammer, but what are you doing about PR?' And he said, 'Nothing. We haven't even thought about PR.' No one ever thought about PR. So I went to see him and switched from that awful but massively paid job to something much, much smaller. When I was there, I launched their anti-fur trade campaign, which became famous, then worked with David Bailey, which was amazing.

What I started to understand was that it hadn't been the PR per se that I'd been hating, but the way that PR was being done. I decided that I would not work in an environment which forced me to do something I couldn't do. But I could still do a form of PR that I believed in, which didn't mean being dishonest – to clients or myself

It would take another step or two before she would be able to put in place exactly the form of PR that she had in mind. But she felt that there was progress and, speeding things up still further, the publicist Max Clifford now appeared on the scene. Cooper has a mantra about meeting everyone once. It is an expansive outlook, encouraged by her father, which suggests that the more people you allow yourself to meet, and listen to, the greater your chances of exposing yourself to life-changing moments. This was one of them.

Like Cooper, Clifford had never been to university, having left school at 15 with few formal qualifications. Clearly, he saw the potential in this entrepreneurial female, and promptly offered her a desk in his office. Cooper regards him as someone who taught her many important lessons about the industry and the nature of celebrity.

I'd got a couple of my own clients and – in a not very dynamic way – started my own business. One bizarre client was a graphologist who wanted to be a fame-junkie, and liked the idea of going to see Max Clifford, which was how I came to meet him. I took the space he'd offered, paid him rent, and that was how I got my Bond Street address – which beat working from my dining-room table at home. It made me think, 'Bloody hell. I'd better be a bit more grown up now.'

I worked with Max for a couple of years... I had a few illusions shattered and any naivety that I had about media was dashed. But he was very good to me. His forte was tabloid media and his ability to understand how to trade stories... made me a bit cynical.

At this time, Cooper was still primarily dealing with personalities in the media, which at times involved hiding in washrooms, under blankets, and being chased along streets by paparazzi. There was a contradiction here, in that Cooper, who places such a high premium on 'honesty', was increasingly operating in a world where transparency counts for little. Something about the 'pure celebrity' PR didn't sit right with her; it was, she felt, 'too much like being a therapist'.

When many people become famous, they can't help but be affected by the machinery of that fame. They follow a dreadful, inevitable path. At first, they don't realise that they're going to go down it, or that their head will be turned, or that they will lose themselves, because it's so hard not to. But the ones that don't are the exception. For many people, everything that you held true as an individual gets undermined or destroyed. As the PR, you end up being the person who is taking them out of situations – physical or mental. After they've said the wrong thing, kissed the wrong person, swallowed the wrong thing, or when they're just having moments of immense self-doubt.

I've always said that if you don't love yourself, you can't be loved by others, and then you'll look for love in all the wrong places. With some of the big personalities, if you get underneath the imagery and veneer,

Stoke will, and Britain should, be relieved to hear it. Bridgewater's own story is the kind that the country needs to hear now more than ever. At its peak in the nineteenth century, the Potteries had more than two thousand kilns on full output, making millions of products each year. By 1970, about two hundred factories were left. Between 1998 and 2008, around twenty thousand jobs were lost. And by 2012, with Britain in the grip of a fierce economic slump, there were only around thirty factories left, the success of one of which is resting on the shoulders of this determined woman who draws inspiration from talking about her mum's old kitchen.

But 2012 was also the year when the Olympics returned to Britain, and Stoke-on-Trent took its place in the unique street phenomenon that the torch relay became in British hands. As it passed the Potteries Museum nearby, tens of thousands of locals braved predictably dull weather, as they had done in just about every other town in the land, to wave in secular rapture at the small figure in white with a stick of gold. A global concept, literally embraced by, and interpreted through the lens of, British enthusiasm. The mood for the Queen's Diamond Jubilee was the same, allowing people a channel for patriotism, optimism, and felicity – at a time when a good deal of the media narrative is of either breathtaking grimness or whingeing curmudgeonliness.

The uplift in mood, at times like these, is Bridgewater's told-you-so moment. She is a fan and vociferous advocate of her country, and it was hardly surprising when the company went big with its unashamedly jolly Diamond Jubilee line, much of which was specially designed by Rice. It was, of course, an outstanding success. But this kind of optimism does not please everybody. The era of austerity has given an excuse to those disparaging anything that hints at middle-class aspiration.

A large majority of people love what she does, just as they loved celebrating the Olympics and the Diamond Jubilee. They love the optimism and the dedication. And that is really what Bridgewater is advocating. 'Britons can be all sorts of things which are hard to understand... but great things happen when they are allowed to express themselves in the way that comes naturally to them,' says Bridgewater. And, in many ways, she has been an inspirational catalyst for that.

Bridgewater never stops banging the drum about the potential in her country. 'After 25 years in business, I don't understand why more people are not doing something more about it.' Signally, Bridgewater *is* doing that something more: with her factory here in Stoke and shops in London, Bicester, and Edinburgh selling ceramics, but also expanding into stationery, gift-wrapping, and even bedding. The Royals have been here (twice) to recognise the fact.

It's so hard to be objective about your own life – your own career – isn't it? You're just in it. I feel very, very focused, but Matthew calls it obsessive: I don't let things drop. But as long as you don't set yourself up, then it's fine, isn't it? Sometimes, you find yourself pretending it's been easy. It hasn't; and it isn't. At some point, no matter who you are, you have to tread on faces and you'll need to have that in you if you're successful. For women, more so than men, it's quite hard to come to terms with that.

At the same time, I think that the brand is very informal and I think that, luckily, I am as well. I think it's what my mum was. Mum's influence is very pervasive; strangely, probably more in the business than in my family life. I feel that I'm trying to capture the spirit of what she made my home life like as a child; what was unusual and special about it. And then turn that into a business. It's a strange thing to want to do really, isn't it?

Mum is still alive, so I can't mourn her because she's alive, but I want to explain her. I sort of feel that when we get this business right – in any aspect of the business – it's explaining her and what she stood for. And that feels very necessary – strangely.

It is hard to define what exactly Bridgewater is battling *against*: government inertia, economic ineptitude, industrial decline, loss of local investment, uncaring fate, lack of room for another plate on the dresser. It could be any or all of these. But, in a way, it doesn't matter. Because she is battling *for* something: and that something is easy to understand. It is the country she loves, and what she is convinced is its reservoir of creative skill and artisan traditions; a belief that when people here put their minds to it, they can generate manufactured goods the envy of the world. 'These people have great skills. It's absolutely daft to fly halfway around the world when what you need is all here… it makes me hot with rage,' she says.

Central to her belief is Stoke-on-Trent, a place that 'really hit me between the eyes': a messy kitchen of a city for this southern bookworm to have adopted back in 1984 straight off the Euston train. Now she will have no bad word spoken against it and its people; she loves it as though she had been born and bred in the place and fights for it most days of her life. She is, of course, an equally odd child for it to adopt, but the city has surely taken her to its heart as she has it to hers. Neither would be what each is without the other. It may be North Staffordshire rather than Red Flag, Nebraska, and the early part of a different century from that of her heroine, but the woman sitting in a warm studio rather than on an arid American plain can, without hyperbole, call herself a pioneer. Not least because she is the type of modern SME entrepreneur on whom Britain's future economic prosperity now rests.

The people for Bridgewater's next appointment have arrived, and it's time to end the interview and leave. She is running behind schedule now, and excuses herself from acting as guide back to reception. 'Forgive me,' she says, 'but I'm sure you know the way back out.' It is the only moment in the entire interview when Bridgewater's faith seems misguided.

———

'The truly important things in life – love, beauty, and one's own uniqueness – are constantly being overlooked.'

PABLO CASALS

———

JACKIE COOPER

(JCPR Edelman)

INTERVIEWED 27 SEPTEMBER 2012

After our earlier discussions with the political guru Tim Bell, we now return to the world of PR, but this time venturing to a different part of the industry, a very different style of company, and a very different style of entrepreneur; to the London offices of JCPR, which stands for Jackie Cooper Public Relations. The eponymous co-founder is our next interviewee.

Since launch, well over two decades ago, JCPR has handled a range of iconic brand 'properties': from Wembley Stadium to the Concorde airliner; from Levi's to MTV; Mars, Microsoft, O2, Wonderbra, Covent Garden, Mary-Kate & Ashley Olsen... Today's client list is a roll call of pre-eminent and familiar household names in both established and emergent markets alike. In 2004, the company was acquired by Edelman – the world's biggest and arguably most successful independently owned PR company – which led to our interviewee, Jackie Cooper, initially becoming creative director of the London business, then global vice-chair of brand properties for the combined international entity.

Here in London, Cooper's name is still over the door. We have come to a tall, shiny building in Victoria Street, which bristles with brisk business and decent suits. We wait in the reception area, perched on large black Alcantara sofas, so deep, you sit with your feet not reaching past the cushion; like Stuart Little, lost among the hectares of opulent fabric. This is PR land, easily (and sometimes unfairly) caricatured as a world of imagery and gloss. In reality, it's not Perfect Curve or *Ab Fab* – but it's not quite not, either.

What is clear, as soon as we enter her office, is that the lady who co-founded this operation does not conform to the slick, Prada-bagged stereotype. There are makeshift photo-collages of gorgeous pouting models (and that's just the men) around the place, but, equally, there is the detritus of office normality too, be it cardboard boxes, stationery, scattered files or IT hardware. In the corner of the room is an enormous globe, so big it probably generates its own weather system.

Jackie Cooper is one of the most sought-after agents in the world. Yet the chances are that you will not have heard of her. Search for her on Google, and you'll find yourself looking at an amiable-looking American actor chap with an Oscar. Check out her YouTube videos, and you might just catch a glimpse of her in the background of an award ceremony. In print, there is a brief chapter about her in a book on *Inspiring Women* (by Michelle Rosenberg). But don't expect much more. Because this lodestar of the publicity world does not show up on the charts; she is the Polaris of self-promotion that does not do self-promotion; someone who wants to make the story, not be it. If you have not heard of Jackie Cooper, it is largely because that's the way she prefers it to be. Which makes this interview an exception to that rule.

I've been quite private outside of my own colleagues and clients. I did rent my first office as Jackie Cooper PR, and the name stayed, but I'm not a fame-junkie, because it's the work that I want to be famous, not me. In fact, it's very unusual for me to do this kind of interview. It was just that with our 25th anniversary party tonight, it seemed kismet, and I thought it was a nice moment to try it.

She takes up position on the black sofa next to the half-size replica of the earth. We perch at right angles to her, on luridly green leather chairs whose Pantone reference does not occur in nature. Her accent is barely modified north London, the voice soft-spoken and easy, and her demeanour has a kind of appealing straightforwardness, all of which serve to draw your attention to her. At the start, she seems more interested in what we are doing than in talking about what she is doing.

It may be politeness or humility, but there is no danger of this being a self-centred diatribe.

Yet when she does get started on her own narrative, it doesn't take long before it is simmering with tales and reflections and thoughts and ideas. Our questioning soon becomes superfluous, because her own questions to herself are better. She abandons anecdotes mid-flow, as she remembers new things to mention; new stuff that happened to her. Maybe it's because she hasn't done many interviews like this before, but her off-the-cuff instant autobiography is unstructured, unplanned, and natural. More likely, it's because artificial parameters and deadlines concern Cooper far less than things that she's interested in and passionate about.

And therein lies a clue to Cooper's success. Everyone says that Cooper is an exceptional listener, able to absorb complex information and subtle cues alike, and cut through to what is pertinent to the matter at hand. Then – *as well* – there is Cooper's ability to generate ideas and inspire them in others. And it is this unusual combination of attributes – an inspirational person who actually listens – that has made her such an in-demand strategist.

Cooper's earliest memory is of moving into the house where she spent most of her childhood, in Pinner in Middlesex. A touch of the profound is there from the start:

I'm six, and standing outside my house watching the removal lorry. It's that moment when you realise your entire life is in a truck. It didn't seem like it was anything to do with me at all. Our entire lives – Mum's, Dad's, mine – were being moved into this strange house and this was to be our new existence. It's neither a bad nor good memory. But at the time, it was an enormous thought for my child's brain to comprehend.

I grew up in that house. It was on the bend of a road and I could see the garden opposite from my window. As I got older, that garden was sold off and a really ugly new house was built there with its own curved wall. On one occasion, soon after I'd learnt to drive, I reversed out of our driveway, to take the cat to the vet. I had this routine of opening the sunroof at the same time as reversing the car with the choke out. This time, as I opened the sunroof, a huge spider fell down onto my lap. So I just jumped out of the car, which of course then shot backwards on the choke, with the cat having a complete fit in the front seat, and the driverless car rammed its way through that horrible ugly front-garden wall and ended up embedded in the doorway.

Cooper has plenty of these kinds of stories – of the slightly chaotic young adult years. Yet you know that now, many years later, she doesn't make many slip-ups. At her level in this cut-throat business, she can unquestionably handle herself in a media street-fight. She says, 'I always want to win and mostly I do,' managing to get these words out with no more aggression than if she were talking about picking bluebells. It's the combination thing again.

I do try and do the fighting with grace and courtesy before being tough or shitty. I'm a fighter. I believe you keep going until you get to where you need to. But this is not about aggression – because aggression is not strength. It's about being resolute and smart and decent to get to where you need to. And knowing how to read the situation or read the people you're dealing with. So that you make it easier for everyone to achieve what is needed.

Cooper's success comes not from the kind of hypocrisy and combativeness for which the media industry has a reputation. Rather, it comes from the opposite set of behaviours: empathy, interest, sensitivity. At times, her look could be mistaken for vulnerability, and you can imagine that you'd hate yourself if you ever upset her. And if you were a potential client, possibly that creates a predisposition in her favour. Thus, the effectiveness of her style.

I was born in 1962: a child of the big era when everything changed. But I don't feel like I was in it at all. I feel like I was disconnected from what happened during my childhood and that time. I wasn't connected to any culture at all until I was about 15. I was an only child, and you end up in a bubble-like unit with your mum and your dad and you...

The interesting part of this experience was that I would read a lot and have always loved being lost in the power of a wonderful story. My imagination was vivid and that remains to this day. I love being inspired by the imagination and not allowing myself to be restricted in thought – or letting account teams or clients be restricted in theirs.

Cooper married a fellow only-child, whom she mentions spontaneously ('a funny, upbeat, brave, generous, and pragmatic soul, who has supported me through thick and thin'). It's as though both she and her spouse share a common insight into the solitary state of being the sole child in the family.

My mum, who's still with us, is a New Yorker. My dad was terribly British, in a sort of David Niven-esque way. He was in marketing all of his life – a brilliant entrepreneur. So the culture that I grew up with was very mixed. I was so very aware of my American heritage – which I'm very proud of to this day. It makes what I do here much easier, because I'm very comfortable with either side of the pond. Plus, there was my dad's business entrepreneurial influence. And that was my world: the three of us; a tight sort of unit. But at the same time, I was painfully shy.

A fair proportion of Cooper's narrative is about *being different*. This woman who has built her business from making people and brands stand out was, during her early years, impeded by her own acute sense of difference. Maybe she is exactly the right person to know how to create difference *and* how to deal with it.

What's the point of doing any of this work unless you make a difference? This career has enabled me to make the most of this trait. And be rewarded for it. If everyone is going to the left, take a look at the right.

Revel in the unusual. I think that's why our campaigns here work. I love the maverick, the brave, the counter-intuitive...

I didn't fit in at school at all. It was a dreadful education. My mind still doesn't work the way others' minds work. School-life was miserable, and I hated it. I couldn't understand anything. I felt like I was lost in a fog. Like everyone else was programmed to know what they were doing while I was different and didn't. The others all came to school with the same sandwiches, but I had American thick sandwiches; they came to school with two pieces of Sunblest bread and one piece of ham, but I had all sorts of weird vegetables in my sandwich. This kind of thing was so embarrassing at that young age. I was in a culture where being different was not a good thing. I longed to be the same as everybody else, but I didn't feel that I could be while I was still in my own skin.

It is a familiar description of adolescent angst, but it seems as though Cooper can still feel what those moments were like.

It was like that until I got to 15, when socially things started to change, and I got my first boyfriend. Friendships changed, going out became more important, and I started to have a life of my own. I loved dancing and used to go to nightclubs. That was liberating. For the first time, I realised that I could be confident at being me.

Cooper had been slowly coming to the realisation that difference can actually be beautiful, and that she had a gift not a handicap. Her questionable attention to detail may have hampered her early academic attainment, but it is balanced by patience and understanding, and by a sixth sense that has made her so valuable.

My head never worked the way other people's heads worked – still doesn't. I'm utterly driven by instinct. I have very sensitive antennae. At school, I had to learn very quickly how to avoid getting beaten up – which had been happening to me at first. I learned how to anticipate things and how to work people out. So to this day, I can go in and read a room.

Having those over-instinctive antennae is brilliant, but it's also fairly exhausting because it means you're quite vulnerable to everything that's going on around you. I've had to learn how to manage that.

Given the nationalities of her parents, the American parent company, her two passports, and the air miles she generates flying between Heathrow and JFK, we suggest that she can fairly be described as a transatlantic spirit. She scoffs at the idea, then demonstrates its validity.

From the age of three, every Easter, my mum would take me back to New York. My grandfather lived there, and my aunt and cousins still live there. I don't have any family here. I always feel like a piece of my heart is in America – especially New York, but I'm comfortable on both East and West Coasts – while still being a London girl. My dad was a Londoner in all the best ways. I was born and brought up in London, and all the big milestones in my life happened in London.

Cooper often mentions the role that her father played in her career. Indeed, he was the first person to moot a future for her in PR, after she had spent years struggling academically.

He was a massive influence on my life. He was my dad, who I loved with all my heart, and a brilliantly wise man. And very entrepreneurial. But that brought times of great success and times of not great success. There were some really challenging periods for us all because of it. One time, his company went bust and we had no money at all and were on social security for some months. I remember one time my dad being utterly flummoxed when his business partner had got involved in some dodgy dealing and embezzled all the money and gone off. Everything was fine one day and everything wasn't fine the next. I remember our world stopping. That's happened a few times in my life.

Then at other times, the company would do well and we'd have a Rolls Royce and go on holiday to the South of France. But during all of that time my dad never bought a washing machine, and he'd take the

laundry in the Rolls Royce to the local launderette. I look back at some
of those moments and I think how peculiar it was.

Cooper never went to university. She says that it was simply because she
never wanted to. She did, however, spend time at a sixth-form college
in Stanmore where, for the first time in her life, she found herself in an
educational environment that liked her and that she could like back: 'an
environment that was vaguely structured and that I could get on with'.

I was now doing stuff with amateur dramatics. I ended up playing
Elvira in Blithe Spirit, *which did a lot for my confidence. And then I*
decided that I wanted to go to drama school – which my parents weren't
that thrilled about. My mum had been an actress in the States and she
thought I'd be on a hiding to nothing.

At that point, my dad had a friend who ran a small PR agency in
Great Portland Street, and I got a job there, on one of those doll's-eye
switchboards where I sat and electrocuted myself for the six weeks.
I stayed in that agency for four years. I loved it. I felt I'd finally got
somewhere. It was a tiny company, called Co-ordinated Marketing
Services, run by a wonderful guy called Wilf Altman. He'd been an
editor on the FT – *a little, short, fat, old-school journalist with a fat*
cigar. He would write out all the stories on the typewriter and then later
on just shout from the office, 'Jackie, what's happened to that story?' It
was great training. I learned as much about what not *to do.*

My instinctive ability to read things was the important thing.
I remember one guy had a go at me and he said, 'You think you're
so much better than us, don't you?' And for the first time in my life,
because I'd never had any confidence about anything, I thought to
myself, 'Yeah, I do! And you *meanwhile are* missing *all the signals.'*
Some people are so into themselves. You have to realise that it's not
about you; it's about others. You need to be attuned to that.

In an industry that is, in some respects, all about being into itself, Cooper
is the very last person who could be characterised as being into *herself.*

Her early years put paid to that. And even after she had shaken off the angst of secondary school, she would not be free from adversity.

My father was 21 years older than my mother. He was born in 1915, and was the same age as many of my friends' grandfathers. He was ageless in his way, and I was never aware of the fact that my father was older, because he never acted older. He was just my dad, who was always sage and funny. But then he had a heart attack and this completely threw me. It was yet another day when my life changed on a pivot.

I was in the office, on my first job and I got a call from my dad saying, 'Don't panic, but I'm in the hospital. It appears that I've had a slight heart attack. The hospital are saying you could come and see me.' So I had to get on the Metropolitan Line to Northwick Park Hospital. I remember that journey, with the train just not going fast enough, and my world in suspended animation. From that day on, the panic attacks came.

It is perhaps a shame that Cooper is not more widely known. She ought to be an inspiration to more than just entrepreneurs and marketers in her industry; for the many who suffer panic attacks, her story is a source of hope.

Panic attacks are often because of a surprise event that you can't control. Then you have another panic attack and then you feel wobbly because you don't understand why you've had another one, and the fear of the attack becomes bigger than the first event itself.

I stopped being able to go to theatres unless I was on the end of a row, which was awkward as we were a big theatre-going family. I told my dad I thought it was leukemia, at which point he thought that I was nuts. So he took me to his local GP, who was the most practical, acerbic, non-right-on doctor you could possibly imagine: an old school, hardcore doctor who just said, 'Well, when did this leukemia start?' Then he asked me about five more questions and told me that it wasn't leukemia. I just started crying and he said, 'Right. Come back next

Monday, and we'll get this sorted out.' You'd never get a doctor to do that today. And he basically gave me a list of things to do, including making me sit in the middle of a row in the theatre. And in the end, I came through.

I still have them to this day, although I can control them now... these days, I'll recognise the first signs. It doesn't leave you. It's your default state – so you get round it by stopping that default. People think they know me and they assume I'm invincible. But that idea is ridiculous. I'm not like that.

The thing about PR people in the earlier era was that it just wasn't the done thing to show vulnerability. Many were quite ego-driven names above the door. So one of the reasons why I wanted to set up on my own was that I wanted to be the antithesis to that. I have always been quite open about my vulnerabilities. It's funny, but I don't think I could have built the business if I didn't have that.

Cooper makes the obvious but telling point that many of the personalities with whom she has worked are equally vulnerable – or weak, or flawed – and that her role, or perhaps her great skill, has been in knowing how to manage this. She says that she is fascinated by different ways of 'helping people through'; driven by her own experiences, of course.

How can you fix anything if you've never felt like that yourself? You learn what it's like. You have loyalty to the people who've helped you get over it, and you try and give loyalty back. And you end up with people around you – colleagues, clients, friends – beyond the norm. You give – and get a great gift back.

After she left her first PR job, Cooper moved to a sister agency working on industrial PR. She describes working in a small agency, ending up doing everything, as being the perfect early training for her. She was put in an office with two female colleagues. One day, they were all sent to do an article with *Campaign* (the advertising industry trade-magazine), about successful women in their particular kind of PR, because, in her boss's words, 'it's not glamorous PR, but you're glamorous women.' Cooper tells how the three women were worried that the slant of the article would be an inevitably patronising one about sex-and-selling – and it was.

I have the article to this day. Campaign *did its archetypal picture on the fire escape with the three of us – it was the eighties so you should see the hairdo – and the headline was 'Sex and PR Persuaders'. I quit.*

To be honest, I did already have somewhere to go, because I'd been headhunted with an offer of ridiculous money. I was still only 23 or 24. But I ignored my instinct, which was telling me not to go there. But I did. And I ended up hating everything about it. Never ignore your inner voices.

There was one day when they told me to go and pitch for the Sanrizz hairdressing salon business and to do it, they gave me the previous presentation to use as a template. They had no sense of going to see what it was the client was needing. They said to me, 'No, no, no. We have our template. Use it.' I had to present a creative brief for a highly trend-focused business, and use the same template as they'd used for the British Woodworking Federation! I just sat there and thought how awful it all was.

I tried to quit, but had stupidly signed a contract with a notice period of six months or something. They obviously wanted to make sure people didn't keep going off. The finance director found me literally slumped over my desk, just feeling completely trapped. I said, 'I need to get out. I can't do this. It's killing me…' So he took my hand and he led me to his office and he just shredded my contract. To this day, I don't know why he did it. He just said to me, 'Go!'

Cooper's next move seems to have even surprised herself. This time, *Campaign* was the trigger for finding a new job, not quitting an existing one. The magazine had written an article about Greenpeace, the international environmental movement, who, in those days, were far less well known than they are today. As a way of raising awareness and their media profile, the group had just employed Yellowhammer as their ad agency. At the time, it was a bold, unprecedented move, and Cooper fancied a piece of that action.

In those days, you expected charities and pressure groups to be dressed in dodgy sweaters and Jesus sandals, but here was a group who were trying to get their issues across by employing what was then one of the slickest, most contemporary, ad agencies of the time, headed up by a real rising star, Sammy Harari. All that seemed remarkable.

On a whim, I just rang up the guy from Greenpeace and said, 'You've employed Yellowhammer, but what are you doing about PR?' And he said, 'Nothing. We haven't even thought about PR.' No one ever thought about PR. So I went to see him and switched from that awful but massively paid job to something much, much smaller. When I was there, I launched their anti-fur trade campaign, which became famous, then worked with David Bailey, which was amazing.

What I started to understand was that it hadn't been the PR per se that I'd been hating, but the way that PR was being done. I decided that I would not work in an environment which forced me to do something I couldn't do. But I could still do a form of PR that I believed in, which didn't mean being dishonest – to clients or myself.

It would take another step or two before she would be able to put in place exactly the form of PR that she had in mind. But she felt that there was progress and, speeding things up still further, the publicist Max Clifford now appeared on the scene. Cooper has a mantra about meeting everyone once. It is an expansive outlook, encouraged by her father, which suggests that the more people you allow yourself to meet, and listen to, the greater your chances of exposing yourself to life-changing moments. This was one of them.

Like Cooper, Clifford had never been to university, having left school at 15 with few formal qualifications. Clearly, he saw the potential in this entrepreneurial female, and promptly offered her a desk in his office. Cooper regards him as someone who taught her many important lessons about the industry and the nature of celebrity.

I'd got a couple of my own clients and – in a not very dynamic way – started my own business. One bizarre client was a graphologist who wanted to be a fame-junkie, and liked the idea of going to see Max Clifford, which was how I came to meet him. I took the space he'd offered, paid him rent, and that was how I got my Bond Street address – which beat working from my dining-room table at home. It made me think, 'Bloody hell. I'd better be a bit more grown up now.'

I worked with Max for a couple of years... I had a few illusions shattered and any naivety that I had about media was dashed. But he was very good to me. His forte was tabloid media and his ability to understand how to trade stories... made me a bit cynical.

At this time, Cooper was still primarily dealing with personalities in the media, which at times involved hiding in washrooms, under blankets, and being chased along streets by paparazzi. There was a contradiction here, in that Cooper, who places such a high premium on 'honesty', was increasingly operating in a world where transparency counts for little. Something about the 'pure celebrity' PR didn't sit right with her; it was, she felt, 'too much like being a therapist'.

When many people become famous, they can't help but be affected by the machinery of that fame. They follow a dreadful, inevitable path. At first, they don't realise that they're going to go down it, or that their head will be turned, or that they will lose themselves, because it's so hard not to. But the ones that don't are the exception. For many people, everything that you held true as an individual gets undermined or destroyed. As the PR, you end up being the person who is taking them out of situations – physical or mental. After they've said the wrong thing, kissed the wrong person, swallowed the wrong thing, or when they're just having moments of immense self-doubt.

I've always said that if you don't love yourself, you can't be loved by others, and then you'll look for love in all the wrong places. With some of the big personalities, if you get underneath the imagery and veneer, the problem is not because they love themselves too much, *but rather because ultimately they don't love themselves* enough.

That's why LA is so scary, because the place is driven by so many things that aren't grounded. I worked for Mary-Kate and Ashley Olsen for eight years – just kids, who were helming a billion-dollar empire. If we were on a shoot, and Mary-Kate wanted to go to the bathroom, she wasn't even allowed to go on her own. The security had to be with her.

Sometimes, the celebrity thing is fun – Cannes, the red carpet, the police escort... to live that life for a few hours is fun. But I've always been so glad that it's not my life and I can just be me. In that puffed-up world, the more you're out there, the more there's participation in you, and the more people have expectations of you. To survive, you have to stick with what's real and sometimes it's easier to run or hide, and we've all done that. If you're lucky, life pulls you up short and makes you stop and look into yourself and say, 'OK. What is good for you? What's real? Because if you're not grounded in something that's real, for you, life will be hollow.

I remember when I got the desk in Max's office, David – who was my boyfriend and is now my husband – took me out for dinner and he said, 'Well, that's it then.' I said, 'Well, what's it?' He said, 'You know, we'll probably be over, because you're going to enter this incredible life of premieres and red carpets...' I thought, 'Gosh. If that's going to happen, I'm not worth having, am I? And actually the opposite happened. It made me run home, because I wanted to know that the arms around me were because someone loved me and believed in things that were true, and were there for the right reasons and not for the wrong reasons.

In business, there are people who have managed it brilliantly. In show business, it's more difficult because the accolades are more fickle and the pressure is more nerve-wracking.

Cooper's achievement has been her ability to turn what she observes as an industry problem into an opportunity. Of course, she still works with personalities and entertainment. But now it is more about developing shared strategies for those personalities and their partner brands – more subtle and less clichéd than using the PR tactic in isolation – where she can call on her experience of what she calls the 'promotion-protection' balance. Recently, she has been working on a new strategy model to deal with it – what she calls the 'prism' methodology. Originally a way of identifying the appropriate values of a brand, it has now been engineered to apply to media personalities and the difficult decisions they constantly face.

We try and articulate in a very reductive way what a brand stands for. But what's been particularly interesting is when we've used it on people. In fact, one quite famous anchor guy rang me up and went, 'Jackie, I've just been offered this job, and I've got my tax bill to pay. But my prism says that I shouldn't do this job.' It meant that he was now understanding what's important to him as an individual, rather than just taking any job that his agent throws at him to pay his tax bill. Now, he's finally having the honest conversation with himself.

In earlier times, when Cooper was starting out in PR, the industry was a mix of commercial work, lobbying, and leveraging publicity for individuals and celebrities. The step up for her career came through matching celebrities and brands. Celebrities were often nervous of the press, but her approach and character, matched with her experience, allowed her to bring the two together, 'so if the focus was, say, fashion, the magazine was happy because they got a celebrity, and the celebrity was happy because they got media without being asked who they were sleeping with. And the fashion brand was happy because they got space that they couldn't normally get.' She describes this as both exciting, and relatively 'easy' work. But the key was that, to the industry, this seemed like a unique approach. With her name on it.

It was in the midst of this early success that her father, having had one heart attack already, now had a serious stroke and became paralysed in hospital. This was one more of those 'pivot-point' moments that she still remembers so vividly.

and I'm as excited at this as I was about Wonderbra. I think the product is potentially a category-changer, but the strategy behind the company is what is really mould-breaking. We've got a whole new way of allowing celebrity and entrepreneurial potential to work together.

It's wonderful to be able to do these things and that people think I've still got something to say. Now I feel like I'm an entrepreneur who happens to be in PR. I never ever want to stop learning.

And in my life, I've learnt that being different is good, not bad. We all just need to find our place. Everyone in the world has got something that they're brilliant at. If I can help people find that, then that will do it for me. Because I was different, and suffered for it, and I'm still different today. But I eventually found something that I could do without feeling that I didn't belong. How fantastic is that?

And I can send you each away with a pair of underpants...

Now Cooper is really late, and she hurries for the door, still thinking and talking about new things she needs to say. Things she feels are important. Things that might help.

Cooper has spoken a lot about how she has always felt different. But that has given her a story – and a skill in communicating its lessons – that can be inspirational for many others: small or great, man or woman, troubled or lonely or panicked through a sense of their own uniqueness. It is in this way that Cooper is making a difference... and will, no doubt, continue to make a difference.

I thought I'd have to stop the business. I was the only child and my mum was in bits. But I had a client – a man called John Rowley, who had left Pretty Polly to set up a hosiery company of his own – and I'd been doing entertainment PR with him. I'd been working with some of the cast from EastEnders, and with Kate O'Mara who was in Dynasty at the time, and he wanted to do a tie-up. Well, I rang him up and told him that I had to stop my company.

John got me to meet him for a drink and I told him what had happened. My dad really liked John and had known him a for a few years – he'd taken him out for his first posh lunch to Claridge's when he was just a sales rep. John recalled my dad always treating him with respect and he said, 'Look, I know your father. How do you think he'd feel if you gave up? You've suddenly got to the point where you've got the experience to do this job. You stopping is the last thing your dad's going to want to feel he's responsible for. You can't stop.' And so I didn't.

It's time for Robert Phillips, co-founder of JCPR, to enter the story. Like Cooper, Phillips is hardly a household name. Sitting, until recently, on the Global Executive Committee of Edelman, servicing a panoply of multinational clients, he has become one of the brightest stars in the PR universe. Unlike Cooper, Phillips had excelled at university. His father was an international fashion agent, who died suddenly, prompting a former client to ask Phillips to take over the reins of the business. Phillips declined (he was still at university), but sold him his 'new' marketing services company instead (which actually did not yet exist).

I was asked by the editor of this yuppie magazine to think about a bridal wear feature and the trade guys recommended I go see Robert Phillips. A guy who knew about bridal was weird. Was he gay? No, he wasn't gay. So I went to meet Robert, who fed me turkey and mustard sandwiches, which I'd never had together in a sandwich before. The conversation moved from bridal to marketing and PR, and Robert just came out with the comment that we were destined to work together for the rest of our lives. He genuinely said that line. I remember telling my dad, who said, 'Oh, he probably just wants to give you one.'

When I'd left Robert that first day, I'd used that great PR exit-line to get you out of awkward situations: 'Call me if something comes up.' But then, in a very, very Robert kind of way, he did – the very next day: 'Something's come up,' he said. This has been a defining characteristic of our relationship for 25 years. 'What's come up?' I said; you know, immediately irritated by him. And he said, 'Sears!' That's so very Robert. He has to be very impactful. He can't just start small.

Long-story-short, we found ourselves on a train to Nuneaton to pitch our business to Sears. No business cards; nothing. I expected just a chat and we walked into a boardroom full of suits. I was 25, and he was 23, and we had to wing it. Robert says he always remembers me saying, 'What you guys need is more sex!' Whatever we did, we walked away with a piece of business. And that was that.

At first, I didn't know if I wanted a full-time business partner. But Robert just dementedly pursued the idea of closer working. In the end, we were really good together; very yin-yang. In fact, there were many reasons to merge the businesses and take our first office in Wardour Street – which was massive. Because my profile was a bit more known from the PR and marketing point of view, we just kept my name. So JCPR it was.

Cooper and Phillips were off and running. But for all their enthusiasm and belief, there was an enormous gap in their business nous. Very soon into the new venture, they began to make what Cooper now regards as 'ridiculous mistakes'. Without any start-up capital or longer-term investment, and lacking managerial knowledge, their debt quickly grew. Soon, they were going cap-in-hand to the bank manager in her father's branch at Moorgate (who Cooper says was something of a 'guardian angel').

Cooper has a strong aversion to debt. As usual, this is based on bitter experience, which she talks about as if it were a recent memory.

When you set up a business, no one tells you that you have skilled at the thing that you do and you have to be skilled at run business. On that, we hadn't a clue. I didn't even have a maths Robert was too academic. Neither of us knew how to run a We had expensive Wardour Street property with staff and and a showroom – all far too ambitious. Plus another pa revamping our offices had leased everything on expensiv owned the most expensive fax machine in the kingdo said 'bye bye' to that third partner.

But my dad continued to be a fantastic supp helping to pay the salaries. He would say, 'It's ver Robert. You have to get more in than you have go

We had a moment where we were outside bashed-up old Renault, so it became known as It was the moment when we said, 'You kno not.' Could we trade out of it? Well, we to and I don't think we actually breathed fo frightened.

And while Robert and I are very both immensely proud and princi principled, and poor'. But I believ that was fundamentally different. obsessively. It was an obsessive

Difference drives Cooper. Sh and that the key to entrepre ity to make something out

I'd set up another bus I was also running a John Rowley – whi That cheque went From then on, u Debt brands yo

―――

'Aye sir, the more they overtech the plumbing,
the easier it is to stop up the drain.'

SCOTTY (*STAR TREK*)

―――

SIR JAMES DYSON

(Dyson)

INTERVIEWED 28 FEBRUARY 2012

———

Some stories begin without any sign as to what is in store. Like this one: a tale of engineering that starts without machines or factories or engineers; a journey to wealth and success that takes us through hardship and failure; a story about an inventor who sells to millions of people, yet starts where there are very few people at all.

Even today, there is not very much at Cley-next-the-Sea, on the blowy north Norfolk coastline, apart from a windmill and a handful of tearooms and arts & crafts shops that close for winter. But in 1956, the place belonged almost exclusively to the sand dunes, marsh birds, and far flat horizon – and to a small boy who had just lost his father to cancer.

James Dyson doesn't need people – he needs to build solutions for people. Lock him up in a solitary confinement cell with only a rubber band and a Lego set, and he will happily emerge with an automatic washing machine. Introduce him to a belly dancer and he will wonder if she suffers from navel fluff and a potential home dust conundrum. This is a man who dreams of inventing and invents while he's dreaming. Yet over half a century ago, wandering around that lonely north Norfolk coastline, the boy Dyson knew nothing of design or engineering or innovation. He just knew what it was like to have to rely on oneself.

It was incredibly remote, because nobody came there. A few people went to Cromer because it was an old seaside town with hotels and things, but the bits I was in – Holt and Blakeney and Cley – no one went there.

It was all discovered later, when people had cars, by people from the Midlands and London. People were born there and died there, but north Norfolk was not a place on the way to anywhere.

We were in an old Victorian rented house, divided into three, and we were in one bit of it, with another family, and then the old lady who owned it and her daughter. It was a pretty dreadful house, not centrally heated, and ice formed on the inside of the windows. There weren't curtains. I think I had a bed, but it was pretty grim.

One of the perils of self-reliance is the sense of being the outsider. You feel different; you act differently. Everyone else is a stranger, so you become strange. Making your own solitary decisions creates reluctance to accept those of others. And before long, a fine line develops between being resourceful and independent and being stubborn and opinionated.

Dyson is the first to admit that he has spent a lifetime oscillating back and forth across that line. It is what has made him what he is, and as he explains himself (in the opening of his autobiography, appropriately entitled *Against the Odds*), 'Misfits are not born or made; they make themselves. And a stubborn opinionated child, desperate to be different… carries the weight of that dislocation for ever.' Time would prove that, for Dyson, such weight would come in handy – essential ballast against the headwinds of vested interests and conservative bankers, fighting him as he invented, designed, built, and sold his creations to a world that neither knew what it needed nor had been given the opportunity for improvement.

It is hard to believe that it was as long ago as 1995 that the Dyson DC01 became the top-selling vacuum cleaner in the United Kingdom, using the (literally) revolutionary feature that replaced the dustbag with the cyclonic vacuum. It had taken him about five years of design, and well over five thousand separate prototypes, along with long, brutal, and expensive legal battles, but with the DC01, Dyson made the breakthrough.

For nearly forty years, he had been on a mission to make his world a better-designed place, which would see his work go from theatres and landing craft to garden equipment and now a vacuum cleaner. That's not

everyone's idea of an upward career path, but, in Dyson's world of non-conformity, it is the height of progress.

I had developed a latent desire to make things around me better, and that desire was the very part of who I was. The important thing was that they were things that I used, so I knew – because I used a vacuum cleaner myself – that I hated the bag. And I'd got to the bottom of the problem with the bag, in that I'd worked out it killed the suction – and I knew that because I was a user myself. So I felt that I could make a better vacuum cleaner for the simple reason that I was coming at it actually as a user.

By 2004, one in four households in the UK had purchased one of the company's vacuum cleaners. In 2011, Dyson achieved sales of over £1 billion, operating in over fifty countries, with 85% of those sales outside of the UK, and employing nearly four thousand staff worldwide. The man's personal wealth is well in excess of £1 billion. And he now has windows with curtains instead of ice.

It has enabled me to stop feeling so frightened. It's allowed me to do gardens and a few other things like buy a JCB. But it hasn't made me any less hungry in business – because this business survives on coming up with new technology and new machines. And if they're no good, business fails. Of course, I don't have to worry about the bank manager, which I did for 40 years after I left college, so it's brought me peace of mind – plus a lot of fun with Deirdre [his wife]. But I don't think it's made me any happier, simply because I was still very happy when we were almost bankrupt. It's an old cliché, but money doesn't make you happy. It's doing exciting things and creating things that make you happy.

And I'm not satisfied; I'm still not satisfied. The moment you've done something, then you're onto the next thing, which is full of new problems that you've got to solve. And then you're onto the next thing. So it's a life of failure and dissatisfaction, whatever your private wealth.

to work together for the rest of our lives. He genuinely said that line. I remember telling my dad, who said, 'Oh, he probably just wants to give you one.'

When I'd left Robert that first day, I'd used that great PR exit-line to get you out of awkward situations: 'Call me if something comes up.' But then, in a very, very Robert kind of way, he did – the very next day: 'Something's come up,' he said. This has been a defining characteristic of our relationship for 25 years. 'What's come up?' I said; you know, immediately irritated by him. And he said, 'Sears!' That's so very Robert. He has to be very impactful. He can't just start small.

Long-story-short, we found ourselves on a train to Nuneaton to pitch our business to Sears. No business cards; nothing. I expected just a chat and we walked into a boardroom full of suits. I was 25, and he was 23, and we had to wing it. Robert says he always remembers me saying, 'What you guys need is more sex!' Whatever we did, we walked away with a piece of business. And that was that.

At first, I didn't know if I wanted a full-time business partner. But Robert just dementedly pursued the idea of closer working. In the end, we were really good together; very yin-yang. In fact, there were many reasons to merge the businesses and take our first office in Wardour Street – which was massive. Because my profile was a bit more known from the PR and marketing point of view, we just kept my name. So JCPR it was.

Cooper and Phillips were off and running. But for all their enthusiasm and belief, there was an enormous gap in their business nous. Very soon into the new venture, they began to make what Cooper now regards as 'ridiculous mistakes'. Without any start-up capital or longer-term investment, and lacking managerial knowledge, their debt quickly grew. Soon, they were going cap-in-hand to the bank manager in her father's branch at Moorgate (who Cooper says was something of a 'guardian angel').

Cooper has a strong aversion to debt. As usual, this is based on bitter experience, which she talks about as if it were a recent memory.

I thought I'd have to stop the business. I was the only child and my mum was in bits. But I had a client – a man called John Rowley, who had left Pretty Polly to set up a hosiery company of his own – and I'd been doing entertainment PR with him. I'd been working with some of the cast from EastEnders, *and with Kate O'Mara who was in* Dynasty *at the time, and he wanted to do a tie-up. Well, I rang him up and told him that I had to stop my company.*

John got me to meet him for a drink and I told him what had happened. My dad really liked John and had known him a for a few years – he'd taken him out for his first posh lunch to Claridge's when he was just a sales rep. John recalled my dad always treating him with respect and he said, 'Look, I know your father. How do you think he'd feel if you gave up? You've suddenly got to the point where you've got the experience to do this job. You stopping is the last thing your dad's going to want to feel he's responsible for. You can't stop.' And so I didn't.

It's time for Robert Phillips, co-founder of JCPR, to enter the story. Like Cooper, Phillips is hardly a household name. Sitting, until recently, on the Global Executive Committee of Edelman, servicing a panoply of multinational clients, he has become one of the brightest stars in the PR universe. Unlike Cooper, Phillips had excelled at university. His father was an international fashion agent, who died suddenly, prompting a former client to ask Phillips to take over the reins of the business. Phillips declined (he was still at university), but sold him his 'new' marketing services company instead (which actually did not yet exist).

I was asked by the editor of this yuppie magazine to think about a bridal wear feature and the trade guys recommended I go see Robert Phillips. A guy who knew about bridal was weird. Was he gay? No, he wasn't gay. So I went to meet Robert, who fed me turkey and mustard sandwiches, which I'd never had together in a sandwich before. The conversation moved from bridal to marketing and PR, and Robert just came out with the comment that we were destined

JCPR was bought in its entirety by Edelman because it had something that Edelman didn't have. That was why we did the deal. The consumer equity, in the bigger sense of the word, was needed by Edelman, and the global reach and intelligent people were needed by us, because, as we were, we couldn't go much further. Some of our people thought we had sold out, because they wanted to stay working for Jackie and Robert and now we might disappear. But Ruth Warder and Sharon Reid now run the business with the original principles and carry the ambition, the sheer love for the job, to this day.

We're running over time with Cooper, but she is enjoying herself – or seems to be – and there is no hint that she is running out of patience or steam. She rearranges her hair, her position on the sofa, and does her slightly puzzled expression. She says she is still shy even today – unless she is talking about brands. The things she is most proud of in life are her marriage and her daughters, Megan and Zara.

She suddenly leaps up to check whether her taxi has arrived, to take her to the company's anniversary celebration, but then, almost as quickly, gets sidetracked by another anecdote and by remembering something she needs to find. She is definitely going to be late, but then thinks of other point that she'd like to add.

...er made a thing of being a woman. I just think you should be ...re, if you can, which is a challenge in itself. I've ended up ...women, just to try to help them be confident – but in who ...eople, irrespective of whether they're female or not.

...ut the inevitable chauvinism sometimes meted out to ...xecutives like herself, but how she has never tried to ... a woman. In the context of the business world in ...asy to understand what she is getting at. She tells ... Dove's Self-Esteem Fund, and how she would ...en there to 'be yourself and find your wings'. ...oman?' is the wrong question, and that the

When you set up a business, no one tells you that you have to be skilled at the thing that you do and you have to be skilled at running a business. On that, we hadn't a clue. I didn't even have a maths O level. Robert was too academic. Neither of us knew how to run a business. We had expensive Wardour Street property with staff and equipment and a showroom – all far too ambitious. Plus another partner who in revamping our offices had leased everything on expensive contracts. We owned the most expensive fax machine in the kingdom. And we soon said 'bye bye' to that third partner.

But my dad continued to be a fantastic support, even at times helping to pay the salaries. He would say, 'It's very simple, Jackie and Robert. You have to get more in than you have going out.'

We had a moment where we were outside my flat. Robert had this bashed-up old Renault, so it became known as the Renault conversation. It was the moment when we said, 'You know, we either let this go – or not.' Could we trade out of it? Well, we took the decision to go for it, and I don't think we actually breathed for three years. I was very, very frightened.

And while Robert and I are very different in many ways, we are both immensely proud and principled. I coined the phrase 'proud, principled, and poor'. But I believed that we were offering something that was fundamentally different from everybody else, and that drove me obsessively. It was an obsessive time, not a healthy time. But we did it.

Difference drives Cooper. She says that she feels like an entrepreneur, and that the key to entrepreneurship is, among several elements, the ability to make something out of a difference.

I'd set up another business. While I was doing the day job of the PR, I was also running an exhibition in designer menswear – actually with John Rowley – which I then sold in a successful deal where I got 50%. That cheque went into our bank and I paid off everything that we owed. From then on, we never missed a target. Never got back in debt. Never. Debt brands you and it's all-pervasive and you don't have any control.

So we repaid the debts, and I could finally relax. And at that point I got Epstein-Barr virus.

Epstein-Barr is dormant in many people, but when activated, it can bring on a severe form of glandular fever, among other debilitating and unpleasant symptoms. It often occurs in university graduates after finals. 'It's when your whole system is so wired and then the system shuts down. It was because I relaxed and that's when the illness strikes.' Cooper was subsequently laid low with ME (or chronic fatigue syndrome), and yet again, life was pitching up and down.

I couldn't do anything. For 18 months. No life; no work; utter misery. The doctors couldn't do anything. I spent a fortune, but no one could help. But then I met this homeopath called Simon Taffler and within six weeks I had my life back. I had to learn how to be different – how to be healthy… Over six weeks, I went on a very strict diet of not eating certain things – no booze, no sugar – to support the remedies. And after that, I swore I would never be that way, like a workaholic, ever again. Robert and I kept going through that horrific period when I think many might have given up.

What have I learnt from that experience? It's this: Have a life. Go home. Be loved.

I remember one time going to a designer launch that we were running and the editor of The Sunday Times *supplement was there, but I could find nothing to say to him. Nothing at all. Because I was so wrung out and I was so exhausted, I couldn't even make the smallest conversation. That was when I realised what trouble I was in. I'd got so geared up just working and working and working that standing around with a glass in my hand trying to have a conversation had finally got beyond me.*

You need to have a life or you won't be a good person at work. Where are your ideas going to come from? Where's the source of your inspiration? So, to this day, I work part-time. Tomorrow, I won't be in the office and every Friday I do something that feeds my brain.

There is something extraordinary in what she has achieved in this respect: in balancing a senior position at a company of the global magnitude of owners Edelman with the kind of personal life that she feels is crucial. After JCPR was sold to Edelman, the companies merged formally in 2007. Now, at last, there is backing, investment, and global reach – which was one of their main justifications for selling the business – and she is supporting initiatives all over the world. She talks about how, so often in her career, she has considered whether she could regard herself as having 'made it'. It is a discussion she often has with Phillips ('probably a hundred times in the last 20 years'), only for both of them to conclude that no achievement can ever warrant that description if you are to keep your motivation and perspective. 'You've never truly made it, nor should you want to have.'

*I'm very lucky in that Edelman is an entrepreneurial organisatio***[*** The schoolgirl Jackie is still the blip, but Edelman embraces th***[*** allows me to be me.*

*Working on global business and finding proper***[*** love or don't know they need, or helping the r***[*** have to work better – it's a great job. Ro***[*** to be a great businessman. He was ***[*** the machinery of the business***[*** now JCPR is still runnin***[*** within Edelman.*

Trailblazing ***[*** with M***[*** practica***[*** what seem***[*** fields – you ***[*** terises what C***[*** Starbucks, Dove ***[*** has been doing thin***[*** attracted Edelman.

real issue is whether one is a successful *person*. And to be that, 'you have to believe, work hard, have a dream and never ever give up. There isn't a short cut to this. Whether you are a man or a woman.'

Despite the position in which she now finds herself, Cooper is keen to stress that her life is still not an idealised one:

Be it at home or at work, it's impossible to have it all, or get everything right. I just try to work smart rather than drive myself into the grave trying to be the perfect mum. There's no such thing. But women have to remind themselves of that and not feel a failure.

Cooper pulls the issues of self-worth and business success back to honesty.

In a way, that explains why I will say the thing that no one else wants to say. It's the importance of honesty. I was on a three-day workshop with Starbucks, and our client – who happens to be a very impressive woman – came up to me afterwards and said, 'What I've heard about you is true. You say the thing that nobody else wants to say.' And she thanked me for it. Before that, I actually thought that I'd lost the client. But I hadn't, and they'd listened. I think sometimes you have to say it. You have to speak up.

I try to be really honest with my clients. I encourage the team here to work on a very human level. I always wanted people to be sad when we left the room... I always said to the team, 'Don't just show up, but really make it matter. Make sure the client's sad when it's time to leave.'

Amidst the fashion photographs, there are some cardboard boxes full of products of some kind. Cooper starts rummaging and comes out with a selection of flat paper packages. She wants to know what size underpants we wear. Cheeky...

I'm working on a company, launching just now in the US, which is new men's underwear brand. We're going to redefine men's underwear

and I'm as excited at this as I was about Wonderbra. I think the product is potentially a category-changer, but the strategy behind the company is what is really mould-breaking. We've got a whole new way of allowing celebrity and entrepreneurial potential to work together.

It's wonderful to be able to do these things and that people think I've still got something to say. Now I feel like I'm an entrepreneur who happens to be in PR. I never ever want to stop learning.

And in my life, I've learnt that being different is good, not bad. We all just need to find our place. Everyone in the world has got something that they're brilliant at. If I can help people find that, then that will do it for me. Because I was different, and suffered for it, and I'm still different today. But I eventually found something that I could do without feeling that I didn't belong. How fantastic is that?

And I can send you each away with a pair of underpants...

Now Cooper is really late, and she hurries for the door, still thinking and talking about new things she needs to say. Things she feels are important. Things that might help.

Cooper has spoken a lot about how she has always felt different. But that has given her a story – and a skill in communicating its lessons – that can be inspirational for many others: small or great, man or woman, troubled or lonely or panicked through a sense of their own uniqueness. It is in this way that Cooper is making a difference... and will, no doubt, continue to make a difference.

SIR JAMES DYSON

(Dyson)

INTERVIEWED 28 FEBRUARY 2012

S ome stories begin without any sign as to what is in store. Like this one: a tale of engineering that starts without machines or factories or engineers; a journey to wealth and success that takes us through hardship and failure; a story about an inventor who sells to millions of people, yet starts where there are very few people at all.

Even today, there is not very much at Cley-next-the-Sea, on the blowy north Norfolk coastline, apart from a windmill and a handful of tearooms and arts & crafts shops that close for winter. But in 1956, the place belonged almost exclusively to the sand dunes, marsh birds, and far flat horizon – and to a small boy who had just lost his father to cancer.

James Dyson doesn't need people – he needs to build solutions for people. Lock him up in a solitary confinement cell with only a rubber band and a Lego set, and he will happily emerge with an automatic washing machine. Introduce him to a belly dancer and he will wonder if she suffers from navel fluff and a potential home dust conundrum. This is a man who dreams of inventing and invents while he's dreaming. Yet over half a century ago, wandering around that lonely north Norfolk coastline, the boy Dyson knew nothing of design or engineering or innovation. He just knew what it was like to have to rely on oneself.

It was incredibly remote, because nobody came there. A few people went to Cromer because it was an old seaside town with hotels and things, but the bits I was in – Holt and Blakeney and Cley – no one went there.

everyone's idea of an upward career path, but, in Dyson's world of non-conformity, it is the height of progress.

I had developed a latent desire to make things around me better, and that desire was the very part of who I was. The important thing was that they were things that I used, so I knew – because I used a vacuum cleaner myself – that I hated the bag. And I'd got to the bottom of the problem with the bag, in that I'd worked out it killed the suction – and I knew that because I was a user myself. So I felt that I could make a better vacuum cleaner for the simple reason that I was coming at it actually as a user.

By 2004, one in four houscholds in the UK had purchased one of the company's vacuum cleaners. In 2011, Dyson achieved sales of over £1 billion, operating in over fifty countries, with 85% of those sales outside of the UK, and employing nearly four thousand staff worldwide. The man's personal wealth is well in excess of £1 billion. And he now has windows with curtains instead of ice.

It has enabled me to stop feeling so frightened. It's allowed me to do gardens and a few other things like buy a JCB. But it hasn't made me any less hungry in business – because this business survives on coming up with new technology and new machines. And if they're no good, business fails. Of course, I don't have to worry about the bank manager, which I did for 40 years after I left college, so it's brought me peace of mind – plus a lot of fun with Deirdre [his wife]. But I don't think it's made me any happier, simply because I was still very happy when we were almost bankrupt. It's an old cliché, but money doesn't make you happy. It's doing exciting things and creating things that make you happy.

And I'm not satisfied; I'm still not satisfied. The moment you've done something, then you're onto the next thing, which is full of new problems that you've got to solve. And then you're onto the next thing. So it's a life of failure and dissatisfaction, whatever your private wealth.

It was all discovered later, when people had cars, by people from the Midlands and London. People were born there and died there, but north Norfolk was not a place on the way to anywhere.

We were in an old Victorian rented house, divided into three, and we were in one bit of it, with another family, and then the old lady who owned it and her daughter. It was a pretty dreadful house, not centrally heated, and ice formed on the inside of the windows. There weren't curtains. I think I had a bed, but it was pretty grim.

One of the perils of self-reliance is the sense of being the outsider. You feel different; you act differently. Everyone else is a stranger, so you become strange. Making your own solitary decisions creates reluctance to accept those of others. And before long, a fine line develops between being resourceful and independent and being stubborn and opinionated.

Dyson is the first to admit that he has spent a lifetime oscillating back and forth across that line. It is what has made him what he is, and as he explains himself (in the opening of his autobiography, appropriately entitled *Against the Odds*), 'Misfits are not born or made; they make themselves. And a stubborn opinionated child, desperate to be different... carries the weight of that dislocation for ever.' Time would prove that, for Dyson, such weight would come in handy – essential ballast against the headwinds of vested interests and conservative bankers, fighting him as he invented, designed, built, and sold his creations to a world that neither knew what it needed nor had been given the opportunity for improvement.

It is hard to believe that it was as long ago as 1995 that the Dyson DC01 became the top-selling vacuum cleaner in the United Kingdom, using the (literally) revolutionary feature that replaced the dustbag with the cyclonic vacuum. It had taken him about five years of design, and well over five thousand separate prototypes, along with long, brutal, and expensive legal battles, but with the DC01, Dyson made the breakthrough.

For nearly forty years, he had been on a mission to make his world a better-designed place, which would see his work go from theatres and landing craft to garden equipment and now a vacuum cleaner. That's not

When you set up a business, no one tells you that you have to be skilled at the thing that you do and you have to be skilled at running a business. On that, we hadn't a clue. I didn't even have a maths O level. Robert was too academic. Neither of us knew how to run a business. We had expensive Wardour Street property with staff and equipment and a showroom – all far too ambitious. Plus another partner who in revamping our offices had leased everything on expensive contracts. We owned the most expensive fax machine in the kingdom. And we soon said 'bye bye' to that third partner.

But my dad continued to be a fantastic support, even at times helping to pay the salaries. He would say, 'It's very simple, Jackie and Robert. You have to get more in than you have going out.'

We had a moment where we were outside my flat. Robert had this bashed-up old Renault, so it became known as the Renault conversation. It was the moment when we said, 'You know, we either let this go – or not.' Could we trade out of it? Well, we took the decision to go for it, and I don't think we actually breathed for three years. I was very, very frightened.

And while Robert and I are very different in many ways, we are both immensely proud and principled. I coined the phrase 'proud, principled, and poor'. But I believed that we were offering something that was fundamentally different from everybody else, and that drove me obsessively. It was an obsessive time, not a healthy time. But we did it.

Difference drives Cooper. She says that she feels like an entrepreneur, and that the key to entrepreneurship is, among several elements, the ability to make something out of a difference.

I'd set up another business. While I was doing the day job of the PR, I was also running an exhibition in designer menswear – actually with John Rowley – which I then sold in a successful deal where I got 50%. That cheque went into our bank and I paid off everything that we owed. From then on, we never missed a target. Never got back in debt. Never. Debt brands you and it's all-pervasive and you don't have any control.

So we repaid the debts, and I could finally relax. And at that point I got Epstein-Barr virus.

Epstein-Barr is dormant in many people, but when activated, it can bring on a severe form of glandular fever, among other debilitating and unpleasant symptoms. It often occurs in university graduates after finals. 'It's when your whole system is so wired and then the system shuts down. It was because I relaxed and that's when the illness strikes.' Cooper was subsequently laid low with ME (or chronic fatigue syndrome), and yet again, life was pitching up and down.

I couldn't do anything. For 18 months. No life; no work; utter misery. The doctors couldn't do anything. I spent a fortune, but no one could help. But then I met this homeopath called Simon Taffler and within six weeks I had my life back. I had to learn how to be different – how to be healthy… Over six weeks, I went on a very strict diet of not eating certain things – no booze, no sugar – to support the remedies. And after that, I swore I would never be that way, like a workaholic, ever again. Robert and I kept going through that horrific period when I think many might have given up.

What have I learnt from that experience? It's this: Have a life. Go home. Be loved.

I remember one time going to a designer launch that we were running and the editor of The Sunday Times *supplement was there, but I could find nothing to say to him. Nothing at all. Because I was so wrung out and I was so exhausted, I couldn't even make the smallest conversation. That was when I realised what trouble I was in. I'd got so geared up just working and working and working that standing around with a glass in my hand trying to have a conversation had finally got beyond me.*

You need to have a life or you won't be a good person at work. Where are your ideas going to come from? Where's the source of your inspiration? So, to this day, I work part-time. Tomorrow, I won't be in the office and every Friday I do something that feeds my brain.

There is something extraordinary in what she has achieved in this respect: in balancing a senior position at a company of the global magnitude of owners Edelman with the kind of personal life that she feels is crucial. After JCPR was sold to Edelman, the companies merged formally in 2007. Now, at last, there is backing, investment, and global reach – which was one of their main justifications for selling the business – and she is supporting initiatives all over the world. She talks about how, so often in her career, she has considered whether she could regard herself as having 'made it'. It is a discussion she often has with Phillips ('probably a hundred times in the last 20 years'), only for both of them to conclude that no achievement can ever warrant that description if you are to keep your motivation and perspective. 'You've never truly made it, nor should you want to have.'

I'm very lucky in that Edelman is an entrepreneurial organisation. The schoolgirl Jackie is still the blip, but Edelman embraces that and allows me to be me.

Working on global business and finding properties that brands love or don't know they need, or helping the properties that they do have to work better – it's a great job. Robert has had to learn how to be a great businessman. He was the one who ended up running the machinery of the business, as well as doing the day job... and now JCPR is still running and trailblazing in the consumer world within Edelman.

Trailblazing indeed. At the time of the interview, Cooper is working with Microsoft on its launch of Halo 4 for Xbox, for which they have practically taken over the entire principality of Lichtenstein – or at least what seems like most of its landmarks (castles, quarries, mines, farms, fields – you name it). It's typical of the kind of innovation that characterises what Cooper loves doing. Whether it is working with Shell or Starbucks, Dove or the London Olympic mascots, the order of the day has been doing things that create difference, and that is possibly what so attracted Edelman.

JCPR was bought in its entirety by Edelman because it had something that Edelman didn't have. That was why we did the deal. The consumer equity, in the bigger sense of the word, was needed by Edelman, and the global reach and intelligent people were needed by us, because, as we were, we couldn't go much further. Some of our people thought we had sold out, because they wanted to stay working for Jackie and Robert and now we might disappear. But Ruth Warder and Sharon Reid now run the business with the original principles and carry the ambition, the sheer love for the job, to this day.

We're running over time with Cooper, but she is enjoying herself – or seems to be – and there is no hint that she is running out of patience or steam. She rearranges her hair, her position on the sofa, and does her slightly puzzled expression. She says she is still shy even today – unless she is talking about brands. The things she is most proud of in life are her marriage and her daughters, Megan and Zara.

She suddenly leaps up to check whether her taxi has arrived, to take her to the company's anniversary celebration, but then, almost as quickly, gets sidetracked by another anecdote and by remembering something she needs to find. She is definitely going to be late, but then thinks of another point that she'd like to add.

I've never made a thing of being a woman. I just think you should be who you are, if you can, which is a challenge in itself. I've ended up mentoring women, just to try to help them be confident – but in who they are, as people, irrespective of whether they're female or not.

Cooper talks about the inevitable chauvinism sometimes meted out to successful female executives like herself, but how she has never tried to be a man or not to be a woman. In the context of the business world in which she moves, it's easy to understand what she is getting at. She tells of the work she did with Dove's Self-Esteem Fund, and how she would encourage the young women there to 'be yourself and find your wings'. She stresses that 'man or woman?' is the wrong question, and that the real issue is whether one is a successful *person*. And to be that, 'you have to believe, work hard, have a dream and never ever give up. There isn't a short cut to this. Whether you are a man or a woman.'

Despite the position in which she now finds herself, Cooper is keen to stress that her life is still not an idealised one:

Be it at home or at work, it's impossible to have it all, or get everything right. I just try to work smart rather than drive myself into the grave trying to be the perfect mum. There's no such thing. But women have to remind themselves of that and not feel a failure.

Cooper pulls the issues of self-worth and business success back to honesty.

In a way, that explains why I will say the thing that no one else wants to say. It's the importance of honesty. I was on a three-day workshop with Starbucks, and our client – who happens to be a very impressive woman – came up to me afterwards and said, 'What I've heard about you is true. You say the thing that nobody else wants to say.' And she thanked me for it. Before that, I actually thought that I'd lost the client. But I hadn't, and they'd listened. I think sometimes you have to say it. You have to speak up.

I try to be really honest with my clients. I encourage the team here to work on a very human level. I always wanted people to be sad when we left the room... I always said to the team, 'Don't just show up, but really make it matter. Make sure the client's sad when it's time to leave.'

Amidst the fashion photographs, there are some cardboard boxes full of products of some kind. Cooper starts rummaging and comes out with a selection of flat paper packages. She wants to know what size underpants we wear. Cheeky...

I'm working on a company, launching just now in the US, which is a new men's underwear brand. We're going to redefine men's underwear,

and I'm as excited at this as I was about Wonderbra. I think the product is potentially a category-changer, but the strategy behind the company is what is really mould-breaking. We've got a whole new way of allowing celebrity and entrepreneurial potential to work together.

It's wonderful to be able to do these things and that people think I've still got something to say. Now I feel like I'm an entrepreneur who happens to be in PR. I never ever want to stop learning.

And in my life, I've learnt that being different is good, not bad. We all just need to find our place. Everyone in the world has got something that they're brilliant at. If I can help people find that, then that will do it for me. Because I was different, and suffered for it, and I'm still different today. But I eventually found something that I could do without feeling that I didn't belong. How fantastic is that?

And I can send you each away with a pair of underpants...

Now Cooper is really late, and she hurries for the door, still thinking and talking about new things she needs to say. Things she feels are important. Things that might help.

Cooper has spoken a lot about how she has always felt different. But that has given her a story – and a skill in communicating its lessons – that can be inspirational for many others: small or great, man or woman, troubled or lonely or panicked through a sense of their own uniqueness. It is in this way that Cooper is making a difference... and will, no doubt, continue to make a difference.

SIR JAMES DYSON

(Dyson)

INTERVIEWED 28 FEBRUARY 2012

Some stories begin without any sign as to what is in store. Like this one: a tale of engineering that starts without machines or factories or engineers; a journey to wealth and success that takes us through hardship and failure; a story about an inventor who sells to millions of people, yet starts where there are very few people at all.

Even today, there is not very much at Cley-next-the-Sea, on the blowy north Norfolk coastline, apart from a windmill and a handful of tearooms and arts & crafts shops that close for winter. But in 1956, the place belonged almost exclusively to the sand dunes, marsh birds, and far flat horizon – and to a small boy who had just lost his father to cancer.

James Dyson doesn't need people – he needs to build solutions for people. Lock him up in a solitary confinement cell with only a rubber band and a Lego set, and he will happily emerge with an automatic washing machine. Introduce him to a belly dancer and he will wonder if she suffers from navel fluff and a potential home dust conundrum. This is a man who dreams of inventing and invents while he's dreaming. Yet over half a century ago, wandering around that lonely north Norfolk coastline, the boy Dyson knew nothing of design or engineering or innovation. He just knew what it was like to have to rely on oneself.

It was incredibly remote, because nobody came there. A few people went to Cromer because it was an old seaside town with hotels and things, but the bits I was in – Holt and Blakeney and Cley – no one went there.

It was all discovered later, when people had cars, by people from the Midlands and London. People were born there and died there, but north Norfolk was not a place on the way to anywhere.

We were in an old Victorian rented house, divided into three, and we were in one bit of it, with another family, and then the old lady who owned it and her daughter. It was a pretty dreadful house, not centrally heated, and ice formed on the inside of the windows. There weren't curtains. I think I had a bed, but it was pretty grim.

One of the perils of self-reliance is the sense of being the outsider. You feel different; you act differently. Everyone else is a stranger, so you become strange. Making your own solitary decisions creates reluctance to accept those of others. And before long, a fine line develops between being resourceful and independent and being stubborn and opinionated.

Dyson is the first to admit that he has spent a lifetime oscillating back and forth across that line. It is what has made him what he is, and as he explains himself (in the opening of his autobiography, appropriately entitled *Against the Odds*), 'Misfits are not born or made; they make themselves. And a stubborn opinionated child, desperate to be different... carries the weight of that dislocation for ever.' Time would prove that, for Dyson, such weight would come in handy – essential ballast against the headwinds of vested interests and conservative bankers, fighting him as he invented, designed, built, and sold his creations to a world that neither knew what it needed nor had been given the opportunity for improvement.

It is hard to believe that it was as long ago as 1995 that the Dyson DC01 became the top-selling vacuum cleaner in the United Kingdom, using the (literally) revolutionary feature that replaced the dustbag with the cyclonic vacuum. It had taken him about five years of design, and well over five thousand separate prototypes, along with long, brutal, and expensive legal battles, but with the DC01, Dyson made the breakthrough.

For nearly forty years, he had been on a mission to make his world a better-designed place, which would see his work go from theatres and landing craft to garden equipment and now a vacuum cleaner. That's not

everyone's idea of an upward career path, but, in Dyson's world of non-conformity, it is the height of progress.

I had developed a latent desire to make things around me better, and that desire was the very part of who I was. The important thing was that they were things that I used, so I knew – because I used a vacuum cleaner myself – that I hated the bag. And I'd got to the bottom of the problem with the bag, in that I'd worked out it killed the suction – and I knew that because I was a user myself. So I felt that I could make a better vacuum cleaner for the simple reason that I was coming at it actually as a user.

By 2004, one in four households in the UK had purchased one of the company's vacuum cleaners. In 2011, Dyson achieved sales of over £1 billion, operating in over fifty countries, with 85% of those sales outside of the UK, and employing nearly four thousand staff worldwide. The man's personal wealth is well in excess of £1 billion. And he now has windows with curtains instead of ice.

It has enabled me to stop feeling so frightened. It's allowed me to do gardens and a few other things like buy a JCB. But it hasn't made me any less hungry in business – because this business survives on coming up with new technology and new machines. And if they're no good, business fails. Of course, I don't have to worry about the bank manager, which I did for 40 years after I left college, so it's brought me peace of mind – plus a lot of fun with Deirdre [his wife]. But I don't think it's made me any happier, simply because I was still very happy when we were almost bankrupt. It's an old cliché, but money doesn't make you happy. It's doing exciting things and creating things that make you happy.

And I'm not satisfied; I'm still not satisfied. The moment you've done something, then you're onto the next thing, which is full of new problems that you've got to solve. And then you're onto the next thing. So it's a life of failure and dissatisfaction, whatever your private wealth.

Dyson's office is in the corner of the upper floor of the company's Research Centre and Head Office at Malmesbury, in Wiltshire. It is some distance off the M4, in the middle of acres of agricultural monotony and very occasional new-build housing developments that have escaped conservation planning. Our destination is the crop of low-level, grey corrugated steel and frameless glass hangars, which, despite a huge white undulating roof (by the architect Chris Wilkinson), still feel rather like any other modern blue-chip electronics factory. That is, until we pass through the security checkpoint and park between a real-life Harrier jump jet and a catamaran. And until we see sinister giant-sized copper anthropoids watching us wherever we turn: they were created out of old industrial water tanks by a local sculptor called Peter Burke, but they have the gait of a mutinous collective about to jolt into self-awareness and take control. Then there is an original Mini, sawn in half to showcase its mechanicals like a 3D *Eagle* drawing that has lifted itself off the page. It seems there should be an original Citroën DS exhibit nearby, but we are told that, bizarrely, someone has borrowed it.

We enter an enormous lobby with glass cabinets everywhere, full of blue and red plastic machines, silver cogwheels, and yellow tubular gadgets. The metal device holding an upright blue see-through plastic cylinder full of clear fluid looks like it's part of the iconic design collection, but actually it's only the water cooler. The site is a working office complex, but it is also a veritable Science Museum: the overspilled detritus of James Dyson's brain, raised on Virgil's *Aeneid* and D. C. Thomson *Commando* comics in equal measure.

Upstairs, we enter an open-plan office space framed by a huge continuous glass window. There are rows and rows of boffins, their desks cluttered with screens and pipes and wires and plastic tubes. It is like the inside of a Borg spaceship or the outside of a Richard Rogers building. In the air is the ambient hum of ingenuity and creativity – or perhaps it is just the air-conditioning fans.

In his office, Dyson is playing with a new thin white rectangular machine that seems to move up and down using thought waves. He explains that it is his new desk lamp, actually designed by his son Jake.

(It's a talented family all round: the younger son Sam is a professional musician, and daughter Emily runs her own fashion boutique.) The room is shiny and modern, but with arbitrary collections of framed awards, Dyson prototypes, unidentifiable plastic artefacts, and aeroplane models scattered on surfaces. An enormous drawing board is in the corner, showing a scale cross-section drawing of what looks like a giant mechanical mouthguard.

Dyson puts down a half-eaten chocolate bar and shows us his iPad: David Hockney has been sending him drawings. Dyson has also been doing his own iPad painting, which he seems to enjoy with the exuberance of a man whose lifelong driving forces of art and technology have now merged in the form of this stylised electronic slate propped up on his desk. There is a simple, but beguiling, Impressionist portrait of his wife Deirdre in among the Hockneys, and you get the first of several indications that his fellow artist and soulmate has been another inspiration, ever since he started taking her off on weekends to Cley in his Mini. They first held hands on a college art trip to Regent's Park Zoo, which we include here for a reason no more meaningful or important than that it makes for a nice image.

Dyson has obviously thought a lot about how he came to be where he is, and has a great deal to say about his own form of occasionally dysfunctional individuality – a character trait that is subtly but immediately in evidence, because he clearly prefers to pursue his own exposition rather than be put off by our line of questioning. This is a man who has experienced every kind of interview, be it with hawkish American lawyers paid by the blood-bag, or with airheaded advertising executives paid to promote image rather than substance. (He is scornful of both, needless to say, because the engineering is the least of those people's interests.)

The long, drawn-out death of his father comes early in the story. After James turned six, Alec Dyson was hospitalised on a near-permanent basis, so any memory of him is very sketchy. His father's absence left Dyson with no one to go to for help, having to come up with his own solutions to life's problems. He suggests that he probably suffered from the absence of a male father figure, at the same time being only too aware of how much his widowed mother did as a single parent, and acknowledging her stoicism in the circumstances. (She was, incidentally, one of the women who pushed small aeroplanes around a large map in the Second World War Bomber Command bunker, answering Bakelite telephones to Lancaster pilots in a Celia Johnson voice.) Being fatherless, from such an early age, was a catalyst of sorts, and in characteristic Dyson fashion, he puts it into a rather unexpected context:

Do you know, I think it's over 80% of British prime ministers since Walpole lost a parent before the age of ten, compared to only 1.5% of the normal population? It had a big effect on me. I was at boarding school, which we could only afford because my father had taught there. So there I was, alone at boarding school – very different, very isolated, very much all on my own. Which I think was an important part of my character. I'm not saying my mother wasn't supportive, but split families and single-parent families are very common now. They weren't then, so I felt very different.

Time and again, he comes back to the notion that he was an individual, struggling with difference by being ever more different.

Having being forced to feel difference, I then revelled in it. At every opportunity, whether it was acting or whatever it was, I'd be different. Even my clothes were different: I had stiff collars, whereas everybody else had rather nasty floppy ones.

I remember the headmaster announced in school that there were vacancies to learn certain instruments, and when he said the bassoon – which no one had heard of – I put up my hand because it was off into the unknown again. I wondered what on earth was that thing; nobody else was playing it, so I wanted to do it.

He still has that bassoon. Lonely north Norfolk kid, maybe. But he also was developing the inner constitution of a prizefighter. It would stand him in good stead years later, when he had to face mean-spirited bankers and rival manufacturers hell-bent on seeing an end to his cyclonic bagless impudence. Not surprisingly, while still at Gresham's Boarding School, long-distance running became his world – a place where he could road-test his fighting skills using his own body and the elements around him.

I rather liked running because I could be on my own. I could have an adventure by myself, out of school, across the country, running along the long wild beaches there. It was all about getting out on my own and doing something; trying out my own theories for how to be good at things... like the psychology of the race, because you have to accelerate when you feel the most tired, because that puts off all the other runners. When you go up the hill, you should accelerate because that's when everybody else would be slowing down, feeling exhausted; that's when you accelerate and apply maximum effort.

The anomaly, the fighter, the individualist... yet there is another side to Dyson that adds complexity to the portrait: the artist and scholar.

At a young age, I won the Eagle *painting competition with a painting I did of Blakeney Point. It had an early effect on me. My art master was very proud, but most of all, it told me I was good at something.*

Dyson is actually rather good at rather a lot of things. He is a learned and cultured man, and he can fire off classical, literary, linguistic, musical, and operatic allusions without blinking. Living in the old house in the grounds of the boarding school obviously left as much of a mark as did the bleak Norfolk winds. Actually, to Dyson, it is all part of the same phenomenon: art and the country. His strongest memory of 1956, he says, is the smell of oil paints. In his reverie, the Dyson 'Billy Casper boy' has morphed into Dyson 'Enid Blyton short-trousered boy':

It was a Swallows and Amazons *type of existence. My father was a teacher, so during the holidays we had the whole grounds to ourselves – with a swimming pool, squash courts, the woods, and everything really, so it was pretty, it was fine, you didn't need money. We grew vegetables and had chickens. It was a very rural, cut-off existence – but that's important, because it fitted with the arts background. My father had been a classics teacher and my mother went to Cambridge later on to read English, and my brother was a classics scholar. So it was an entirely arts background, with our only bit of news being the Sunday papers, which started arriving with a colour supplement about the time that Armstrong-Jones got married to Princess Margaret. But up to that point we were totally cut off. We had no telly and we didn't listen to the radio much either.*

Arts and the country. Many years later, he will decide on lavender and pink as his colour scheme for the G-Force vacuum cleaner, claiming as inspiration the morning tones of the Provençal landscape from his time in southern France – the same colours that inspired the French Impressionists, which leads him to call his early design the 'first Impressionist vacuum cleaner'. Art, design, vacuuming – it's all the same animal.

As he tells his story, a pattern starts to emerge. Dyson enters each phase of his life in a state of uncertainty, but invariably emerges the stronger for it. From Norfolk, the misfit boy travels to the capital and – weirdly enough, for a Norfolk teenager at the time – enters the Byam Shaw School of Art in Kensington. A place he says felt less like an art school and more like the staging post for London debutantes; the spam fritter had stumbled into a world of dessert wines and canapés.

But it was also a world where there was fun to be had, along with an opportunity to be grasped for someone who knew self-reliance.

I think I was the first person from my school ever to go to an art school. My headmaster had actually told me I'd be better off without a degree round my neck. And it did turn out to be great fun. It was a very independent place run by a man called Maurice de Sausmarez, who towards the end of the first year called me into the office and said, 'I think you should be a designer.' So I said, 'Well, what's design?' You see, I didn't actually know what design was. He said, 'Oh well, there's furniture design, there's stained glass, there's interior design, there's industrial design...' So I chose furniture design because I thought I knew about chairs because I'd sat on them.

From there, I got into the RCA, without a first degree – because they were allowing one or two students in on an anti-elitism programme, into the architectural department. It was called interior design but actually it was architectural. One of the lecturers was Tony Hunt, a famous structural engineer. I remember going to the first lecture – engineering – thinking it was going to be really boring; but I was riveted.

I became fascinated by seeing how structures work. Buckminster Fuller [the famous American engineer] was there, as was Anton Furst who designed the Batmobile and did the whole thing for Star Wars. *All the sort of things I'd stood for in my prior life suddenly went out of the window.*

And just as this was happening, I then met the theatre impresario, Joan Littlewood – quite by accident. She would ask anybody to do anything and she asked me to design a theatre for Stratford in east London. So I did a mushroom-shaped building in Buckminster Fuller's style, using an aluminum triodesic system of tubes that would be made by Vickers. I went there and they showed me a film of this man pulling up his huge factory roof by hand made out of the same system. I said I wanted to go and meet him. So I drove down to Bath and it was Jeremy Fry who owned a firm called Rotork. I asked him for some money for this theatre I was doing and he said, 'Absolutely not. We're not going to give you a penny. But you appear an interesting designer, so I will give you a few things to design.' In fact, he asked me to design a boat that he'd invented.

Thus was born the Rotork Sea Truck – a kind of fast, flat-hulled landing craft. Fry was a millionaire industrialist, but the thing that singled him out was that he was a confidently instinctive *doer*. On meeting Dyson, he did the obvious thing – employed him and put him in charge of his pet project. And this attitude to risk has been adopted by Dyson – don't over-interrogate the issue, or else it becomes an even bigger one: just do what needs to be done to achieve what needs to be achieved. Dyson could, and would, make the Sea Truck happen. And he would also make it less ugly.

Fry needed someone with an eye for aesthetics. Someone who could, if not exactly turn the Sea Truck into a Princess yacht, at least make it a bit less painful on the eye. Rotork paid Dyson £300 for his final design work, but by 1970 had set him up with a subsidiary company making the peculiar flat-bottomed water-going craft. Or as Dyson called it, 'the fastest piece of plywood in the world'. Now all he had to do was sell the thing.

I got the thrill of making and going out and then selling a completely different piece of technology in an outlandish shape. It was a very unusual thing. Someone described it as a Welsh dresser, skimming across the water. But it took two Land Rovers at 40 miles an hour and you could land on the beach – so it was a very, very useful thing.

Dyson was learning on the job, and by making mistakes. At the same time, Dyson the salesman neither looked the part, nor felt comfortable in the role.

I was 23, coming out of the Royal College, with flared trousers and flowered shirts, and now I was having to go and find out who wanted to use these boats and why. If I put a suit on to go and do selling, I felt as though I was denying my birthright. I mean, we despise selling in England; we despise salesmen. Whereas in America, it's a very esteemed profession.

But, in time, I discovered that selling is absolutely fascinating. And exciting, because when you get a sale, it's absolutely thrilling. But also I found it really interesting to understand what people wanted. Selling isn't about talking – it's about listening; about asking questions.

Many years later in 2012, with his vacuum cleaner business a worldwide success, he still insists on his workforce not bothering with shirts and ties as a point of principle.

By 1973, Dyson was talking with Special Forces worldwide: taking part in weapons tests and seat-of-the-pants sea trials, with option packs offering anything from armour-plating to desert-enabled wheel kits. The British were – in a foretaste of vacuum cleaner deal-making to come – one of his most conservative and 'blinkered' (his word) clients. But the business was a success. Within five years of trading, the company was selling hundreds of the new craft, now much more sophisticated. And made, not from plywood, but from the latest plastics, and making millions of pounds for the British economy.

I did that for five years, loved it, and went all over the world, selling it. It was very exciting and great fun. But I felt slightly remote. I wanted to do something that everybody used every day. I had helped design something for people with whom I had nothing in common. It wasn't part of my life building assault craft or smuggling-boats or whatever they are. It's not what I did. I wanted to get back to doing something that we all use every day.

From military landing craft, then, it was time to look at garden equipment. From one end of the spectrum to the other.

But this part of our story will not, be warned, end particularly successfully. In 1977, Dyson's new venture, Kirk-Dyson, was selling Ballbarrows – barrows that have a large red ball rather than a wheel around the front axle – in shops and garden centres throughout the UK. There are fundamental advantages to having a ball at the front of a vehicle that you push, especially when it tracks round a corner or follows a curve. So the Ballbarrow was in that sense a success. Yet it is likely that the barrow in your garden still has a wheel and not a ball around its front axle. So what happened to the idea? To get this far, the company had borrowed too much money, and paying it back, at the level of interest applicable in the seventies, was unsustainable. The tension led to infighting between the board members, and Dyson was forced out. He had proved that he could design a machine and launch a company from scratch – and learned in the process that business can be vicious and soul-destroying. 'Like giving birth to a child and then losing it,' he says.

From the sea to the garden to the dining room, where the Dyson family's Hoover was playing up and the holiday was being cancelled. The Dyson family were now in a bad place. They had moved home to be near the Ballbarrow factory, and, with only his wife's teaching income, Dyson's debt was in danger of dragging them under. They could not even afford a replacement for the vacuum cleaner, which kept losing its suction; in fact, they could barely afford the bags.

At this low point in Dyson's story, let us pause and reflect on the way the lights of invention come on at the darkest of times. Think of lonely Barnes Wallis, skimming pebbles across his deserted pond, or a solitary James Watt, boiling his kettle. We are now approaching Dyson's own eureka moment, and a demonstration of invention's serendipitous nature. Indeed, at this point in the interview, he breaks the narrative to make a general point about his team's later 'discoveries'.

Take our hand-dryer, for example. We didn't actually set out to design a hand-dryer. But we were developing something else and just noticed how it scraped the water off your hands. So we immediately saw that it would give us a better hand-dryer, because it's fast, it doesn't use the energy of having to have a heater, and it doesn't damage your hands. What we're always searching for is that magic technology that makes something work better and solves things you get angry about.

Back in the late seventies, Dyson is sick to death of the blocked, suctionless Hoover Junior and the bags that he can't afford. He is in the garage, cobbling together, like a *Blue Peter* presenter, some old Cornflakes packets, Fairy Liquid bottles, gaffer tape, and redundant home appliance spares. The rest of the city gradually take to their beds, switch out their lights, and close their eyes...

And in the morning, there, in the centre of the garage, is the world's first prototype bagless cyclonic vacuum cleaner. Dyson is back in business.

When we went to sell it to the shops, they said you'll never sell a vacuum cleaner with a clear bin: it's ridiculous, seeing the dust. But you see, I had used it myself, and I had actually liked seeing the dust: I got a morbid pleasure from it, a bit like a German lavatory. I knew that I could take that risk. I think that I understand things that I use in a way that I don't understand things I don't use, like wheelchairs and Sea Trucks. It's about understanding what I'm doing when I use the device, and then being able to take a really risky decision because I understand it and know exactly what the risk is. I can't go to wheelchairs and know how to do a revolutionary wheelchair, because I don't know what it's like to use a wheelchair.

(He mentions the wheelchair probably because his erstwhile sponsor, Jeremy Fry, wanted Dyson to start designing them – presumably riding on red balls; but that is a tale for another day.)

There were plenty of people out there who wanted Dyson stopped: anyone who sold vacuum cleaner bags for a start. And, of course, there was still no investment, but plenty of debt. Before it got better, it would get far, far worse, and there were betrayals by American companies, leading to huge legal actions, and continual, hurtful, and short-sighted rejections from companies in Europe. In one incident, Dyson visits – incognito, mystery-shopper fashion – the John Lewis store in Bristol to see if they will sell him a Dual Cyclone. The sales assistant suggests that Dyson would be better suited to an alternative German model, on the grounds that it is made of superior plastic. Dyson can stay quiet no longer, reveals his true identity, calls the store manager, and at some point during the ensuing argument, avails himself of a ball-peen hammer and invites anyone there to attempt to smash each model to pieces. Guess which one loses the game.

The turning point was when he finally persuaded the Japanese retailer, Apex, to sell his technology. At the time, an American company – with whom he had been dealing previously – was suing him for a lot more than everything he owned. He was, he says, 'broke, hungry, and depressed.' The Japanese deal was the one he simply had to close or face financial, mental, and spiritual ruin.

Dyson has much to say about international business dealings, and how he endured months of futile cultural induction courses, learning the language, and bowing and smiling, to achieve nothing but ever-greater humiliation and retreat. Japanese businessmen, he learned, are not always as honourable as we are often led to believe, and he found himself in meetings, not so much being listened to with serious intent as being a source of chauvinistic ridicule. He became known as the large, smelly, unattractive *gaijin*.

Then the penny dropped. He stopped trying so hard. That is, he decided to be more like himself. 'They will never ever like you,' he says, so you have to stop being so desperate to please them. (Paul Smith would take a small train set into meetings with Japanese businessmen, and would begin to play with it when he got bored. Of course, they just assumed that this was normal *gaijin* behaviour, no less insanely Western than eating Cornish pasties or peeing in the bathtub, so it never mattered much.) Everyone gets on better when you just act yourself. It's not a bad piece of life-philosophy at the best of times, and the change of approach worked. In 1986, Apex signed a deal with the tall rancid one who happened to make the piece of kit that they wanted. It took him out of the crippling debt into a healthy profit. And it enabled him finally to set up his own manufacturing facility at Chippenham, Wiltshire, in 1993. As sales took off, Dyson had to move, in 1995, to nearby Malmesbury, the current home. Then, in 1996, the main bulk of the building had to be re-extended (the wavy roof part) to deal with ballooning demand.

In time, and backed by an advertising campaign of which Dyson himself actually approved – based on the idea that a bag was counterproductive – the Dual Cyclone became the fastest-selling vacuum cleaner ever sold in the UK. Even then, however, the struggles didn't end.

Finally sensing that Dyson was onto a winning idea, his competitors began to replicate his design, and the company still has to devote time and money to a robust defence of its patents. Dyson has seen enough American legal actions to launch his own US TV mini-series courtroom drama, but ultimately, he has faced them all down and been the one who blinked last.

His extraordinary story has, no doubt, made Dyson the prolific thinker that he is. The man is frequently in the press, advocating more engineers and investment in research and development. He has written books on design, set up various awards and foundations of his own, and practises a level of philanthropy that often goes unnoticed or unreported. He has also been tireless in defending himself against the threat of industrial espionage. He has, inevitably, received awards such as the Prince Philip Designers Prize and the Lord Lloyd of Kilgerran Award; he is a Fellow of The Royal Academy of Engineering, a Knight Bachelor, and in 2011 was appointed Provost at the Royal College of Art.

Meanwhile, he has ambitious plans for Dodington Park, his hundred-or-so-room stately pile in Gloucestershire, designed by Capability Brown; a place he apparently first visited on a school trip, and said – as boys tend to do – that one day he'd buy it. However, unlike the rest of the class, and £20 million later, he did just that, proving again that he was different from the rest. But you sense that money is of relatively low interest to a man whose head is full of operatic scores, Impressionist paintings, and yellow plastics. He is driven – but not by money for its own sake. If anything, he was almost exactly the same man when he didn't have any.

He is far more interested in what he wants to do than what he has done, and is in full flow when the delightful and delightfully un-PR-like PR lady tells us it's time to leave – although he will likely continue buzzing with his ruminations long after we have gone. Dyson's idea of a legacy is not the simple desire to see his name immortalised. It is more subtle, more complex than that. Instead, he wants to appropriate the generic, in the way that Hoover has done for so long, and plays with the fantasy that one day, people might say that they need to 'Dyson the carpet' – and that this will have been achieved, not through the momentum of a marketing phenomenon, but through the intrinsic excellence of the machines.

In this sense, Dyson is a romantic. He believes that good, and good design, will triumph; and that after years of uncertainty, fear, debt, panic, sleepless nights and suffering loved ones, there comes a time when, as he describes it, 'You come out of the darkness.'

Even now, I quite enjoy being on the edge, which is why I haven't sold up or sold shares. Because most people in my position, like almost any British entrepreneur, they sell out because they're worried it will fail. But I haven't done that. My wealth is tied up in the business. So I don't want to sell even one bit of it, because I want the control. I want to be free. Free to do what I want to do.

Problems inspire the man – which is fortunate, given the number of lonely struggles he has had to face. Clearly, the lives of inventors were ever thus: he has known two colleagues who have tragically committed suicide. Yet even when Dyson developed viral meningitis ten years ago, he emerged from the crisis intent on turning problem into solution, and began sponsoring schools and hospitals fighting the disease. He doesn't look like a man who has been that close to death. Sitting there, munching on a chocolate bar, it's hard to think that he is near to a pensionable age. In fact, he looks decades younger than he is. Perhaps it's the choc-bars. In any case, what people think of him is very low on his list of priorities. His next puzzle and product are not.

I believe the engineering is the most important thing, so all we worry about here are our next inventions; what we're going to do. That's all we have to worry about. We don't worry about what other people think of us; we don't have to worry about what investors think. We just have one thing to worry about and that's the technology.

Isambard Kingdom Brunel is one of Dyson's heroes (a father-by-proxy being another way Dyson looks at it). The great British cigar-smoking engineer and aesthete in the silly beaver hat was known as being arrogant, rude, stubborn, and solipsistic, which are four adjectives that have also been used to describe Dyson – fairly or not. That is probably why the Great Western Railway and various implausibly dimensioned suspension bridges and transatlantic steamships got built (along with Brunel's possible need to compensate for being a short-arse). Like Dyson, Brunel had to battle against financiers and prejudice, hostile elements and awful luck.

Dyson accepts the criticisms of his own temperament, but he excuses himself, and why shouldn't he, given what he has overcome and what he has achieved? As we close this chapter, it is appropriate to quote Dyson's words, taken from his autobiography: 'Now, with a hindsight that proves I was right, those faults of mine seem less criminal... When all has come right, the kind of man who persisted despite constant ridicule from the controlling forces will be said to have possessed vision.' Dyson has a powerful sense of when he is right – because he has experienced what it is like to be wrong. That is the fact of engineering life.

Everything, or almost everything, I do fails. Almost everything an engineer or a scientist does fails, because when you get success you stop. You've done it. That's what I learnt working with an engineering company. And that it's a bit like long-distance running. You start out not knowing where you're going to end up. You start with an idea, you develop it, you develop it, and you develop it, and it's failures all along. And eventually you end up in a place where you had no idea you would be when you started.

Dyson has learned what was beyond the horizon when he stood in 1956, uncertain and alone, on those long remote beaches at Holkham or Cley or Blakeney Point. What the small boy couldn't then see has turned into the brilliantly realised vision that the man would see and did see – and still can.

And there is still not a bag in sight.

'The sun does not shine upon this fair earth
to meet frowning eyes, depend upon it.'

CHARLES DICKENS (*NICHOLAS NICKLEBY*)

SIR JOHN HEGARTY

(Bartle Bogle Hegarty)

INTERVIEWED 2 NOVEMBER 2011

Dickens knew how to think up a name. And if he'd ever needed one for an advertising agency, in the gloomy alleys behind Regent Street, he might well have called it Bartle Bogle Hegarty – the names of its two marketing masterminds, and a third, a dapper artisan with enough hair curls for all three. This sundry trio could just as easily have been a fiction etched by Phiz in 1852 as a reality photographed for *Campaign* magazine in 1982.

BBH's work has given us some of the most iconic advertising of the last thirty years: Nick Kamen washing his Levi's; Häagen-Dazs as a sex aid; a German car factory aphorism (*Vorsprung durch Technik*); the Johnnie Walker walking man; Boddington's Vera; a fluffy puppet called Flat Eric; Lynx pheromonia; the rapping Yeo Valley farmers... Nowadays, there are offices in London, New York, Singapore, São Paulo, Shanghai, and Mumbai, their reception areas decorated with coveted industry awards. This company has been built on a foundation of insightful strategic planning and sublime creative output. And the figure who, over the last three decades, has taken final responsibility for that creativity is Sir John Hegarty.

To get to the London office, we turn under Liberty & Co's Tudor-timbered arch into the constricted passage of Kingly Street. Down here, among old pubs and pawnbrokers and the backside trade entrances of Regent Street chain stores, we find number 60. The entrance opens out onto a long wide nave of floor-to-ceiling glass windows, behind which are the open-plan galleries, decorated by gamine and understatedly hip advertising executives busy at their 27-inch Apple Cinema Displays, sipping espressos. Behold, then, a cathedral of the advertising era.

John Kevin Hegarty is one of the industry's most highly regarded statesmen, and if he is not quite a household name, you feel he ought to be – although he was once on *Desert Island Discs* with Sue Lawley ('Here, Mr Hegarty, we strip you of everything...'). These days, his work isn't confined to advertising, because in his spare time he runs a burgeoning wine business ('Don't get him going on that,' we are mysteriously warned by people in the agency, pre-interview), as well as consulting on BBH's new venture capital enterprise. In between all this, he has been touring various festivals with his book, and attending countless industry events to receive awards. At an age when Hegarty is eligible for a bus pass, all this is some going.

The list of awards and accolades is startling. Standing out on a mantelpiece heaving under the weight of gold statuettes, shields, and mounted pencils are the D&AD President's Award (a prize he shares with people like Jonathan Ive, Alan Parker, and Neville Brody) and the Lifetime Achievement honour from the esteemed CLIO Awards in the US. Then there is the One Club of New York's Creative Hall of Fame, where he sits alongside the luminaries of American creativity, like Saul Bass, Steve Jobs, Leo Burnett, and Bill Bernbach.

We meet him in his unspectacular office, along with a knee-high black wooden sheep called Zag (the BBH motto being to 'zag when others zig'), on which he often rests a foot in press photographs – a symbolism that you can unpick at your leisure. From his window can be seen the end of Carnaby Street – a symbolism that needs no unpicking at all for this man who was a child of, and takes inspiration from, the sixties.

One of the first things that he does when we meet is to show us the scene from his window – outside of which, down below, they're putting up street decorations for Christmas – with the finger-pointing glee of a child who has noticed twinkling coloured lights for the very first time. Now in his late sixties, Hegarty feels that his psychological age settled at about 37, which seems a vast over-estimation. He has the excited gaze (and perhaps the hairstyle) of a 1960s art school 20-year-old whose psychological age settled at around eight. Despite the facial cragginess, he still looks youthful – like a teenager who has had the wrinkles airbrushed in – which he puts down to keeping his hair and not getting fat. But above all, it's the enthusiasm that comes through. He doesn't just love life, but loves everything it contains. You get the impression that if you pulled out a biro from your pocket he would say, 'Wow, that's amazing!'

His charm is an easy one. For someone who claims to 'never look backwards', he does a great line in nostalgic reminiscence, taking a storyteller's delight ('creativity is telling stories') in tale after tale, inviting you to share in the fun. It is clear that, over time, the Irishman's niceness genes have not been neutered by the rather less nice Soho advertising mores; the Irish working-class sense of proportion is still there; and the Irish-Catholic sense of being humble, charitable, and unpossessive – even at your own dining table.

I was born in Edgware, brought up in Mill Hill East, and went to school in Finchley. I came from a working-class Irish family – my father was a gardener – and I think actually that helped, because we were outsiders, and this made me an observer. I went to an English Catholic School and I would go and watch people in an English environment, so to speak, then come home to an Irish environment. All the time you knew there was a difference; the way language was; the way we spoke; the way we talked. All the time, there was that sort of sense of being an outsider. It was something that gave me a useful, twin perspective.

I certainly came out of a household where any airs and graces would be just laughed at. It's an Irish sense of proportion. My father's view of life was that if you could sing a song, tell a joke, or drink a pint of Guinness, then you were an honorary Irishman; and as far as he was concerned, that was that. He was a tremendously open man.

I remember in the mid fifties, my father going to church on a Sunday morning followed by going to the pub, then he'd come home for lunch. Occasionally, he would just come back with some black guys in tow. Strangers, workers, they were coming in from the Caribbean, but they used to get very lonely. They would walk up the Edgware Road, into the pub, and drink Guinness, so my father would talk to them. If you drank a pint of Guinness you were OK in his book, so he'd ask them what they were doing about lunch, and then, without telling my mum, just arrive home with these guys. So it was quite normal to have Sunday lunch with a few strangers there around the table as well. Which was actually fantastic. And completely innocent.

You wouldn't dream of doing this nowadays, but we were exposed to a way of living life as it should be. I count myself very lucky to have had that experience; a truly cosmopolitan atmosphere where everyone is welcome as part of your family at your dinner table.

He suggests that this kind of exposure has been a major factor in his success. He has a dislike of pretension and airs and graces that, over the years, has been evident in work for which he has been responsible: the idea of taking off your Levi's in the same launderette where you're going to wash them; the model who smears her face with beer froth in lieu of expensive body lotion; the couple who take sensual pleasure through their ice cream. In their day, these ideas were iconoclastic and dramatic, turning convention and social logic upside down. The process is rather more orthodox creative practice these days, but at the end of the eighties, when Nick Kamen and Brad Pitt began demonstrating a product by using it as a prop for their bodies, this was Hegarty kicking orthodoxies up in the air, just as his rock 'n' roll heroes had done in the fifties and sixties.

As with his Celtic forefathers, Hegarty's open-smiled bonhomie sits alongside a rebellious streak: his kicking back against the unquestioned order of things will be familiar to many lapsed Catholics. Hegarty's brand of apostasy, however, meant doing this without raising his voice – without even getting out of his bed.

I had a Catholic upbringing, but I've admitted to being an atheist. At about the age of 15, I realised it was all bullshit. Early one morning, my mother said to me, 'John, what Mass are you going to?' and I just came out and said, 'I'm not.' She said, 'Why?' and I said, 'Because it's all rubbish.' And all she said was, 'All right, John,' and closed the door.

People ask me if it was difficult giving up Catholicism and I say, it was very easy. I just turned over in my bed and went back to sleep.

That religious upbringing was something to kick against, because it was so wonderfully ridiculous. At school, we used to play games in Religious Instruction lessons, where we would ask the teacher how it was that if Christ says all men are equal, yet we still ought to marry a Catholic. I loved questioning accepted beliefs, and I think that if you're going into a creative world, it's very important you know what it's like to kick against something. You've got to have an opposition. You've got to have something you're breaking down. Creativity is about breaking things down and rebuilding something.

During the interview, Hegarty keeps referencing dualities: English and Irish, Catholicism and atheism, order and chaos, kicking down and building up, tragedy and comedy; the importance of contrast and juxtaposition. He sees much of his creativity as being a form of constructive dissonance, whereby unconnected elements are brought together to achieve a surprising and striking result.

His belief that dissonance leads to creative energy seems founded on his being immersed in the spirit of the sixties, to which he returns frequently. He often says that he was lucky to be born in 1944, just so he could be a child of the ensuing epochs:

The sixties were a fabulous juxtaposition between what had been and what was changing. We knew the wind of change was blowing, and we knew we were inheriting the future. Up until that moment, everybody aspired upwards. Even in the forties and the fifties, young kids looked like their dads. We were the first generation who didn't want to look like our dads. We wanted to be like ourselves.

But the amazing thing was that, at that point, we didn't have any media that was talking to us. Can you imagine that now? No media, no voice for the youth, no clubs as such. We had to kind of go off and find it. Or even make it yourself, if you could. There was no radio that played rock 'n' roll, television was deeply boring, and it wasn't really until the early sixties that we got That Was The Week That Was, *and only then did you think that, my God, this world is changing. We used to have to listen to* Housewife's Choice *to occasionally hear a Buddy Holly song. You might try and listen to Radio Luxembourg, but it would fade in and fade out.*

So you had this kind of seeking out things so you had to know where things were. You had to go and find them and explore and that made you part of something. You attached yourself to something and made a judgement about it – whereas today, you just go on YouTube, and it's there, taken for granted. What we've lost today is that sense of seeking something out. And of making it yourself. That's why the sixties were the origin of a huge creative energy.

Hegarty ET-fingerpoints back to the street outside. 'It was all happening down there in Carnaby Street. It was opening up and you knew it was a brilliant moment. It was just phenomenal. Amazing.' Appropriately enough, he is currently reading Keith Richards's autobiography, *Life*, and recounts the story of Lennon and McCartney bumping into the Rolling Stones on the Charing Cross Road and deciding, on the spur of the moment, to let them record a version of 'I Wanna Be Your Man'. A moment of pure spontaneity and impetuous creativity – the kind of thing that he has been talking about and, he feels, defined the era. 'Imagine that today. Imagine it. My lawyer will talk to your lawyer. Our manager will do this and then we've got to do that. Then we'll get the contracts drawn up. To think, they just went, "Yeah, here's a track you can have…" Amazing.'

Of course, there have been growing pains, and Hegarty talks about times in his early career, when he was not always quite as laid-back. He talks about his days at Benton & Bowles as being 'an endlessly uphill struggle', and later periods of 'distrust and disillusionment' at TBWA.

When I first started, I was an archetypally oversensitive creative person, in that, if I created a piece of work and the account man would come back from the client and say it had been rejected, I used to throw a fit and scream and shout and do all the usual things you're expected to do as typical creative people. But I never really liked being like that. I used to feel horrible about doing that and I couldn't work it out. Until I remembered my old tennis coach.

Hegarty goes on to recount the story of an incident in his early twenties, in which he was having a tennis lesson from a man called F. H. D. Wilde, a Wimbledon mixed doubles finalist from the 1930s, who was helping him with his backhand.

I was very weak on this, but finally, after practising and practising I finally hit this just beautiful backhand straight down the line, off the front foot. Fantastic. I did it just once. And straight away, Frank Wilde walked up to the net and just said, 'Very good, Mr Hegarty. We'll now move on to the overhead smash.' And I'm thinking, 'But I've only hit one...' but Frank had already turned and was walking away from me. He shuffled; he'd been injured in the war, so he shuffled away. So I say, 'Shouldn't I be trying to do it again?' Frank stopped, turned round and, I can hear it to this day, he said, 'Mr Hegarty. If you can hit one, you can hit a thousand and one. If you please, we will move on to the overhead smash.'

And in that single reflection, years later, I realised what he had been saying to me was not to go and keep on doing the same thing. You know you can do it. Believe in what you can do, then go and do something else better. Once you understand this, and apply it to having creative ideas, you know that you've not just got a diminishing pot of 500 great ideas, so if just one is rejected, that's 499, then 498, then 497 left... where you can imagine the exact time when you're going to run out of every one of your ideas and have to quit the business. That was what was sending me berserk. That fear of an end. But at that moment, I saw that the pot of ideas is limitless. If you can have one, like Frank said, you can have a thousand and one, or an infinite number, and that is the sudden realisation of confident certainty. Shouting at people is a lack of confidence; a sign of panic that you think you can only do a

*fixed number of ideas and then you'll dry up. But actually, you won't,
so move on.*

For many of us, age can soften the angst of youth. Hegarty claims that
he has also mellowed over time, yet he seems to have avoided some of
the downsides of growing older. He admits, though, to being prone to a
'residual recalcitrance'.

*I've never really craved material things. Once I got the money, I still
didn't go crazy over a watch or a car or something. I did actually get
an Austin Healey 3000 Mk III when I was 23 because I thought that
if you're going to have a sports car, then have it when you're 23, not
when you're 63. But I wasn't hankering after it or anything like that.
I never have done.*

*I've found that for me, the great thing that success and wealth bring
is the ability to say fuck off to anyone you don't want to have to work
for. That to me is the most brilliantly powerful thing that you can earn;
the one thing, more than anything material, that I wanted to purchase.
There is nothing worse that the inability to say it, and being forced
to do things you don't want to do. If I don't want to do it, then now
I don't do it, and to be in that position is a great privilege.*

True to the sentiment, BBH eventually parted company, after a very long
relationship, with Levi's – amicably, it seems.

Ask Hegarty why he still works after all this time – when he clearly
does not need the money or the fame – and his answer is that he does
it because he wants to; because he likes doing it. Not ultimately for the
money; not ultimately for the applause and the glamour; not for valida-
tion from others.

*People say I have a great skill at putting myself in the shoes of the
consumer. That's bullshit. How can I put myself in the shoes of a person
I've never met in my life? I've got no idea who they are, what they
do, how they think. It's just absolute crap. If I have an idea, it's what*

*I believe in and if I'm right, I'm right, and if I'm not, I'm out of a job.
J. K. Rowling was asked what aged child she had in mind as her reader
when she was writing Harry Potter, considering he goes from age 8 to
18, and her reply was that she just wrote it for herself. That's what you
do. And you've got to have the courage to do that. It's a kind of naivety.*

*As a creative, you shouldn't be writing for a 25-year-old or a
50-year-old, you should just be writing it for yourself. Did you know
that when you draw a picture of a person – free-draw – you draw
yourself? You draw who you are without you realising it; you just draw
yourself. So when you go to a [fashion] designer you should always go
to a designer who is shaped like you...*

Hegarty sees self-motivation, self-confidence, and common sense as
bedfellows; as part of the philosophy of being serious about not taking
anything too seriously. That attitude requires certainty; the 'ignorant certainty' that he sometimes mentions; the sense that what he does means
everything and nothing. Put another way, it's about keeping things in proportion, he feels: 'If Johnnie Walker suddenly closed down tomorrow,
people's lives wouldn't change; they'd drink Bell's or Whyte & Mackay
or whatever.'

*I heard the story about a writer trying to do an interview with a famous
US musician, so he flew all the way to Los Angeles, and once he got
there, this guy just decided there and then that he didn't feel like being
interviewed any more. And I thought, you know, he writes half-good
songs – about three or four have been great, the rest were pretty rubbish
in my view – but he behaves like he just cured cancer or something. It
just pisses me off, that. You have to have a certain nonchalance about
what you do. You have got to keep it in proportion.*

*I remember years ago, when I was at TBWA in Covent Garden and
there was an art bookshop on the corner of Long Acre. Andy Warhol was
coming to do a signing and I couldn't be there and one of our art directors
said he was going to go and take a can of Campbell's soup and see if he
would sign it. And I said, 'Don't be stupid. Of course Andy Warhol won't*

sign it.' But he did sign it, and, you know what? He didn't care. That was the thing. Andy Warhol had that nonchalance. He didn't care. His attitude was: 'Yeah, sure, you want that. You want my signature on a soup can. Fine, this is my signature, fine. What do I care? Here you are.' That is a sense of proportion, not just deciding on a whim that you're gonna spoil things for some poor interviewer just doing their job.

If the early days' anger has mellowed into something resembling serenity, Hegarty still expresses frustration at how the gravity of the marketing world acts as a drag on creative expression. He is scathing about the use of market research to judge creative material, and remains convinced that one of the most astute decisions on which one of his two co-founders, Nigel Bogle, insisted was that the agency only ever pitch with its focus on strategy, and never by presenting creative material. 'If we really believed in the superiority of our creative product, we shouldn't give it away for free.' Above all, he genuinely feels that the creative mission is 'not order out of chaos, but the use of chaos to create order'.

I remember being about four, at pre-primary school, and we were given paintbrushes for the first time, and I painted a great house, but I splattered paint all over the place, had paint everywhere. And then the teacher suddenly asked for everything to be cleaned up, and I thought, my God, I'm in the shit. I've painted all over this, so how do I clean it up? I thought, I know what to do. Some of the paper was black, so I think I'll paint all the rest of the paper black. So I got the black paint and I painted the whole thing black and then handed it in, ready for somebody else to use again. And I can now remember the teacher looking at all the paintings; a house, another picture, and then my picture came along with all these black brushstrokes. And I can imagine the teachers contacting my mother, telling her that we have a seriously disturbed child here and we need to talk about his mental state. And then of course afterwards I realised how, in innocence, you can get something completely wrong. But it was a lovely bit of creative ignorance. All that black.

He looks around his office, full of black furniture and black paintings and black crockery and a black sheep, and wonders if we're going to analyse his subconscious, and then just laughs at the idea that we might.

I have held on to a sort of ignorant certainty. Having gone to art school, one of the great things you're taught there is that there are no absolute answers in creativity. It's not a science. It's not an equation. So if you believe in something, then it's right; that's it; that's fine; no one can say it's wrong.

This isn't anarchy. Hegarty is not interested in disruption without purpose ('Irreverence for its own sake is dangerous,' he often says, and gives as an example the Benetton campaign that featured gratuitous photographs of a birth and AIDS-related death), and although he espouses many an egalitarian principle, you get the impression that the pragmatism of a self-made businessman wins the internal squabble: 'Socialism is obviously right, but it can never work in practice, can it?' Again, we see that Hegarty is a duality of forces, but one that gets those forces the right way up to be successful.

In his book, he goes out of his way to praise the other two founding members of the BBH partnership for having the sense and intelligence to get the right balance: 'Having partners you trust and have faith in is vital... I was incredibly lucky having two partners who understood that principle – both John and Nigel, apart from being supremely talented, were brilliant at that. They trusted me with the creative work and I trusted them with the business and strategy. They made sure the creative process wasn't interfered with, was given the freedom to express itself and, most importantly, was respected.' He stresses that 'none of us is as good as all of us' – a line that could be his Irish father speaking again, after a Sunday lunchtime Guinness.

Our interview passes by quickly, impelled along by the relentless enthusiasm of the man-child. *Enthusiasm* is the order of the day, and Hegarty offers us a piece of factual trivia that he has probably used in countless interviews and presentations; a point about the etymology of the word, which, he explains, literally means being with God. 'Isn't that just amazing?' This is his personal life-credo. Enthusiasm is next to godliness. He's now on a roll:

You've got to keep trying things, and trying more things. If you keep repeating the same thing, it doesn't matter how hard you try, you'll never succeed. But if you're open to things, then things come to you. They don't bounce off you and go away. They get absorbed by you and make themselves part of you.

It's hardly surprising, then, that he has been doing other things lately. Not least his beloved viticulture, which he caveats by telling us how hard it has been turning from West End commerce to Languedoc farming. He runs the enterprise with his long-standing partner, Philippa Crane, selling under the title of Hegarty Chamans without any undue self-consciousness ('If I kept it as Domaine de Chamans, the property I purchased, you'd have forgotten it in five seconds.') His French vineyard has allowed him to put his money where the mouth goes, and it has been a learning experience that he still relishes, despite the challenges ('If you're thinking of doing it, don't.'). The venture allows him to put his creativity to the ultimate test, this time, not growing ideas from client briefs, but growing a real product from the land; a neat symmetry, mirroring his Irish father's gardening job years ago. He says, 'My first piece of wine advice to you is this: Drink only good wine, drink it with respect, and it will pay you back for life.'

I think it is really important to have good taste. That's part of creativity. I don't know where it comes from: why do you like that piece of music versus that piece of music? Why do you like that building versus that building? Why do you buy your jeans there and wear them like that and put that jumper with that shirt and do that? I think I picked that up from art school in the sixties. It's a form of thinking about things in a certain way. I was surrounded by people who thought about the way they were, how things looked, sounded...

I can remember there was a couple of shops in London where you could get 501s and you went and got them, just round the corner here where the London Palladium is. But these things were important and you thought about them in detail. That's why you were aware of that piece of furniture versus another piece of furniture; why you wanted the walls painted white.

I think taste is crucially important to success. It governs virtually everything that you do; every decision that you make. Look at someone like Steve Jobs at Apple, who would micromanage to an extraordinary degree just because he knew that his taste was right and that it was crucial. The typeface had to be right and those things matter, even if it made him a really obsessive, intolerant man in some eyes.

That's why I think the fashion industry is so interesting and why we all ultimately love fashion. I love the way that if Karl Lagerfeld just says something needs to be blue, it's right – because he says so. I love that sort of commitment to just doing what he thinks is right.

Even at the end of our time with him, and with his PA stressing over his next appointment, Hegarty is not flustered. We need to let him go, but he wants to wish us well with the book, as though it were his own venture.

It feels as though he sees *everything* as a part of life's excitement and opportunity. Indeed, there is something about Hegarty that suggests he isn't altogether convinced that he is actually living a real life – being, instead, in a dream, about to wake up back in his bed in 1950s Finchley. Although if he did, he would probably raise his head from the pillow, smile, and say, 'Wow. That was amazing.'

And then try something new.

———

'To be alive at all involves some risk.'

HAROLD MACMILLAN

———

ROBERT HISCOX

(Hiscox)

INTERVIEWED 1 AUGUST 2012

Robert Hiscox is the eponymous founder of Hiscox, an incorporated insurance underwriting empire listed on the London Stock Exchange, that provides cover for every kind of risk imaginable, from biblical-scale apocalypse to leaking-tap accidents. You could be forgiven for thinking that a man now entering retirement, who has given his working life over to an insurance company, would go out of his way to circumvent risk or lessen its presence. Not one bit. When we meet, he has just returned from safari in the African bush hunting the Cape buffalo – and risks do not come much more striking than this.

It's the most dangerous beast on earth and it's big, ugly, and plentiful. The hunting is carefully controlled, so that you're only allowed to kill the old bulls. If you kill a female, you get fined. I love Africa and the people and being uncomfortable and dirty in the bush; I love the way of life; the Boys' Own *stuff. And like everyone else, once you've done it for a time, you end up wanting to experience an actual charge from a buffalo. They tell you to beware of what you wish for, and you can see why they say this. On a recent trip, I had it happen: I finally faced something running at me trying to kill me. I've had motorcycle accidents and things, but this was the most awesome experience of my life...*

In somewhat safer circumstances, Hiscox has asked us to join him over lunch in an upper-floor office of the City of London building that bears his name. The view is dominated by 30 St Mary Axe, otherwise known as The Gherkin – an enormous ogive structure, more or less next door, which from this angle looks less like a variety of pickled cucumber and more like a soil-planted glass rugby ball in a string-bag. The iconoclastic Lloyd's building is on the corner, intestines and vital organs dangling all over the outside of its metal torso, with the Heron Tower having sprouted on the opposite side. In between the jumble of oddly shaped glass sky-scrapers in this financial quarter, serious people hurry their take-outs back to their desks. The City is not what it used to be, and, on the streets, these buildings now cast cold shadows of austerity. For the insurance industry in particular, 2011 was a year of multiple troubles, with a run of extraordinary disasters in Asia and the US, and world financial crises hitting on a weekly basis.

Yet when we meet him, Robert Hiscox is smiling. Unlike many of its competitors, his company has managed to turn in a pre-tax profit of £126 million for the half-year (reversing a loss of £86 million previously), premiums are running at £1.4 billion (for 2011), dividends are up, and a major new television advertising campaign is about to break. He smiles when he greets us at the lift, smiles at the end of every sentence, and can be seen smiling in just about every press photograph there is of him – so it is difficult to work out whether he thinks that things are really good at the moment or if this is just his default expression. Perhaps the answer is a bit of both. Whatever the case, not for him the steely sinister frown and focus into the Venetian blinds favoured by most company supremos for their publicity shots. Nor the hunched weighed-down look of the suits on the street. This 69-year-old Lloyd's grandee, of the older, impeccably turned-out and well-mannered generation, has mastered the art of being the perfect host and gentleman. 'My philosophy is always to be cheerful,' he says. Which doesn't, it is worth adding very quickly, preclude him from telling things exactly as he sees them.

The smile is decidedly not that of the yes-man. Anything but. Hiscox has, for most of his professional life, and for some years before that, been ever ready to tell people just what he thinks – in the politest possible way, of course. Which is what happened during his address to the London 2012

Insurance Day Conference, when he gave Sir Mervyn King (Governor of the Bank of England, and arguably the most powerful non-elected bureaucrat in Britain) and Hector Sants (then head of the Financial Services Authority) not so much a kicking as a hefty punt right over the stadium roof. Charm personified, Hiscox let rip against the impending control of the insurance industry as part of the financial regulatory system. How could this be right, he opined, given their lack of experience? How could it be that the financial institutions that got their economic predictions so wrong, the Bank of England included, are being given a supervisory role over the one part of the financial sector that had actually avoided much of the toxic opportunism? 'Can we stop the master-servant attitude, especially as the servant is often far more qualified than the master?' he concluded. For Hiscox may smile, and he may charm, but he does not play the quiet diplomat.

I do understand how hard it is to get good people to regulate, because anybody good in the regulators gets pinched by private enterprise. But the result is that currently we are told what to do by inadequate people and that ought to stop. We ought to get good people seconded.

It is easy to see the reason why this man has succeeded, and, as part of the same equation, easy to see how he might have been underestimated by the unwary. Hiscox neither looks nor sounds like an intimidating individual, nor someone who would upset vested interests. Yet the City's longest-serving executive of some 48 years has developed an ill-fitting reputation as a 'difficult character' (his own words). Too bad. For someone who likes nothing more than fast unruly motorbikes and large horned bovines chasing him, the scowls of the establishment seem inconsequential.

I found out very early in life that it was fun to break every rule in the book. At school, I wanted the freedom: the swimming at night in the lake and things like that; providing you didn't get caught. When I first arrived at Rugby, I did get caught, and was beaten for it. From then on, I decided that I would exercise all my cunning to avoid being beaten again, and, to a large extent, I succeeded. My housemaster disliked me and I disliked him because he was a sarcastic sod, but his accurate comment on my last report was that I'd made life far more difficult at Rugby than it need have been.

But I was, and still am, anti-establishment, anti-authority, or at least anti-mindless authority. Hence all the publicity I've had recently about being anti-FSA. Most people just give in and go with the flow. But if somebody starts to push me around, I won't stand for that if I believe them to be wrong. I've been a company chairman, so I've been master of my own destiny for a long time, and for me to be told what to do by somebody who has little or no experience is quite hard.

My father was always very respectful, but I don't fear senior people. It's why I'd get absolutely nowhere in politics, because I'm too honest and outspoken and could never have been a diplomat. I say what I think, even if the mouth moves ahead of the brain in these situations sometimes. Someone once told me, 'Robert, there is such a thing as an unspoken thought.' I took the criticism, and realised that I ought to keep my mouth shut occasionally. But I seldom do.

The insurance world is a tempestuous one, up one minute, down the next, where predictions need to be made about the most unpredictable of things. Hiscox explains how experienced African trackers cite the unpredictability of the bush as its greatest danger, but respond by backing their own judgement, and respecting their environment, not trying to systematise things or take instinct out of the process. Hence what he dislikes about the impending changes in the regulatory system. He wants *balance* between strict regulation and flexibility, and warns of its opposite: rigidity, insensitivity, and a lack of common sense. It is a familiar pattern in the way the establishment tries to regulate the unpredictability of modern life.

Risk has become a dirty word. All this health and safety nonsense, trying to legislate against anyone having an accident. The Financial Services Authority wants no business to be a risk. But life is about risk.

Having ridden motorbikes and skied fast – I like risk. But I know the odds, and if you do, you can decide if a risk is worth taking, rather than have someone from Health & Safety tell you what you can and can't do. When I was young, we climbed trees, we bicycled around streets; how did we ever survive? It's so very dishonest, the nanny state trying to take risk away from us.

I was there when George Osborne made a speech about how we must get less litigious, and I just wanted to jump up and tell him that it's the politicians who've created that problem. Health & Safety is causing considerable litigation. If you contravene the regulations – which are so prolific and contrary to common sense, you can't possibly know them all – you're prima facie guilty and will be sued.

In his speech, Hiscox spoke of a 'very, very frightening world' where 'technocrats will abound, but candidates with... common sense, business ability, and intuition could be ruled out'. Back in the 1990s, Hiscox played a key role in rescuing Lloyd's of London from collapse, by using these very qualities – an 'epic' challenge, which he regards as his greatest achievement in a long career. Part of the solution was to recapitalise, and establish the Equitas Group, whose job it was to reinsure the bad syndicates that Lloyd's had accumulated; a solution that today's regulators would not be flexible enough to allow; the implication being that, had the same thing happened today, Lloyd's of London would be left to fail.

Times were different then. Hiscox puts the problem that Lloyd's experienced down to poor underwriting and a lack of the right kind of regulation.

In my early days in Lloyd's, it was full of very honest people like my father who thought it was a very honourable profession. Your word was your bond and you made verbal promises or wrote scribbled policies on bits of paper, and you always stuck by your word. He'd have been mortified in later years, in the eighties, when we discovered considerable dishonesty. The majority of people were like him and were absolutely honest and therefore didn't think regulation was necessary.

But then you had the villains who were cheating, so they weren't going to impose regulation because that's the last thing they wanted. I had enough financial nous to see how the villains operated, and when I got into Lloyd's, I saw immediately who was cheating, because when you have 83% taxation and somebody is running a yacht and an aeroplane on earned income, they're cheating.

Hiscox reckons that the disasters of 2008 were visible a mile off, and takes issue with Sir Mervyn King's claim that no one could possibly have seen what was about to happen. In his conference speech, Hiscox hit back with a list of the numerous figures – Dan Healey, Jonathan Ruffer, Goldman Sachs, Warren Buffett, et al – who *had* predicted the catastrophe. 'It all seems trees and no wood to me,' Hiscox said in his concluding comments.

Common sense, balance, flexibility, and honesty – this is the Hiscox lexicon, and it is pretty clear where he gets it from:

My father was devoutly religious. And my mother was a Scots-Irish Presbyterian who never went to church, because she didn't feel that, in order to worship, you necessarily had to be on your knees. I was never aware of my parents ever doing a dishonest act, which is an incredibly good upbringing to have. My mother had strong discipline being from Ballymena, while my father was a very gentle man. They'd met at a party at the Windmill Theatre. He was very respectful and modest, whereas my mother was a farmer's daughter from Northern Ireland who was very earthy. It was a frightfully good cocktail.

The context of my early life was the war. As a child, I was acutely aware of it; people talking about the doodlebugs, the shelter in the garden, the soldiers and tanks, and feeling very small. My father had been in the RAF, and all his friends had been in the war; all our advisers had been in the war, our stockbroker had been in the war, as had our solicitor, dentist, and even my housemaster at Rugby. His judgement of a man was whether he'd had a good war or not.

At the start of the war, my father was 32, which was too old to be called up. He had just started a new syndicate, his first child had been born in 1939, and he was in a reserved occupation as an underwriter at Lloyd's, so he didn't need to enlist. But on the day of declaration, he still signed up and went because he just felt he ought. It's something I'm rather proud of him doing.

Robert Ralph Scrymgeour (it's a Scottish name, and means 'sharp sword') Hiscox was born on 4 January 1943, into a family that was, he stresses, not well off. He is keen to correct any preconceptions that he was born rich, and puts his meritocratic success down to being energetic and ambitious, and the set of strong values imbued by his parents; packaged in what he feels was a remarkable upbringing and education.

My father's father died just before he was born, and there was little family money. And tax was incredibly high after the war. My father always told me that he had given me the best education that money could buy, but he could not leave me any money – and I told him that I was deeply grateful for it being that way round.

I matured early, and, at eight, got sent for one term to a girl's school because I was too advanced for my primary school. Having two sisters, and an open and natural mother, I was totally used to girls, so I enjoyed it. I've always found women easier company than men. I was very close to my mother, and I think I'm a woman's man, not a man's man. I've never stood in a pub drinking beer, talking to men. When I first came to London and saw my friends going out and standing in a pub drinking beer, talking to men, it bemused me, because I thought girls were rather better company. My younger sister said to me one day, 'Robert. If you look them in the eye and listen, you can have any girl you want.'

I peaked at 14, by which time I was physically the same size as I am now. They said I was the strongest boy they'd had at my prep school for many years, and I was passing the exams relatively easily, and I was clever enough not to have to worry over lessons. Then I stopped growing, and went from being the strongest for my age to nothing much at all. But that was very good for my character.

I didn't really want to go to university, as I wanted to make money, but I took an exam to get into Corpus Christi, Cambridge, which, to my surprise, I passed. I was quite idle, and did minimal work, but it was just blissfully hedonistic, like being Sebastian Flyte. I did economics for one year, then law, and came out with a 2-2. My father said that a 2-1 shows you tried to get a first and failed, but a 2-2 shows you had a bloody good time. I wasn't at Cambridge for the intellectual side, although I thoroughly enjoyed the law. But I spent three years in the company of extremely intelligent people, and mixing with the brightest people in England sharpens you up no end. I also mixed at Cambridge with some very rich people, and, having not much money myself, that gave me a real insatiable desire to make money as I do like the good things in life, and money gives you freedom. I'm very naturally ambitious.

Ambition often features in Hiscox's commentary, and there is no mistaking the philosophically conservative mood-music of self-help and self-responsibility, and a dislike of what he sees as collectivist dishonesty. He keeps a photo of the doyenne of self-made entrepreneurialism, Margaret Thatcher, in his office, next to a picture of a Cape buffalo, and – completing this politically incorrect triumvirate – a large dead squirrel in a glass.

I have definite heroes: Winston Churchill, because he gave England its spirit during the war, even if he was a micromanaging nightmare. And Mrs Thatcher, of course, is my goddess. I was sitting in the City of London being taxed at 83% in the pound, trying to build a business and everybody was cheating, because if tax is that high, you cheat. I had got a job offer from overseas, and was going to emigrate in 1979 if she didn't get into power. But she did get in, and she brought a work ethic right back into this country. Suddenly, you saw this commercial engine starting, with people going in early to work and staying late.

I would walk round the office telling people to go home, because I thought you should have a decent work-life balance. I used to tell them to go and play tennis or go and see the family or something. I don't make decisions well at the end of the day, so I used to say that long hours only prove lack of competence to do the job in the right hours. But then I realised that their friends were all working late as well: if you weren't, you weren't a player. That's how it worked. If an investment banker still gets home before ten at night he's failing.

Delegation is the secret. I never understood why investment banks didn't employ twice as many key people and pay them well, instead of half the number being paid obscenely. But then I underestimated the greed. Ambitious as I am, I don't believe that I'm greedy. Enough is enough, and I like a life balanced between work, family, and my outside interests.

Greed can be very destructive. When I was backing other syndicates in Lloyd's, if there was a greedy underwriter who took 3% commission instead of 1% or he had a hugely high salary, I generally avoided him. If people became obsessed about what they could get out of the business, and put their own interests ahead of the business or the customer, destruction inevitably followed, as it did with the banks. I don't mind a person who's paid an awful lot of money if he is very good, but if they're just paid, regardless, I despair.

Not surprisingly, Hiscox seems to enjoy the trappings of success. But it's all kept in perspective. When it's not, he doesn't stay quiet for long about it.

I think the banks got greedy and stopped caring for the customer. Brian Pitman [chairman and chief executive of Lloyds] was a great hero of banking, and he made Lloyds Bank efficient, but in doing so, it got nasty to the customer. It was all about shareholder-return, and so the customer suffered. You got call centres and you got treated badly and it was one-size-fits-all. Once you disregard the customers and get obsessed about what you can make out of them, you start to abuse them. That led to toxic instruments being sold to customers, which were going to do them extreme harm in the bigger deals, and small customers being mis-sold

*policies which were incredibly lucrative to the banks. How could any
bank sell a useless product with a bad wording to their customers and
take 90% commission? Outrageous and disgustingly greedy. Here our
job is to insure people with a policy at a fair price with a clear wording
which will make them whole when they have had a loss. If you have
that attitude and care about the customer, and give them a reasonably
priced product that works, you'll build a decent business in the long term
without a huge crisis every 15 years like the banks.*

*The fact that there are only four or five big banks in this country
is not good. If there were lots of regional banks, it would be much
healthier. Terry Leahy is partly right when he talks about economies
of scale, and how big is beautiful, and how you'd never have had the
internet or Amazon if it weren't for big business. And I agree that some
big businesses are much better than lots of small ones.*

*But I can also see how smallness has its place. I love the revival of a
small business that has come from the internet. You can have a room
this size in Sutton Coldfield and sell worldwide through the web with
the appearance of an international business. I love it when you ring
them up and they say they'll check in the warehouse, when you know
they're operating from a one-room cottage.*

Hiscox has five sons from two marriages, his first wife being an American.

*I was incredibly fond of my first wife's grandfather, who was the most
un-greedy type and a great mentor to me. He had been a very successful
businessman, but lived a good life and never saved a penny for a
rainy day. He was very open about his finances, and having been very
generous to us early in our marriage, it was a pleasure to help him
when the seventies stock-market crash came.*

*I find the openness of Americans about their finances very refreshing.
I had another very successful American friend, who retired at 65 from
being President of Citibank with quite a modest income, as he had
acted with total integrity and never owned shares in any business they
did business with. He needed to build up his 'net worth' to have the*

quality of life he wanted, and started to try to build capital. He used to
have dinner with me two or three times a year, and he'd always tell me
how his 'net worth' was growing. In Britain, we have this thing about
never talking about money – which is our way, but not theirs.

It was the mid sixties when Hiscox first entered the insurance industry
straight from Cambridge, working for a small insurance broker for a year
before joining his father Ralph's business (Roberts & Hiscox), initially
working as an underwriter of fine art (a strong interest throughout his life)
and personal accident insurances. In an era where there were no com-
puters or calculators or risk-algorithms, success was dependent entirely
on mental agility, be it in dealing with clients or in calculating complex
aggregated liabilities in your head, and it was in this respect that Hiscox
junior thrived. He very quickly developed some business thinking of his
own, such as in underwriting art as a separate and cheaper insurance
product rather than as an element of household or marine insurance; a
move that was a huge success. Before long, he had become emboldened
enough to disagree with his father about the more strategic and profound
elements of the company's direction, which included a desire to see the
Roberts family partners bought out. 'I was deemed arrogant, but I think I
was just confident,' he has suggested.

There was no doubt that the company was struggling with the market losses suffered by Lloyd's in the mid sixties. In 1967, Hiscox senior
became chairman of Lloyd's while Hiscox junior started underwriting
and effectively steering the business. And then, suddenly, in 1970, Ralph
Hiscox died. His son was only 27.

I was very close to him. He was in Scotland – a country that he loved.
What was really nice was that he had sent us a postcard saying he
was having a wonderful time, but then died the next day, so we got it
posthumously. He was not a well man, but he died happily. I went up
there and I cremated him and came back down with his ashes. I always
said that he went up in the front seat of the Jaguar and came back down
in the boot.

At the time, my father was only a 20% partner, and there was always going to be a battle. His very good friend, to whom I'll always be grateful, came to me and told me to try and make it into a Hiscox business. My father had done all the work, but the Roberts family had been his backers, and he was undyingly loyal to them, so he never would have pushed them out himself. We had a bit of a battle, and the hierarchy of Lloyd's was not keen on a 27-year-old running a Lloyd's agency, but in the end, I said to Anthony Roberts, 'Look, you've had your time. Do you believe this business has a future?' He didn't, so I just asked him to let me have a go to see if I could make it all work. He was a decent man, and at that point, he just gave up fighting. I took control and from then on had some sensationally exciting and happy years.

It was a huge privilege to be in charge of a business in Lloyd's at such a young age. It was such a fun place to work, but it was bloody amateur. There were a lot of very thick people there – Hooray Henries, Tim-Nice-But-Dims, put in by their fathers paying £13,000 to get them made a Member of Lloyd's which gave them an income so their firms didn't have to pay them – whereas I was an ambitious graduate, so I had the advantage. The great myth is that Lloyd's was full of Old School types, when actually, it was the Cockney traders who were the most successful.

Quite soon, the name of the new company became an issue. I'd often thought that we ought to have a clear identity, so we got management consultants in and they told us to cut out the 'Roberts' and go with 'Hiscox' alone. In fact, it had been quite a contortion anyway being Robert Hiscox of Roberts & Hiscox. One of my partners, who I was deeply fond of, sat there saying it's a great mistake to put your name above the door because you are branded by that brand and it can be a curse on you. But that's the point. You are directly responsible.

The brand is how we behave, and I still feel personally flattered and proud when people say it's a nice company and it behaves well. I might be blunt, but I've never been devious. When asked about this company, I say that I hope it feels human. When I get letters from people complaining or praising, I get back to them because, if they get a reply from Mr Hiscox of Hiscox, it gives the business a human feel to it. I've always wanted to run a business this way. It feels right. So we changed the name and became Hiscox. It was a shock for about a year, hearing my name used corporately, but now it doesn't even register.

It is very clear that the name is, quite literally, a priceless thing for Hiscox. Indeed, he could easily have sold the company to the American conglomerate Chubb, which bought a 27% stake in 1998, and he could, in doing so, have made a killing. But he didn't, because he didn't like the idea of being bullied into a sale.

I personally cannot be bought. Some people get paid to do things they would never normally do. When it's been tried on me, I've just felt insulted. I've never been bribe-able, because it would be so humiliating to know that you'd done something purely because of some money. The same principle applies with the Honours system. I'll never get an Honour with my inability to hold my tongue when faced with some childish politician. If you behave obsequiously to the right people and give money to the right charities, or do a bit of work for the right quango, the gong gets pinned on the chest. I am totally incapable of grafting like that.

I have never sought approval. I'm not a man who sacrifices his opinion to the wish of the majority. That's one reason why I've found Cameron and Osborne deeply disappointing, and said so. I pay about 50% or 60% of my income to people to run the country who couldn't organise a sandwich-run; who seem to have no intuition or plain common sense, and are lacking in business acumen, but who are desperate for approval. You can't be like that in business.

At this point, Hiscox quotes Edmund Burke's famous lines to the electors of Bristol in 1774: 'Your representative owes you, not his industry only, but his judgement; and he betrays, instead of serving you, if he sacrifices it to your opinion.' Hiscox says he'd like those words engraved on the desk of every MP in Westminster.

Cameron just looks over his shoulder to see what the people want and does it. He shouldn't. He should be running this country. I told him that and he lost his temper with me in 30 seconds. I don't get on well with politicians and few of them seem to have good judgement.

The next course arrives, a hedonistic Pavlova, which would not suit anyone with arteries that were not like a racing-car's fuel pipes. Hiscox says he's a pudding kind of guy. After which, he eats the chocolates. He does not give the impression of someone who has ever expended more than one minute worrying about health, but that belies the fact that he has had some ups-and-downs when it comes to stress and illness. He is a restless individual – 'I like everything done well and I'm never satisfied,' he says – and probably burns off most of his calories in nervous energy before he even loads his rifle or fires up the motorcycle. It's a restlessness that extends into a search for spiritual equilibrium. He goes to church, but his metaphysical view is extremely broad.

I'm prepared to believe in anything that seems to work. For example, if anybody argues against feng shui, I just point out how people sit in the same seat every time or sit in the best seats in the cafe looking out of the window. It's just the ancient art of Chinese placement and human beings feeling comfortable if they're in a certain place. I've had people to my house to get rid of negative energies. I used to get a headache sitting in a certain seat in my house, so we had a dowser in and it worked. I have acupuncture. It's wonderful; you can get rid of pain straight away. They can do open-heart surgery with acupuncture, so it works. Nobody knows why. I think orthodox doctors have killed more people than unorthodox, so what's the problem? I mean the standard of medical care of the average GP is appalling and I've seen them make mistakes because they sit there doing mundane stuff all day long, and cannot possibly keep up with the latest medical advances.

Hiscox can speak from experience because, in 1996, he was diagnosed with cancer.

It would have killed me if I hadn't had it cut out. It makes you look at life and realise you're lucky to be alive and you just savour it more, doing things like big-game hunting. At first, you think you're going to die, so I gave far too much money away. Three days after the diagnosis, I was lunching with a wise friend and he said, 'Robert, it will be life-enhancing.' I could have hit him, but a few days later I realised he was right. I decided to savour life and never do anything mundane or ugly. I'm only sitting here now with you because I want to be.

I kept the cancer secret for 18 months and tried to cure it with alternative medicine. That was an odd period in my life, because everyone in this country says, 'How are you?' when they meet you and you are thinking, 'Actually, I've got cancer' – just as you reply 'Fine'. In the end, I chose the knife and antibiotics. I had the operation and it turned out it wasn't a tiny cancer at all and if I had stuck with alternative medicine I probably wouldn't be here now. But it did get me incredibly healthy and made the operation much easier. When I had the operation, bish, bash, bosh, it was a real bloody affair: they cut you right from your top here right down to your bum and the loss of blood can be phenomenal. But the surgeon said it was so easy because there wasn't an ounce of fat in there. If you're going to have a major operation, get fit. I recovered very fast and I touch wood that it doesn't pop up again. We live in a sea of cancer, trying to get into all of us all the time and you have got to keep the immune system in tip-top condition. Stress does bad things to the immune system and I think three years as deputy chairman of Lloyd's during the crisis years lowered my guard and let it in. It was a grim time with people being financially wounded and my whole business and domestic life was threatened as I had unlimited liability.

I'm still not a good sleeper. I don't know if it's to do with worrying. I do find that little things become monstrous things at night. I envy the people who just put their head on the pillow and go. So I'm now trying to get rid of the tyranny of the diary, where I've things to do all the time and meetings are being constantly written in. I want to get back control. I recently took my wife with me on a business trip, which I've never done before and I realised that you can actually enjoy the trip much better this way. Normally, I'd go to an airport, go to an office, out of the office, back to the airport. I've been to Munich twenty times, thirty times, and never seen the city. But with my wife, I can do two hours in the office and then spend the rest of the day enjoying myself. That was a whole new experience.

As was becoming the High Sheriff of Wiltshire, an office Hiscox took in March 2011, being sworn in at a rather bizarre Old Saxon ceremony that hasn't changed much since someone called Edric started it all off in 1066.

In Saxon times, the High Sheriffs were the most powerful men in the county because they raised tax for the Crown and imposed the law. They got curtailed because they behaved so badly and now the position has no power at all, but it has history. It's the oldest secular appointment after the Crown in England, making you the Queen's representative for the law in the county, so you're supposed to attend hangings and things. All it does nowadays is mean you're invited to everything, so you can go and look into things, and can help charities and see how the county runs.

It was very good for me because I was one of those businessmen who believed that business was wonderful and that the other monopolistic world was hopeless as they've got no bottom line – like the army, the police, the civil service, the councils, the politicians. Well, I learnt that it is different: [but in that] they do jobs that we would find very difficult to do; I started to understand the difference in the workings of the county administration [compared to business]. I got about a lot and I tried to help. I finished in March this year. It made me busier than I've ever been in my life.

A trawl of the local press shows that Hiscox was certainly not inactive during his year in high office at Marlborough, immersing himself in local events and responsibilities – from organising steam rallies to tackling local crime. These days, he has a substantial country pile in Wiltshire, along with another residence in Kensington. He occupies these with his second wife, Lady Julia Elizabeth Meade (third daughter of the 6th Earl of Clanwilliam, no less).

Hiscox does, of course, have substantial wealth, including over £20 million in company shares alone, and a vast art collection, acquired over decades, scattered around his properties. 'Art is an integral part of the culture of Hiscox. We insure it, we own it, and we encourage it,' he declares on the company's website. The thing is that, for Hiscox, art is far more than an investment or a simple hobby. It is yet another route into adventure and risk. His collection – which includes works by Andy Goldsworthy (who built him a Millennium Arch at his house), Lucian Freud, Frank Auerbach, Damien Hirst, John Virtue, and also contemporary ceramics – is famously radical. The couple's friend and art advisor is Ivor Braka, the eccentrically long-haired Chelsea millionaire, or rock 'n' roll art dealer as he is sometimes called in the press, who is no stranger to controversy. And not so long ago, Hiscox actually sat for the performance artist and sculptor Boo Ritson, known for smearing household emulsion all over her subjects before she begins a portrait. For Hiscox, art is not a 'safe' pastime.

I love buying art, and my ultimate luxury is having a store so I can buy a 10 ft by 10 ft painting and not worry where to put it. I have been constantly frustrated that I don't see a fraction of the art I would like to see and am fed up with looking at images on my computer instead of taking in the real thing. So cutting back my business diary to spend more time with all this is very exciting for me. I think having had no money in your youth means you appreciate much more the things it brings you in later years. I have the self-made man's pleasure, whether I enter the drive to my house or when I buy a £10,000 painting.

When I was young, I wanted money for the freedom it gives you, which was one of the reasons I loved riding a motorbike. I've got an instinctively good feeling when I've got my leg over a motorbike. You're never going to be delayed. The thing is that money gives you the freedom to go where you want, and do what you want, but I never wanted it for its own sake. I don't understand people who just get richer and richer and get a kick out of that, rather than acquiring beautiful things or helping other people.

At school, the comment was always that I could have tried harder, but I've lived a very balanced life. I have not worked these huge hours. I have always had lots of hobbies and a good personal life. If you are totally wrapped up in your work it's very hard for your family. I think my five children are all well balanced. That's the achievement.

Achievement it most certainly is. In 1993, when he was deputy chairman of Lloyd's, Hiscox brought in Bronek Masojada from management consultants McKinsey to ensure succession. Now the company has well over one thousand employees, including, Hiscox claims, some of the most inspiring people in the industry.

My life's work has been to surround myself with people who are brighter than I am. If I have done one good thing, it's employing very strong people. To be able to bring on the next chairman and chief executive is, I think, the great achievement. And then, I can get out gracefully. Most people can't do that; it's their baby and they can't leave it behind, so it dies with them. Better if you can breed continuity. Bronek's been here for 19 years as chief executive, and the new chairman [Robert Childs] has been here 26 years. We all feel we're trying to build something, which I'm sure Paul Smith and James Dyson feel as well, and there's no greater goal.

I want this business to go on, and stay healthy. Because it has got my name on it and I am very proud of that. It's my life's work. Now, it's time for me to leave it. I'll be here on and off, but it's time for me to take the hand off the tiller. It's like a family. I love my children, and although we train them to be independent, it hurts when they go away. I have got a 44-year-old son and a 40-year-old son, and I love them and their children, but I don't want to live with them and they don't want me to live with them either. Well it's just like that with the team here. They've grown up, and they know how to run this business without my

*constant presence. Personally I've had a very good life, so my ambition
for the business is the same as for my children. I want them all to go on
being healthy and happy. I think I was born ambitious and now that's
my ambition.*

As we have said, when Robert Hiscox took over as head of the partnership in 1970, he was warned about renaming the company after himself.
That, it was claimed, would mean too much responsibility on one person.
And that, he felt, was exactly why it was the right thing to do. The Hiscox
advertising strapline is 'As good as our word'. And as he steps towards
retirement, Hiscox can make an entirely reasonable claim to have been
just that.

Lunch over, he smiles, and bids farewell, heading off for a spot of tennis. He likes to be outdoors, facing a challenge. A risk. A buffalo.

*My son was a pretty good shot and had hit it, but the bullet was deviated
by a small tree and just creased the heart of this beast. It ran off, and
we ran after it, but I can't run so fast, so the others got about thirty
yards ahead of me. But this thing was waiting for them in the bushes
and just charged my 16-year-old son and the professional hunter. I saw
it and fired two shots at it, and they fired five shots at it and it went
down at their feet. But then it got up again. It only had one front leg
working, but it still got up and turned and saw me and now charged
at me. I fired at it, but got the worst sound in the bush – just the dry
'click' – because in my desperation when it was charging my son, I'd
not properly chambered the next bullet. I just thought, 'Fuck, I've had
it.' It all happened in slow motion.*

*I jumped left and by sheer luck, with one broken front leg, it couldn't
jink that way. If I'd jumped the other way, it would have easily got me
as they are fantastic killers, and not only jink but move their horns
widely to either side. You mustn't run, or you'll die. I mean there's not
much you can do really, other than try and climb a tree or lie down or
curl into a ball and play dead, but even then it'll trample you and gouge
you and bite you.*

I've never taken cocaine or [other] drugs – I'm a very boring fellow – but this was easily the most exhilarating experience of my life. For about three hours afterwards, we were jabbering idiots talking about what had happened. I always say fear is a much-underestimated emotion as you tingle all over with nerves and get a knot in your stomach, but then you conquer it, which is a good feeling. If the action starts, adrenalin kicks in and everything goes into slow motion. It's a powerful feeling, and then if you escape or succeed, dopamine comes flooding into the system – and that, I am told, is exactly the same chemical as cocaine. There cannot be a bigger high. Plus, you're in Africa; there's the sky in the evening and the exhaustion, and sitting in a camp swapping stories. It's the only time I'm a man's man. It is basically primal; you're back to being the hunter-gatherer.

Back home here in the UK, outside the window, is a country in debt and depression. A respite is around the corner, however, and the 2012 London Olympics will prove to be one of the most successful events the country has ever known. Ten years ago, most of the Cabinet argued against making the bid, on the basis that it was all too great a risk. In the end, it was the minority opinion that prevailed, the risk was taken, and the rest is history. All of which goes to show that a life without risk is no life at all.

Which has been, and still is, Robert Hiscox's guiding principle.

‘And if we sip the wine, we find dreams coming upon us
Out of the imminent night.’

D. H. LAWRENCE (*BIRDS, BEASTS AND FLOWERS*)

TONY LAITHWAITE

(Laithwaite's Wine)

INTERVIEWED 19 NOVEMBER 2012

You will be hard pressed to find a more numinous product endorsement. The manufacture of wine at the Cana wedding was the first miracle that Jesus did – and (according to Christopher Hitchens) the only one worth doing. You don't have to go trawling very far through religious folklore to find that wine is close to godliness: for those who nurture the land, an eternally rejuvenating gift from on high (and the old vines do actually recycle extremely well if properly tended). No question, the grapevine trumps the grain when it comes to associations with the deities. To paraphrase Martin Luther: if men make beer, the gods give us the wine.

And it's easy to feel, on meeting wine entrepreneur Tony Laithwaite, that those same deities knew exactly what they were doing when they put this man on this earth. Were you to bump into him, a stranger, in a queue at the post office or at an airport check-in, you would probably guess that he is a wine maker; put him in a vineyard and he looks like he belongs there – in the way that French existential philosophers look like they belonged in street cafes on the Boulevard Saint-Germain.

All of our subjects in this book have had a compelling passion for the work they do and the challenges that they have set themselves. But just as something is spiritually unique about the product involved here, so is something correspondingly unique about its producer. What we encounter here feels different from the passions of our other subjects; from the way that Dyson is consumed by engineering or Warburton by his baking – and we are certainly not undermining what our other interviewees believe, or have achieved, by making the observation. But in this case, it feels like the connection between man and vine has an oddly elemental quality – something that is a little more than *merely* right. This can't fail to cross one's mind, talking to this unassuming, soft-spoken chap with glasses – at his modest office near the banks of the River Thames at Henley – hearing him refer to a 'business for life'.

They say that the only way to make a small fortune in wine is to start with a large fortune. People don't usually make money out of wine. You go into wine because you like it. And that was my attitude. My plan was to have a lovely life, just swanning around in vineyards and so on and so forth. A lot of people I know have wanted to build up businesses so that they could just sell them on. That was never my idea, and it wasn't Barbara's [his wife] either. If we made some money as we went along, all well and good, but it's the wine itself that gives you the reward... that's where it starts and finishes.

In 2010, world wine consumption was the equivalent of nearly 32 billion bottles, and global sales are currently showing year-on-year growth, with the UK being the world's biggest importer, and sixth-largest consumer (China just having overtaken us in that department). In the UK, our wine consumption is actually declining; but if people are drinking less, they are also drinking better, so at this stage, few in the industry are what you might call unduly worried.

The UK's biggest wine company is eponymously named after our man Laithwaite and his wife, Barbara. In fact, according to some analyses, they are the biggest wine merchants in the world (excluding supermarket retailers). Trading under his own name and several other subsidiaries (Averys of Bristol and *The Sunday Times* Wine Club being the more well known), Laithwaite and his wife have built up a company with turnover in excess of £350 million annually (which in very broad terms works out at around 50 million bottles), with usually at least 2,500 wines in stock, and directly employing well over a thousand people worldwide. Last year, they had sales of over £80 million in the US, working with partners there, including *The Wall Street Journal*. The Laithwaites *make* wine too, being owners of a collection of vineyards and wineries in Bordeaux and Australia.

The interview doesn't start according to plan, or doesn't really start at all for a while, because one of us has been driving round much of Berkshire for the last hour trying to find the right place, but Laithwaite is calm about the delay. He is a man who savours time like he savours his wine.

The property is a large old high-ceilinged terrace, now stylishly converted, like the boutique hotel next door, with thick walls that soak up the sharp edges from people's voices and dull any street anger. In reception, which was probably once someone's drawing room, sits Maxine, his PA, friendly and professional in equal measure, typing on what you feel ought to be a mechanical Remington, but of course isn't. Laithwaite's daughter-in-law, Kaye, completes the tableau, making us tea and bringing posh crackers. It could easily be a smart country legal practice, and a far cry from where Laithwaite started off, in industrial Lancashire.

My dad was from St Helens and my mother was a teacher from Bolton. A lot of the time it was my grandmother looking after me, and she had a corner shop – an Arkwright's sort of thing – where she baked and sold cakes. One grandfather was a jobbing builder, and I loved his carpentry shed, with its wood smell. The other grandfather was in the building trade too, with a fantastic carpentry shop as well. It was all sheds; everybody had sheds. In fact, now I like sheds more than buildings; I've an obsession with them. My grandmother used to sit and tell me stories about building things. In those days, the notion of do-it-yourself was the norm – rather than going and getting a job done for you by someone else. I was always stealing bricks from the building site for my make-believe houses.

Neither my mother nor my father did anything entrepreneurial. But for me, it seemed natural to be that way inclined. In fact, the whole business thing came upon me like a sort of madness.

Laithwaite didn't start out with the 'madness', of course. Neither a madness for entrepreneurship, nor for wine, for that matter. In fact, the fascination that got the bottle rolling was actually based on a kind of teenage Francophilia.

For some reason, I was very French-ified. I loved Maigret *on television; I liked* Gigi, *the film, and all things French. It just seemed so sexy. France was cool. You're going back to the mods 'n' rockers era, and I think my dream was to get a scooter and cruise round Paris, the south of France, St-Tropez, wow! It was a cool thought – really cool. I mean, France for me seemed like the centre of the world. I'd this little wine book and the photographs were all sort of beautiful, happy girls in vineyards. So it had just made me want to go harvesting grapes. I still get loads of young people contacting me wanting to come and do that.*

As luck would have it, my grandmother met a little French lady who was lost in Windsor, who she befriended. And Leina, the French lady says, 'If your grandson wishes to come to France, I will look after him.' So when I left school, I had a three-month gap, and went over and she and her husband took me in. Unlike my family, they were both entrepreneurs. He was very clever and had started a scaffolding business; she was manufacturing these woven fences from an idea that she'd seen in England. They were two French people being very entrepreneurial, even in the 1970s. And all the wine growers I then eventually met were all being very entrepreneurial as well.

For this reason, Laithwaite associated France – after the romantic imagery – with entrepreneurship. It seemed only a matter of time before the third and final component of his life's work, wine-selling, would enter the mix. Immediately after leaving school, and inspired by both his own interest in France and his father's love of wine ('I think he got into wine quite early on – especially for a northerner, because northerners didn't do wine in them days'), Laithwaite returned to France, this time to Bordeaux, where he worked in the vineyards and washed bottles. 'It was great... exotic, fabulous food, and there were the girls as well...'

However, before anything definitive took place, Laithwaite needed to return home where there were still harsh realities to face, as he attempted more orthodox routes into gainful employment:

I got into Durham [University] on two Es and a D. How did I do that? I thought I was clever, but the examiners didn't. Anyway, I still got in. But I didn't bother when I got there. As far as my mother was concerned, university was the treat you got for actually getting there, and that was my attitude too. I spent my time on doing set decorations for the college and university dances, with all the great groups that played, like The Who and the Small Faces – you name it, we had them. I liked doing the lighting and all that stuff. I spent my time on that and came out with a Third – in geography – so I wasn't going to just walk into a job with a crap result like that.

Even before university, I was an awkward sod. I went to Bishop Vesey's Grammar School in Sutton Coldfield, when we moved there. I was good at sports, like sprinting and decathlons and rugby, and got to be a bit cocky. In sixth form, there were only about forty boarders and we had a great time because nobody bothered us; it was like a mini university. I was pretty self-confident by then and some masters queued up to tell me that I was useless. Although one or two masters thought I did have something, and I owe them a lot.

Even by the time I came out of university, I still had the massive chip on my shoulder. One of my main motivations was to show the bastards. I went to a job interview at Grants of St James in Burton-on-Trent. I took my final geography dissertation – which I'd written while I'd been in Bordeaux – on the wines of Saint Emilion, which I thought was very profound. I showed it to the director, and told him I wanted to get into the wine trade, but he tossed it back at me, and said, 'The best thing you can hope for, laddie, is running an off-licence in Carlisle.' So that was that. Thank God.

It's difficult to tell whether Laithwaite's failure to land a job was down to potential employers thinking him unsuitable or an inner reluctance on his own part to defer to the career norms. You get the feeling he's still not sure about that himself. What he does recall, however, is a sense of destiny stepping in and taking him back to Bordeaux, and his previous employer there. The seminal moment is near:

I went back to Monsieur Cassin – the guy who had employed me in his winery – and back to washing bottles for a bit. And he really did help me. Monsieur Cassin became my mentor – he and his wife. They were much older than my parents; an elderly, childless, French couple. And I became their surrogate son.

They taught me French, they made me speak it, and they told me all about the culture, which I was already in love with and just fell even more in love with. And above all, they taught me about the wine. He gave me a job and then he pushed me to go further afield. So I tried to get [more permanent] jobs in Bordeaux, but without success. Then one day, he asked me why I didn't just sell his wine in the UK. We were driving back from the winery and it really was like a light-bulb moment – on the road to Damascus in his 2CV. I saw the vision immediately. I'd go round and do tastings; or write to people and offer to have a guy come and give a tasting; and lo and behold, they'd buy the wine. I just thought, Wow! I could do that. And so we started composing the letters immediately. We must have sat there in that car, parked in his garage, for hours. I remember Madame coming out thinking we'd gassed ourselves.

Straight after the harvest, I returned to England. My grandmother gave me £700 to start up, and then a little while later gave me another £7,000 through my mother. You needed a bit of funding and the banks would certainly not have given any money to someone like me, would they? I wrote a really good mail-order letter, which I've still kept somewhere – very mail order. I think I ripped it off somebody. I sent it out, got a couple of replies, did a couple of tastings, and got two orders. And one of my dad's friends at the golf club bought a bit of wine as well. I took a Christmas job to ease my way through, but then, in the New Year, I did more tastings, and gradually, it got going. I was about 23 by that time.

Laithwaite frequently reminds us that his is a joint venture, with wife Barbara his invaluable partner. 'It's a two-person thing, and she is the business head,' he says. They actually didn't get married until some time after they had started working together, in 1975 ('to everyone's relief,' she has said). Like many things in the Laithwaite tale, timing is every-thing: just as he returned from Bordeaux, his future wife re-entered his life (having been there once previously):

We'd met before at university. I went out with her sister, Helen, who picked me up at Freshers', and I went out with her for a term. Then, at a dance, she introduced me to her little sister in her miniskirt and it was just lust at first sight – and she could clearly see what I was thinking. Barbara came to Durham the following year and I tried it on again, without getting anywhere; she wasn't having any of it. After I'd just started the wine thing, Helen, who'd returned from South Africa married, invited me to her party. And obviously her sister was there – and this time, we did get together.

Barbara would come out for weekends to Windsor and see me trying to flog wine. A lot of people had thought I'd never get anywhere, but she believed in it. She kept saying I was selling too cheaply. She was a statistician. So one day I just said, 'Well, if you think you're so bloody clever, why don't you come and do it?' So she did. She had an amazing job doing JICTAR audience research, but she just packed it in. They said she was mad to go from that to working for me in a caravan under a railway line.

But she sorted me out. She discovered that I hadn't kept any accounts for two years. I didn't know what accounts were: I didn't know you had to do such things. She dealt with all the things to do with people and money and law and the business. I just threw the lot at her. But luckily she was the right person and more than capable of doing it.

Barbara took one look at the accounts and saw that it didn't make financial sense, so she made me put the price up. Basically, you had to ask the right price for your product. Not too much; not too little; and

*going up a bit each year to cover inflation and cost of living. Cassin
had tried to drum that into me. All very French.*

    *And, in time, we began to earn enough to live on. At first, we didn't
really try and make profits. That wasn't a priority. Anyway, at that
time, the top rate of tax, if we made good profits, was going to be 98%
super tax. So what was the point in making a big profit?*

In his first year, Laithwaite concentrated on selling the produce from
Monsieur Cassin. He describes how he 'just sat there in the UK', sending the orders over to France. Then, in due course, he expanded his
range of suppliers; slowly at first, concentrating on several of Cassin's
winemaking friends and associates. These wines would be sent over
by ship-consignment to Shoreham-by-Sea (on the Sussex coast) for
distribution.

*But the dockers used to nick a lot. I came to the view that it would be
much better – and actually quite nice as well – to drive down and get
it myself.*

It was one of those moments when the necessity to solve a problem leads
to a decisive opportunity.

*My aim now was to make enough to live on and allow my holidays and
my treats to be part of the job. And I used to love bombing down through
France in the old Ford Transit with the stereo thudding away – 'Brown
Sugar', all the way down to Bordeaux. Then I'd go round my five or six
friends, load up, go through the customs rigmarole in Bordeaux, and
then back and more customs rigmarole in Southampton.*

    *By the time it had got to 1970, I was feeling that I ought to be not
working from home. So I went and got an office – a room in Windsor.
But then I couldn't afford that, so I asked the landlord if I could have
the cellar underneath instead. He let me have that for about £1 a week,
and I put all my wine in there and worked out of that cellar. I was
doing the van, and it was going quite well, with quite a lot of orders for*

Christmas gift packs and stuff like that, so then I pushed the boat out and got a lorry: you know, an artic; a whole sodding artic – a 40-footer. But then I realised I didn't have anywhere to put it.

I had this friend called Merv – a real Del Boy – with a lock-up, which he let me use. But the lorry couldn't back into the lock-up because it was too big. So we would park it in a lay-by near Windsor Racecourse, and Merv in his van and me in my van would ship the wine up the road from there. We'd have all this wine coming off the back of the artic, and the police would come, like whoosh! I lived in that lock-up for a few months. We had to sleep in there with the wine because there was no security. Then, finally, I got the railway arch, over at Windsor Station, which gave us loads more space.

Laithwaite explains that it was a good time to start in the wine business, which up until that point had been 'quite monolithic'. Smaller local growers would sell in bulk to merchants, through brokers, who would aggregate stocks and sell on to a merchant in the UK, who would, in turn, sell to wholesaler and retailer. With resale price maintenance (RPM) and exclusivity agreements, the climate was hostile to newcomers. But that was now changing. RPM was abolished, and, at the same time, over in France, Monsieur Cassin was creating a mini-revolution of his own, becoming the first co-operative to sell directly to a supermarket in Bordeaux. It all caused a 'massive scandal', says Laithwaite.

The UK wasn't in the EEC at that time, but in France it was all change. All of a sudden, there were these small entrepreneurial growers who weren't happy just to sit there and wait for their stuff to be bought in bulk; they wanted to put it in a bottle and sell it themselves. That was perfect for me. Roll-on-roll-off ferries had just started, so I was able to drive over direct to them. I called myself 'Bordeaux Direct', just to emphasise that I only bought estate-bottled wines.

It meant that now, there I was, based under a damp railway arch, trying to compete with the big established guys whose stated belief was that Châteauneuf-du-Pape and Nuits-Saint-Georges were nothing more than styles, and that the individual wines had nothing to do with the places they originally came from. But customers would now see that, with me, when they got my Saint-Emilion, it hadn't been faffed around with, and tasted very different from the disgusting stuff mass-bottled in the UK. By comparison, my wines were authentic and I made a big song and dance about this.

As part of that song and dance, Laithwaite contacted *The Sunday Times* – a paper that had been running a series of exposés, including one on the wine industry. Sir Harold Evans was one of the most influential of that paper's editors (serving 14 years in that position – a long stint in that industry's terms), introducing its now familiar crusading, campaigning style of journalism. Catching his attention was a coup for Laithwaite.

I sent a letter to him, which I've kept, and I told him that it wasn't fair. My letter might have been slightly witty. Or maybe he'd known I'd been to Durham and Harry Evans was Durham. I only ever met him once in my life at a dinner, but he was an amazing guy. I don't know why he printed it, but he did – along with my address, following which, we got hundreds of replies asking for the wines. It was something that people could relate to: little old me; this guy who goes in a van and gets the wine directly; it really appealed. So I sent out a list and that was that.

Then a customer of mine [and business investor], who was really well connected, approached The Sunday Times *again on our behalf, and they let me do a special offer for the readers, then a second offer, and both went hugely well.*

Unfortunately, success very nearly, and very quickly, turned into a disaster. The business investor seemed at first to be someone with whom they could build a fruitful partnership, considering the help that he had already given them. The Laithwaites were encouraged to build the relationship, and in due course, he was sold 25% of the company shares. But all was not what it seemed, and their new associate was not quite the well-meaning business 'angel' they'd assumed. In fact, it turned out he was working towards owning the whole business himself.

He did all sorts of nasty stuff to us. Then he got into tax problems, needed money very urgently, and sold his shares back to us, just in time. Basically we were very lucky to be able to buy them back.

We only just squeaked through. Monsieur Cassin helped a lot. When we got the shares back from this guy I let Barbara keep them because she'd done the negotiations: she and our lawyer. They finally got them off him. I can remember I was in France, in Tours, when I had the phone call – we didn't have mobiles then. That was like getting out of jail. Monsieur Cassin had a small percentage but then he wasn't really interested, so we bought his back too, and so basically it was just the two of us that then owned the company.

And we've never sold a share since. It was just too traumatic. This guy had been trying to take my dream away; he just wanted it for himself. They were my wines; it was my writing; it was my thing; and I was never again letting anybody else try to take it away.

When he talks in this way, there's some strong emotion in his eyes: a real sense of protectiveness, remembering a time when he had come very close to losing the very thing that defined Barbara's and his life.

So no more dealings with the City and no searching for large capital investment. Laithwaite mentions that he has the 'mild paranoia of entrepreneurs, alone in the jungle; to survive, we have to spot threats early; to stay there we have to be basically mad!' In those early years, after facing some treacherous problems, the Laithwaites developed the simple modus operandi of reinvesting profits as and when they came in, and doing, in the main, what they 'sensed' was right for them and their ambitions in wine.

'It just gradually grew and grew and I went further and further afield...' An admirable and romantic ideal, but one that could well lead to problems. Laithwaite has always had a largely free-spirited view of running a company: he likes to get his hands dirty, quite literally. 'My obsession became – and still is – about keeping it all close. So much is about your friends, the wine producers, the customers, my lot, the people who truly count…' But the absence of a half-decent management structure, coupled with relentless expansion, meant that, by the early eighties, with turnover past £10 million, logistics were becoming more and more troublesome. The idealism could only go so far.

I just found that very hard and started getting chest pains. It was a very stressful period and I'd taken a few risks, including a couple of ridiculous mailings – which you should never do – which hadn't worked. So it had been a bit hairy-scary. The business had grown, and we were getting towards £15 million, but without taking on anybody of a high seniority. We were trying to do too much ourselves.

At the same time, Laithwaite's other company buyer was killed in Spain.

In those days, as a buyer, you were doing a job which involved a lot of driving and he just forgot and went onto the wrong side of the road. He was a young guy who'd started helping me out from school, and he joined us and became like my other buyer, doing the bits that I couldn't get to. But he had this terrible car crash in Spain on a buying trip – which could easily have happened to me; and it did happen to other merchants. But I took some blame and then I was ill.

Laithwaite had, in fact, suffered a form of heart attack. It was a wake-up moment.

The specialist told me to stop work and sell the business. He was very brutal about it. He said, 'You can't carry on. You've got to stop or you'll die.' He told me to go and have a nice walking tour of the south of France. I told him that I did that anyway. So I ignored him and wouldn't sell it. I was scared, though – I had three little boys – and I did pull right back. Barbara carried on running it and for the first time, we made a decent profit, because I wasn't interfering. I wasn't coming up with bloody wonderful new ideas all the time. She focused on the important matters and made a good profit.

Despite his reluctance to follow the cardiologist's directives word-for-word, Laithwaite knew he could not go on in the same way. As an immediate priority, a new and properly staffed management structure was needed, with more coherent and longer-term strategic planning.

In 1991, a full board was recruited, including managing director, wine director, marketing director, finance director, and head of IT. Before, the company had been successful: now, the effect was spectacular.

We went to something like £50 million by 1994, then £100 million and more. Amazing, really. But basically, there was no new invention after that. It was just perfecting what was there. All the systems, the continuity, all the mail-order techniques; they just focused on that and followed the growth pattern. Then after one year, Barbara and I became non-execs, except I kept working and writing and I did carry on travelling.

The new managing director was Greg Hodder, someone for whom Laithwaite is full of praise: a 'clever, progressive guy', who was responsible for taking 'this rough diamond of a firm and making it the company it is'. But Laithwaite and his wife had been running the company for nearly two decades, and letting go was a culture shock, even if they were trying to make it a 'proper business'. The arrival of Hodder was probably the right medicine, but not a sweet-tasting one.

There was conflict, I'll tell you. It didn't work very easily at all. We were like two cocks. I can't complain: he was good and he did his stuff. I felt that it was his job to run it, yet it was still my business, and I found it hard to let go.

But the business wasn't in good nick. We'd grown all right, but we hadn't kept up with the market, and the market had been changing all the time. When we started up, supermarkets didn't do wine; then they started but with poor wine and they didn't know how to sell it. But then all of a sudden, the supermarkets became really good. And there were other merchants starting up as well. They'd seen a bit of what could be done and were doing it. So it was a call for us to change too.

Hodder wanted to accelerate the growth of the company, but the way in which he planned to do it was not always consistent with Laithwaite's own views. He says it was like a marriage, whereby both of them had to compromise. He even brought in a mediation expert from the London Business School, to manage the relationship. 'The results were positive,' he says, 'and showed we wanted it to work.'

By the end of the millennium, the company was showing a turnover in excess of £100 million. Much now had been improved, but not the name, Bordeaux Direct, which, given the range of products, made very little sense. It was time for a rebranding exercise. Laithwaite admits that a great deal of expense was committed to bringing in branding consultants to come up with the mould-breaking title of 'Laithwaite's Wines'.

Bordeaux Direct had been registered by someone else who tried to blackmail me over it. But by that time, it was limiting us, because a lot of people were assuming, quite logically, that we weren't selling anything but Bordeaux, despite us selling a lot of other stuff including some Australian. Anyway, everybody had starting using 'Direct' – Waitrose Wine Direct, Sainsbury's Direct Wines – they're all direct this, direct that, everybody's damn direct now. So we thought we'd drop it.

We went through all sorts of alternative names, with Laithwaite's fairly well down the list below all kinds of crazy, stupid-sounding names. That was when all the gas companies were giving themselves fancy names and stuff. However, in the end, the logical thing you had to say was 'Laithwaite', and we concluded that probably the most defensible title was, in fact, just my name – you can't really copy that. But I actually found it quite difficult to agree with it, because I'm of a generation and an upbringing where you don't brag. I kept thinking that all my mates will be saying, 'Look at that show-off Laithwaite. Bloody hell.'

Laithwaite dislikes snobbery of any kind, and hopes that he would never be regarded as behaving in that way, despite his wealth and the perception that wine can sometimes be a vehicle for one-upmanship. In fact, he sees wine as the antithesis to pretention, in that you largely get what you pay for, the quality is transparent, and people either know what they're talking about or they don't. He believes that you can't bluff too easily with wine, despite the stereotypes, and adds that, in trade circles especially, people know exactly what is what. Those who try to use wine to show off only make themselves look idiotic, he feels.

Socially, I don't appear to take wine all that seriously. I'm fond of saying, 'It all tastes the same to me.' Because, when I'm working, I'm intense on it, so when I'm not working, I just want to drink, frankly, without thinking too hard. I have a terrible cellar at home. When I'm relaxing, I want someone else to choose what's a fantastic wine. If we ever have to do photographs of me, 'Tony, in his private cellar', I have to have somebody do it up first.

I went to the pub last night, and drank wine... the first one was dreadful; the second one was fine. But that's how it goes. I don't really let it get to me any more. That's the last thing I'm bothered about. I don't want to be going down there and being rude. I'm happy to drink what's there. It's fine.

As for doing all these business lunches, I gave them up a long time ago. Actually, it was because I was always sick. I'd get so nervous, I just threw up all the time, which tends to ruin the event somewhat. It's just that, if I'm working on something, and trying to do a deal with you and sell to you, then I'm going to be all keyed up. Under those circumstances, I can't actually eat. You're just too tense to eat.

These days, Laithwaite need not be tense about too many things, and he can certainly afford to eat. His personal wealth runs to many millions, and the 2012 *Sunday Times* Rich List put the family at 410th in its UK rankings.

Wealth has allowed me not to have to bend the knee. Although, I think maybe that came right at the beginning, because when you set out on your own, you don't have to anyway, do you? Of course, you have to be nice to the bank. But that was what drove us to wanting to do direct selling to customers. I did sell to Marks & Spencer for a while when they started in wine: I supplied them with champagne and stuff. But then they said you're making too much money and you'll have to take a cut in your margin. So I thought, stuff this for a game of soldiers. That was that. Now I've got thousands and thousands of individual customers who matter most of all.

Individuality is important to Laithwaite. The younger family members are all following on in the drinks' trade, but each in his own way: one son, Henry, has his own vineyard, while the younger son, Tom, also helps out; Will has his brewery; all have various schemes for the future. Meanwhile, Barbara has said that she has never been as personally interested as she is now, especially since they have bought a château near their home in Bordeaux. Meanwhile, back where they started, in Windsor, the Laithwaites have become the tenant farmers of the Royal Family on a 4-hectare plot in Windsor Great Park. After planting 10,000 vines there in 2011, their first harvest is due soon, and that really is generating excitement. It's all a far cry from the kind of 'progress' being seen in some sections of the industry, which Laithwaite has set himself against. He's especially concerned about the new industrialisation of wine.

Now, it's proper grape varieties being industrialised. You're talking Chardonnay and Sémillon and all that stuff, but increasingly on bigger and bigger scales. In Australia, it went that way fast, with vineyards and companies swallowing each other up. So now 80% of Australian wine comes from four groups. Is that level of industrialisation good? Well, the product is good, and some people like it. But maybe that's the most worrying thing of all. You can make industrial-scale wine that's quite good and if you package it up in a fancy way, people go for it.

But I want the little guys to carry on, because that's what I enjoy, and they're doing things of character and meaning. People basically may want a bottle of Chardonnay for a Friday night at £5, but I want to say, 'Yes, but try this at £15, and appreciate the difference, and what it means.'

The little old guys who just made wine and hoped somebody bought it are dying a death, and their properties are being taken over by more successful farmers who are becoming a bit bigger, but hopefully not too big. So small-scale wine producers are not altogether dying out. It is becoming quite professional, so if you want to be a successful wine producer now, you've probably got to be very good at winemaking. You've got to have all the viticulture skills, which are complex, then you've got to have vinification skills and ageing skills. And then you've got to be good at packaging and marketing and you've got to get on a plane and fly to Japan. Your little peasant farmer can't do that.

What I hope is that plenty of people will keep buying interesting wines. In fact, these days there are ever more interesting wines appearing, and it's getting more and more complex, with lots of wine tasting, so there'll be more and more shops like ours where you go in and you taste proper wine, with proper wine merchanting. Even if there's Tesco, just down the road, doing bottles for £4.

Compared with the early years, Laithwaite has allowed himself to let go of aspects of the firm's management. Yet his ambitions for it remain as strong as ever, not least in terms of the expansion of the retail business, and there are now over a dozen shops, including a prestigious flagship store at Vinopolis at London Bridge. 'I would hope there will be more – I like that one so much.'

There is a new global CEO in place, Simon McMurtrie, and UK MD Glenn Caton. International growth is a key element of the plan, along with all manner of innovative investments. Direct retailing involves a significant degree of customer churn, but a company recruiting around

200,000 new customers each year has to be doing something right. Almost a quarter of the company's business is now in the perplexing United States market (having acquired Lionstone International, a wholesale and import business in Illinois). The US may be a tricky market, but its wine consumption has grown every year for almost two decades. In addition:

Making our own wine is going to become more important, definitely. It's happening. Years ago, Monsieur Cassin told me he wanted me to buy his vineyard in the underestimated appellation of Côtes de Bordeaux, Castillon. It was a small one of three acres. He goes, 'Tony, one day, you will buy this. I will help you. I will give you good price and I will replant the vineyard. We will show the world that Castillon can make wine as good as Saint-Emilion.' Well, we bought it, and started running it, and I loved making the wine. I could go down there every harvest and do a different kind of work, plunge grapes, and do different things. It was fabulous. That's what this is all about.

At first, we didn't have premises, so we converted a barn and cut down into the caves below. But the wine wasn't very good. Then an Australian I'd met came and told me I was doing it all wrong. He said he would show me, and he did. The year after, he sent me his mate and then the following year, we had a whole bunch of them. The idea was to put them in there to clean the whole thing up. We gave them barrels and chilling equipment and whatever they needed and, lo and behold, they transformed the wine. So suddenly, rather than me having to spend months trekking round the world trying to find the best wine, we'd just make it. In the Dordogne, nobody could make white wine to save their life, but put some Aussies in there, and two years later, they've won the Macon Wine Show with a white wine from the Dordogne. Half of Burgundy had a fit over that. We invented the name, 'Flying Winemakers'.

Eventually, we created Le Chai au Quai [on the banks of the Dordogne] – a place made up of the old riverside merchant cellars, mostly abandoned. We brought it back to life and filled it with hundreds of barrels. So we have a big winery now, making lots of wonderful wines – and it's great fun.

If you add all that together, wine production is now key for us. We've got our guy, Jean-Marc, who, for example, goes to Moldova one week and helps make wines better there, and last week, he was in India helping them make better wine. They have wineries there, but they haven't quite got it yet. In fact, I've got two fantastic winemakers who have got experience in so many styles and places, and they can just deliver the wines. It's a bit like having guys who are music producers who can make hit records. I've got the wine producers, who can go into a winery and produce something that sings.

And that's the music that Laithwaite loves to hear. Since the very early days sitting in his Transit, to the present day sitting in Vinopolis, this man (and his remarkable business-savvy wife) has been singing the praises of how wine should be, and how more people can enjoy it more…

That is: how the gods intended.

'… a certain casualness which conceals art and creates the impression that what is done and said is accomplished without effort and without its being thought about. It is from this… that grace largely derives.'

BALDASSARE CASTIGLIONE (*THE BOOK OF THE COURTIER*)

DAVID ARMSTRONG-JONES, VISCOUNT LINLEY

(Linley)

INTERVIEWED 18 DECEMBER 2012

You have met David Linley before. At least you have if you have been reading these chapters in order. Because he has already enjoyed the briefest of cameos during Emma Bridgewater's story, where he was accompanying his pal, Matthew Rice. Perhaps we might start this chapter with a little fun and hear that story told from Linley's perspective:

We were at a trade fair called Top Drawer in the Barkers, Derry & Toms building in Kensington, where we were exhibiting our paper range. I think she [Emma] was exhibiting her Brixton pottery. Anyway, we went past her stand and Matthew said, 'Oh, I quite fancy that.' He wasn't talking about the pottery. And I went, 'OK, off you go then.' And so he did. And never came back. And now he's become Mr Stoke-on-Trent.

The place we've come to now is not quite Stoke-on-Trent, and, with the greatest respect to that fine city, has no more in common with it than with the island of Krakatoa. We've arrived at the global headquarters of Christie's fine art auctioneers in King Street, St James's, and the chairman of Christie's UK is our next interviewee. David Albert Charles Armstrong-Jones, Viscount Linley, is the co-founder of the Linley interior design and furnishings brand. To keep him busy, the man has also written numerous books on interior design and lectured all over the world, and let's not forget that he happens to be heir apparent to the Earldom of Snowdon, nephew to Queen Elizabeth II, grandson of King George VI, and fifteenth in line of succession to the British throne.

King Street is busy as we drive up and our taxi driver finds it difficult to pull in as there are long shiny black German saloons and Range Rovers parked everywhere, most of them with their drivers still at the wheel and engines running. The building is fronted by black iron railings, and above the doorway to the magnificent stone edifice is a prominent flag, giving the place the aura of a small European state embassy. A grey uniformed doorman guides us into a grand lobby, of which the central feature is an imposing carpeted staircase so wide the designers probably had to factor in an allowance for the curvature of the earth.

Linley co-founded his own company with Matthew Rice back in 1985, originally running it from a characterful store at 1 New King's Road, not that far from where we are now. He is no longer majority share-holder, but almost thirty years later the company still thrives, making beautiful, high-quality furniture and home accessories, in his trademark style of wood marquetry. 'British craftsmanship at its best' is the man-tra, and these days the company has a retail presence through three shops, in Mayfair, Belgravia, and the Burlington Arcade in Piccadilly, and is doing bespoke commissions too. The brand colour scheme is a distinctive bright blue 'to create a positive initial image'. His new major-ity shareholder, wealthy yacht broker Jamie Edmiston, has spoken of their ambitions to be a British super-prestige brand, analogous to Continental premium marques like Louis Vuitton or Hermès, both of which similarly came from the bespoke tradition. Linley and Edmiston have together expressed a desire over the next few years to take the brand abroad, targeting new markets where there is a growing interest in authentic, exquisitely crafted products, and an increasing ability to afford them.

Linley was brought up surrounded by arts and crafts. He has a kind of spiritual fascination with wood, and is rarely more impassioned than when he talks about it. He told the BBC, back in 2002, that he had felt this way...

…ever since I first picked up a piece of wood. Every piece is different. The nature of the wood; the way that you work it; the knowledge that you need to build up to use it properly. It's a warm material. It's very tactile, and people love to touch it. So often you go into antique shops and it says, 'Please do not touch.' That's wrong. To me, the joy is to run your hands along the top, the side and underneath…

It probably goes right back to his early childhood, often spent in a place where things were being made and the ambient temperature was cosy, earth-warm and nurturing.

I was born of two very artistic parents, and my father had this workshop in the basement under the drawing room. I remember it from when I was four or five. There was always the lovely warm smell of cigarettes, red wine, and sawdust. It was a place where everyone met. There was a wonderful working atmosphere around the house, with designers and famous people coming and going. There was no sitting down, just all this excitement of things being created. Making things was so cool; whether it was my father designing the London Zoo Aviary with Cedric Price, or the Investiture of 1969 for Carnarvon, which had this amazing canopy. The day before the event, it flew off, and I think that was probably my earliest memory of somebody being quite cross.

Back at Christie's, we have reached the top of the large staircase and duly entered the boardroom, where they hold personal previews for many high-net-worth individuals. They have wine evenings too, spent trying out different renditions of Château d'Yquem (a Linley favourite) – that kind of thing. ('Wine is that wonderful combination of status symbol and investment. Hopefully, it will appreciate, but if it doesn't, you can drink it.')

We're not kept waiting at all. With impeccable timing, a pair of double doors open, and Linley glides in, suave and smiling, preceded by an air of relaxed elegance in which he has bathed that morning. You can glean straight away why the man is sometimes described as a smooth operator, but this oversimplifies how he works. In truth, there is nothing pretentious about his practised approachability. It is impressive, not dislikeable, and only the most curmudgeonly would interpret it as insincerity or refuse to be drawn into his rhythms and cadences. Not least, because Linley is fun.

As we do the interview, he is careful not to say something that might be recycled mischievously at some later date, but there is often a sense of a joke or naughty anecdote bubbling under the surface, and he delivers some great throwaway lines. You feel that, at less guarded times, he can probably be an absolute hoot, but having met us only a few minutes ago, he probably feels it would be wise not to risk a media firestorm if he puts his foot in it. When it boils down to it, he's a Royal, after all.

In fact, when we start, he self-effacingly tells us that he has no idea what he's meant to be talking about. He starts telling us about interviews he's done and unusual requests he's had:

I was once asked onto Strictly Come Dancing, *although I'm not sure what exactly I was going to have to do. At one stage, we thought we might have a bit of fun with it, and told everybody in the business we were going to do it, but, in the end, it didn't happen.*

You can see why they thought of him. Linley's personal styling is quite something. Today, he is in a grey Savile Row suit, worn over one of the black John Smedley polo necks that he seems to wear all the time, and which, he says, he buys in bulk, ten or fifteen in one go. Whether it's the dress sense or the conversation, there's just no friction. When he arrives home at night, he probably unlocks his door in one single movement without the key touching the sides of the barrel.

Maybe it's something to do with precision. He talks of his father instructing him in the best of woodcraft etiquette and, as an example, making screws line up perfectly, or inspecting the underside of furniture to see if it was as well made below as in the visible areas. Woodwork or living: it's all the same beast. In the sixteenth century, it would have been what the courtier-diplomat Castiglione called the art of the sprezzatura: matching perfect behaviour – in speech, dress, and manner around court

– with an impression of 'unstudied nonchalance'. Perhaps it is because, from an early age, he was exposed to something special.

My first memories are of living at Kensington Palace. We were on the first floor of the building, looking out into a courtyard designed by Wren. I was just sort of nosey and liked seeing who was visiting the neighbours. I was intrigued by the bigger cars, the smaller cars, the convertibles, the Rolls Royces, the smell of five-star fuel. It was a narrative of who was coming to dinner. Because we weren't allowed to go down there ourselves.

Really amazing people were coming through the house at the time, because my father was photographing them. Then, they'd come back for drinks afterwards or dinner, and in the evening I'd be watching people; the mink, the jewels, the long dresses. We would try and guess who they were: Cleo Laine, Elizabeth Taylor, Frank Sinatra... They weren't regarded as 'celebrities' in those days, remember. Not like today. They were seen as people who were bloody good at something and therefore notorious I suppose. The C-word didn't come in till really quite recently.

Linley was born in 1961, the son of the Queen's sister, Princess Margaret, and her husband, Antony Armstrong-Jones, the 1st Earl of Snowdon. The glamorous marriage was rarely out of the public eye (including giving the public their first ever Royal wedding to be broadcast on television), and, given the pressure, it was not altogether surprising when the parents split up after 18 years. Yet Linley says he never felt affected by it at all, and most of his memories are of an immensely happy childhood. 'They were incredibly grown up about the split,' he says.

His mother, nonetheless, was one of the most controversial of recent Royal figures, whether it was down to her romantic links with other men or her penchant for a cigarette or two (which eventually caught up with her in the form of a serious lung illness). For Linley, the title of Viscount is his by courtesy of his father to the eldest son, but he will in due course become the 2nd Earl of Snowdon in his own right. Royal titles in the UK only currently pass through the father, so he has no immediate right of succession from Princess Margaret. That suits him. He purports not to know much about how near or far he is in succession terms, and likes to say that he is 'not technically royal'; and that – quoting his mother – his 'children aren't royal either. They just happen to have the Queen as an aunt'. He has a story about when someone once bowed to him, triggering a sharp reprimand to them from his mother, 'possibly because I enjoyed it a little too much'.

The office is furnished impeccably. His PA brings in three glasses and a bottle of Hildon water, on a drinks tray that looks like it was made by a small man with spectacles who polished a lump of rare rosewood until it eventually reached the right shape. His oak kneehole partners' desk is large enough to take a drone landing. And most impossible of all to ignore, on one wall, is a gigantic painting of his mother, Princess Margaret, by the world-famous Milanese painter Pietro Annigoni. We ask him about it, in passing, but all he says is the name of the painter, as though nothing about it is a big deal. Which makes it about the biggest not-a-big-deal deal that we're ever likely to encounter.

This particular painting has world fame and some degree of notoriety, and has made the national news on several occasions since its creation. Linley's mother did no less than 21 sittings for the portrait in 1957, after which it hung for years in the Kensington Palace home. When she died, and money was needed for her £3 million death duties, her most valuable effects were put up for auction at Christie's, including the portrait, generating a frenzy from overseas collectors. Anticipating that the painting would be lost to an overseas buyer, Linley had three exact replicas commissioned, at which time was revealed all manner of secret flourishes and esoteric details inserted by Annigoni into the painting's background – such as a hidden heart hanging in a glass on a branch, symbol of the young Princess Margaret's tragically doomed romance with the much younger commoner, Captain Peter Townsend. When Lot 793, as it was, came under the hammer, the winning bid of £680,000 turned out to be from none other than Linley himself. Perhaps he had been driven to keep hold of the work because of the newly revealed sentimental significance.

Or maybe it was because of his fascination with anything with a secret or two in its origination.

Because Linley adores things with secrets in them: paintings, boxes, chests of drawers. He tells us how he is constantly trying to get his designers to think about how to make pieces more fun by adding extra clandestine touches: 'like a secret drawer to a desk, or a perfect tray that slides out of a safe'. The impulse was there by the time he was in his early teens at school, where he once devoted an entire week to making a cigar box for his grandmother (when his peers had all gone away on O-level study leave), incorporating his beloved secret precision mitre dovetail joints.

These days, his company will happily produce insanely intricate bespoke pieces that hide spaces known only to the owner and designer. And he was excited recently when he discovered a hand-bound antique copy of Bram Stoker's *Dracula* that included a trickle of blood (in red leather) hidden inside the back cover. One of his favourites from the shop is the Time Table, a clock-topped piece in rosewood and sycamore with drawers lined in gold leaf and velvet which can only be accessed using a series of secret levers (and retailing at £19,500 in case you now fancy one). Items like this – with stories to tell from secrets to be revealed – seem, more than anything, an expression of his own sense of fun, enjoyment, and ingenuity.

Secrets engage people in furniture in ways that wouldn't normally happen... My grandmother [the late Queen Mother] made everything fun as a child and liked challenging us to look for secret drawers in furniture. There's a Jacobean piece up in the Castle of Mey in Caithness. You can still see it; it's still there. One of the drawers comes open off the corners, and one rainy day, she challenged us to find the secret drawer. I still remember how exhilarating it was to find it, and how clever was the design. We found the drawer, and inside, a letter that she'd lost. At that moment, in my mind, furniture became fun, and my interest really started.

But I'm naturally interested in the secrets of how things work, be it

in cars or watches or how you make a dovetail joint or how you make
a mortise and tenon or how an engine can be made smaller – any of
these kinds of things.

My first car was a 1964 Mini 850 which my father bought for me
at a cost of £190 in 1979. But I like motorbikes best. To me, they're
the ultimate form of engineering expression in miniature, which then
delivers the freedom that you feel in riding. I've still got my dad's old
bike – a Triumph Tiger 100 – which originally belonged to Peter Sellers.
He and my father were great friends... We sometimes put it in the shop
and have it as an ornament. It's a beautiful thing that's kept going by a
lovely, brilliant man with a fantastic workshop called Ned Smile, who
found the right nuts and bolts and restored it for me.

A modern motorcycle leaves people cold because its form follows
function: air-tested through a wind tunnel and very efficient, with a
little button and it starts brilliantly. But do you think it impresses the
girls like the old-fashioned ones did – the Nortons and Triumphs, made
by people in sheds without any design?

Linley isn't a particularly tall chap, but he has aged well, and looks fit
and healthy. It would be hard to say for sure, if you didn't know, whether
he had yet reached his fifth decade. And we must mention Linley's
accent, which is an intriguing one. It's good-school southern RP for
most of the time, of course, but there are moments when he likes to get
Estuary-chummy, shorten his vowels, and use the historic-present tense
in the manner of Tony Blair speaking to a group of Asda shoppers. 'Look,
so this bloke says to me, you know, "Dave," he says...'

At school, Linley was far more artistic than he was academic, veering
towards the creative arts that gave him a sense of liberation that other
subjects didn't offer.

I'm sure these days you'd be able to say I had some amazing fault or
disease, but, in truth, I was probably just thick. I wasn't naughty; I was
experimental. There was a gang of us who made things, and drew things,
and I guess we would push the envelope a bit. We would try to make

anything, including controlled explosions that weren't quite controlled and glow-plug engines and all that sort of naughty boy stuff: things that I think are not allowed anymore. Being a child nowadays is getting harder, because everyone's watching everyone doing everything. I'm always trying to get my own children to experience a bit of danger in their lives, because without that, they don't know where the parameters are. Growing up means experiencing risk.

When he talks about the future generations, especially in Britain, Linley probably deserves a much wider audience; indeed, he has quite a lot to say about the way we encourage young people, including helping the many potential entrepreneurs in the country who can't or won't follow a conventional path but still have strong talent. It's a familiar refrain from the people we have interviewed.

Society expects people to have a tag after their name. What do you do? I'm a banker. I'm a lawyer. That's great! But I think the next generation should be just as eager to say, 'I'm an artist' or 'I'm a craftsman' – and for people to also say, 'Well done!' Actually James Dyson is quite outspoken on this. There are the four strands to life: the academic strand, the sports side, the music, and there's another side, which is design, engineering, art – expression through making. And that seems to be suffocated at the moment. All I'm asking is why that is.

Maybe it's political. Which obviously I'm not. But if the government gave a break to people like inventors, writers – like they do in Ireland – you'd have a burgeoning community of people who make a valuable contribution to society. If you look at the way that Dyson started, he was working with Jeremy Fry in his shed and Jeremy was the patron. We need more patrons, so why not encourage people to be patrons? You know – give an old shed over to some 17-year-old and see what comes out.

This whole subject area has a resonance for him. It probably chimes with his own determination to build his career doing what he loved best, rather than wait for any kind of Royal halo-effect to see him along. He may not have been academic, but there was an early inclination towards self-employment, trading, and making his own money:

My first shop was selling sweets out of my tuck box under the bed. That was an industry based on self-survival. We were all under a period of starvation most times, so by having food, it was an absolute given that you'd sell it, and so we did very fast stock turns. I think my greatest achievement was to sell a teacher an illegal Mars Bar. Even the teachers were starving. The Mars Bars were 8p in the local shop, proper old size, but most boys sold them for 9p to make the margin. I sold them for 9p too, but what no one knew was that I had an agreement with the catering manager and was buying them at the cash-and-carry price of 4p.

The retail instinct was one thing, then, but it was also apparent from an early age that Linley would end up earning his living from working in wood. At first, his dream was less the high-end imagery of Chelsea fine-furniture boutiques and Savile-Row-suited staff, and more that of a big old barn in the country, with bearded men sitting around in woolly jumpers and corduroy trousers. But the ambition was forming, nonetheless.

It all started with my form teacher at Bedales, David Butcher – an amazing man. All my form meetings were in the workshop, where the smell of wood and Clan tobacco used to waft around. It sounds weird, because you've got all these sharp things whirring around, yet that workshop environment was extremely peaceful. And by the time I was 14 and 15 and 16, I was seriously making things – and loving it.

It was a welcome distraction. Because, around the same time, his parents were divorcing, with the inevitable disruption for the children. Linley and his sister, Sarah, lived alternately with Princess Margaret at Kensington Palace and with their father at Launceston Place. 'Sometimes we were in a big house, and sometimes we were in a small house. Sometimes lots of people would be looking after you, and sometimes you looked after your-self,' he has said. While this was all going on, Linley began thinking about his next move, and his early experiences working with wood at Bedales triggered consideration of a new and excitingly relevant school that had just opened in Dorset. 'You didn't do gap years in those days. I didn't want time off, but just wanted to get on and learn about making things,' he says. And to this end, he spotted the perfect opportunity at the John Makepeace School for Craftsmen in Wood at Parnham House, which, at the time, had launched a two-year residential course. The place has long since closed down, but not before sending out many students to become top designers and craftsmen.

A friend of mine called Stuart Padwick went and came back and told us how fantastic it was. So all the design year went to look around and it was very exciting. John Makepeace had bought the place and set it up as a new concept, but I don't think he has ever been appreciated for his contribution to people actually making things again. We were very lucky. We had a lot of really good makers in our group and several of us are still making today.

I had great teachers: a man called Robert Ingham; and a second-year teacher, Greg Hasland, who was a born-and-bred artist so less formal in his approach. We always teased him for being a bit of a hippy. We'd say, 'Teach us something!' and he'd say, 'Just do what you wanna do, man.' But the philosophy that we learnt in that year was all about perfectionism. I remember cutting down chisels to get to the right size for the dovetails, which were half a millimetre in size. It was getting your mind down to those precise limits.

We made things straight out of fresh-cut sycamore and ash oak. We went and cut trees and made amazing carvings out of wood. We were very modern, very sculptural, very colourful; utilising materials in a different way. Which I then discovered had already been done in the seventeenth century, called marquetry. And I knew that it was exactly what I wanted to do.

When I left Parnham House, I went straight to a co-operative which

I shared with three other craftsmen, and then two others came with me to the second one which was in Betchworth in Surrey – a lovely nineteenth-century wooden workshop, so cold in winter that it split the chisels if you left them by the window, and so hot in summer. But it was an amazing place to make things. And we then moved to Gloucestershire. All that team are now up in Whitby – favourite place of Jeremy Clarkson for some reason, I read at the weekend.

Before long, Linley was doing rather well for himself, and there was burgeoning demand for his work. At the same time, he had got back with an old Bedales friend, Matthew Rice, by then a practising artist and designer.

He was the best artist that I knew. I don't want to be rude, but some designers think only in the narrowest terms about the product. Matthew doesn't. He's an artist. And he worked really quickly, which is what I like. I was spending a lot of time on my motorbike selling and promoting and Matthew would then do the drawings and that's how it worked. He was unlike any of the other designers I'd worked with before that, who took ages, faffed about and were all 'maybe this, maybe that'. With Matthew, it was like, bang, done, that's it!

The idea for a shop came when we were making furniture for Miriam Stoppard. I sort of knew that we needed a physical retail presence, and then, one time, she very sweetly invited us down to her home for tea, and we were sitting listening to her, and she said, 'Come on lads, you've got to have a shop. Get forward!' And I just went, 'Yeah!' So basically, having left Parnham as David Linley, furniture designer and maker, I then became David Linley, retailer. That was October 1985. Roy Strong [art historian, director at the V&A, and cultural commentator], who opened the launch event at Christie's, very generously called our work the 'antiques of the future'. It was a really amazing time because we had a great group of people come to us. It was extraordinary the support that we had.

And hilarious the cock-ups. Once, we designed a lovely drawer on a stand of six beautiful turned balustrades, taking eighteenth-century balustrades as the idea. Anyway we sent it off to the workshop and it came back with two legs at the front and one at the back, instead of three at the front and three at the back. But you could easily have misinterpreted it. But it was through those kinds of errors that actually we became more decorative designers than furniture designers.

With Linley and Rice now having set up shop in the King's Road (actually, it was the less fashionable end – the *New* King's Road – more Fulham than Chelsea), the company's reputation went from strength to strength, and commissions flooded in from the great and the good. If Elton John wanted a gigantic 12-foot Palladian-style bed or a monumental chest of drawers for 250 of his spectacles (to be made out of sycamore), or if the G8 summit in Birmingham needed a huge new boardroom table for the top world leaders, this is where they would look. 'People would come in with extremely odd requests... but we could generally make anything that we put our minds to.'

We could have called it 'Linley and Rice' but he didn't want that. We called it 'David Linley Furniture' – a blue shop, with two windows at the front and one at the side. We put 'David' and 'Linley' on the front, and on the side, we only had room for one name, so we put 'Linley'. Over time, we tried different things, but it would always be distilled back down to what we started with which was essentially 'Linley', which is what we have now.

I'll never forget the feeling, in 1985, when I came round the corner on my motorbike on the King's Road in the morning and I looked up and they were just putting my name up on the shop, and I thought, 'Bloody hell! This is now public.' I nearly fell off my bike. At that point, I knew that there could be no getting away from the responsibility that this was my work.

He says the same emotion hit his wife, Serena (Stanhope, heiress to the Earl of Harrington – the latter having commissioned him to make another gigantic table back in 1992), when she opened her own eponymously titled shop ('Serena Linley – Provence') in Knightsbridge. He explains that he often tries out his own ideas on her. 'You need someone to tell you that you're not brilliant all the time,' he has said. Their Chelsea home is a temporary staging post for some of the items from the Linley shops, which are housed there for a while to see how they perform aesthetically and practically, and then, having served their time, they are returned. 'I sometimes come home to find that my chairs have gone, or a desk.' It's clear that Linley's life is not always a thing of permanent fixtures and fittings. He used to ride to work on an eccentric sit-up-and-beg bicycle with a basket over the front wheel, but the gods of sport and style even changed that. 'Somebody stole it. I'm now on a 1973 oval-tubed racing bike, but it gives a different kind of pleasure.'

Linley has always kept one dwelling in town, although he is known for easily becoming bored with his properties. He and Serena have two children – Charles and Margarita – and two dogs, Smudge and Shaggie (a Dandie Dinmont terrier that, he says, makes him laugh, but represents a breed that is sadly about to disappear). Next on his list of favourite things – which you might imagine comprises some very classy items – are the trees that he loves to plant in his garden and the very first desk he ever made, at which he still sits at home.

Still living and trading in the borough, Linley is ever the Chelsea man, in several senses of the word. For a start, he follows his local football club of that name (the football passion being shared with Jussi Pylkkänen, president at Christie's, and a Manchester City fan) and has been a follower since the 1970 FA Cup Final, when he went with his mother to see them draw with Don Revie's Leeds United, both teams kicking the living daylights out of each other as well as the dodgy pitch. In those days, Wembley finals brought the country to a standstill, so the interest in the first replay for 58 years, held at Old Trafford, was unsurprising. The boy Linley travelled up for that match too, this time with his father, and despite an unexpected 2-1 win for his team, one of the pair of them spent most of his time staring up not down. In an interview with the *Financial Times*, he recalls his father 'looking at the lights, and the rain coming down in front of them, working out how we would have photographed it. I don't think he looked at the match once.'

His father once inhabited the very epicentre of glamorous media-focused swinging London, and Linley now has built up his own quite extraordinary address book of the famous and fabulous, many of whom want a custom-made piece of Linley craftsmanship. Among the many, his regular 'named' clients include Mick Jagger, Kelly Hoppen, Jo Malone, Ralph Lauren, David Tang, and Oprah Winfrey, and he has recently teamed up with friend and chef Tom Aikens to create a range of kitchen accessories. That is only a small part of the most eclectic of CVs. He has fitted out the Metropolitan Museum of Art in New York, done numerous commissions for corporates like PolyGram or Credit Suisse, entire suites at Claridge's hotel and the lobby at the Savoy, along with kitting out private jets and country-house-sized yachts. He refurbished the Goring Hotel (used by members of the Middleton family before the Duke and Duchess of Cambridge's wedding), and has even done bespoke upgrades for Bentley.

Well, we did ten with them. I know Richard Charlesworth who's their head man around London. He looks after all the ultra-high-net-worth individuals [VIPs, sheiks, rock stars], and I was talking to him about the market that they were going for and the exclusivity that they had. I just suggested differentiating the cars more with limited editions or stuff like that to give people an identity to focus on. Then I went up to the factory with my designers. They went, 'Why are we coming to a car factory, Dave? We make furniture?' [Linley's Tony Blair accent has come back.] And I went, 'Well, this has got nothing to do with furniture. This is just fun.' And now I've taken them to Aston Martin and Rolls Royce and Morgan and McLaren, and to me, it's all about the adventure of making. I've got this new designer called Alex Hull, who's great, and he was delving into the McLaren carbon-fibre parts bin and getting excited about how we could make this or that. It's just how ideas happen. It's what we do so well in this country, and too few people appreciate really quite how amazing we are at doing it.

Coming with the territory, however, is a propensity to court controversy from time to time, and Linley has not been neglected by the tabloids, with the sale of his mother's effects, for example, provoking some criticism. Then there was the incident at the Château d'Autet, his nineteenth-century hunting lodge and guest annex, set in 650-acre grounds in the Luberon area of France – found for him by Peter Mayle, of *A Year in Provence* fame. Here it was where Kate Middleton, the Duchess of Cambridge, was scandalously photographed sunbathing without her top on. These days, of course, you can be behind a lead-lined wall below the horizon and a paparazzo with a modern telephoto lens will still pick out a stray nose-hair. But the whole incident highlighted how there is always the possibility of making headlines of one kind or another, even in absentia.

None of which seems to unduly worry Linley. Indeed, his biggest concern is the familiar lack of time that comes from having so many passionately burning irons in fires. It is clear that, as well as the Linley business, Christie's is both engaging and challenging him.

I don't have any personal time. I mean I love working here [at Christie's] and I love working with Jussi and I love the intensity of what we do here. But it leaves me very little time at home.

In the old days, you had a market where people came and bought and sold: it was a time when people wanted things, people kept things, people died, and people sold the things. Whereas now, because it's so much more immediate, and you've got internet bidding, and you've got all these sorts of things that encourage people all the time to trade, there's so much more on offer all the time. Being a chairman here is rather like being a theatre impresario. If you have a dark night, you've got to think of a solution.

The things that happen here on a daily basis are enormous. I'm not the outgoing gregarious type of person. One's always full of self-doubt – especially when an item doesn't sell. But my key to success is being able to delegate, and let people get on with what they're good at. I would never go into any other departments here and tell them what to do. I just ask how I can help, or free up people to work better in the way that they want. But what I don't like is indecisiveness.

What I do have is currency around the world. If the UK chairman says, 'I'm coming to see you,' it has a greater resonance than me just staying in the UK saying that I've been down to Pontypridd to view a lovely desk. So I do go to the new markets. We've just come back from Azerbaijan, where we took a relatively large display. A few years ago Jussi and I went to Abu Dhabi. We took an enormous display. I go to all sorts of places, whether it's Turkey or newer smaller markets, like Kazakhstan or Armenia. Supporting their local artist base through education is, I think, just as important a thing as trading. Whether it's studio visits or having a closer relationship with the museums, helping in terms of their fund-raising or attracting newer audiences. That's where I can add value, just sort of bringing something new.

One area where Linley does add value is in publicity. As we have seen, he is a figure who can court attention – most of it, the positive kind – and in whom there is always an interest. Back in 2002, Linley became yet another of our subjects who featured on *Desert Island Discs*, although even here, he did it in a novel way.

My mother and father did the show with Roy Plomley and so I'm the only person in the world to have been on it whose both parents have been on it as well. It's my significant differentiator, or whatever you call it. However, at that point, when I went on, my mum was very ill. She died that week. It was not a good time for me, so if you listen to me on air, I'm very, very low and all the songs are very plaintive.

These days, Linley does not sound low. In fact, he's high on new ideas. The new Linley catalogue is full of sumptuous furnishings and superb craftsmanship, but there is a strong sense of innovation in there as well. Like his latest scheme, which seems to be about making the lightest chair in the world, not in wood, but using strands of carbon fibre, and binding them together with gold, 'to make a rather beautiful combination of old and new'.

Or polished silver nickel which would bind the thing together, be really splendid, and it would almost defy gravity in the sense of how thin the piece would be to the whole weight. And you might say, well, what's the point of having a light chair? Well, there is no point – except it's fun.

It's time to leave, because his next guests have arrived. As a final question, we ask what will happen with this hair-diameter carbon-fibre-and-gold chair when you swing back on it. The answer seems fair enough:

Nanny always used to say to us, 'Don't swing back on your chair!'

And with this unimpeachable edict from formidable authority, Linley shakes our hands, wishes us well, and shimmers from the room.

———

'We have a task before us which must be speedily performed. We know that it will be ruinous to make delay... We will labour *now*. Alas, it is *too late!*'

EDGAR ALLAN POE ('THE IMP OF THE PERVERSE')

———

JULIAN RICHER

(Richer Sounds)

INTERVIEWED 23 NOVEMBER 2012

We are in a large hangar. It is one of several outbuildings in the grounds of a beautiful mansion, somewhere in the North Yorkshire countryside. In this hangar are drum kits: that is, rather *a lot* of drum kits. At a quick guess, maybe thirty or so: Yamaha, Pearl, Premier, Ludwig, Mapex – most of the famous makes in black, red, blue, yellow, white, cream – with barely enough floor-space to walk between the glittering silver-framed instruments. And then, just for good measure, there's a scattering of other musical paraphernalia: amps, keyboards, microphones, a pair of wooden conga drums; a leaning tower of original LPs awaiting a breath of air to knock it over.

At the far end, seated and playing one of the drum kits, is a man with longish curled hair and an open-necked white shirt. And he *can* play. It's an accomplished solo rendition, like he maybe knows what he's doing or he plays in a proper band. He interrupts his practice, laughs, and gets up from the stool. Julian Richer is not a tall man; but he is most certainly larger-than-life.

Our latest interviewee is the man behind the UK's largest hi-fi retailer – a company with 51 high-street stores, over four hundred staff, and a 2011–12 turnover of some £138 million (generating almost £5.7 million profits). On the go since 1978, Richer Sounds has, for a long time, been the not-very-well-kept-secret of the millions of audio (and latterly AV) enthusiasts who choose this brand for its strong point-of-sale expertise, which it still manages to provide within a competitive pricing structure.

That he can do this in such a fierce market is testimony to the founder's business acumen and gritty pioneering instincts.

With a headline-friendly name like 'Richer', he had to start an audio company – and get rich with it – just so that the pun would not go to waste: the 2011 *Sunday Times* Rich List put his personal fortune at £115 million, which is quite something for one whose origins were on the humble side.

His original shop at London Bridge now has the highest sales per square foot of any retail outlet in the world, according to *Guinness World Records*. Richer is also the owner of the Empire Direct website (having bought the rights when the original electronics company of that name went into administration) and 51% shareholder of another electronics development and distribution company called Audio Partnership. He has two honorary degrees in recognition of his business success, and until 2006, was a director of the Prince of Wales's charitable trading company, Duchy Originals, which led to his being awarded the Lieutenant of the Royal Victorian Order (an honour conferred for services to the Royal Family). Just to complete this inventory of achievement, he is, as well, a generous philanthropist, a highly motivating business speaker and writer, and – yes – he has his own thriving band, in which his wife is the lead singer.

These days, he avoids media attention, but has welcomed us to his North Yorkshire home for the interview, and allocated a couple of hours, although to do this guy justice, we'd ideally need a couple of weeks. He is a person who has, in the cause of entrepreneurship and other passions, been burning candles at both ends since before he hit adolescence.

Certainly, had we met him when he was a teenager, we would probably have said the same larger-than-life thing about him. In fact, his teachers and parents and schoolmates did. Richer's talents weren't to be found in PE and games. And unlike some of those unsporty peers who would lope around the empty changing rooms wondering how to fill the time, the boy Richer occupied himself running a fledging business enterprise from the back of a white Mercedes wedding limo.

I was lousy at games. So I hired the limo for the Tuesday and Thursday afternoon, partly for my ego, and partly because I could get my stock in the back. I had a big wad of notes and I was buying up hi-fi stuff like there was no tomorrow – doing it up and reselling it. I had this business at school selling to the kids, plus a guy in Liverpool selling for me, and my dad doing the same for me in London. I kept books and everything, and having started off with the initial £10, in a very short time I was up to £4,000.

Richer is not our only interviewee to have built up from scratch a top UK retailing enterprise; nor is he our only multimillionaire; or large-scale philanthropist. But he has to be, by a very long stretch, the one who started his entrepreneurship at the youngest age. At 14, when most schoolboys are in a testosterone-induced stupor, Richer was trading hi-fi hardware in sufficient quantities to be generating regular three-figure monthly profits, and within a decade, he would have built up one of the most successful home-grown electronics enterprises that the UK has known. Heaven only knows what he would have been like had eBay been around during his teens.

Richer thinks that retailing was in his blood. Or at least in the ether of the family home. As he says in his partly autobiographical treatise, *A Richer Life*, 'If you sawed me in half, it would say "retail" all the way through me like a stick of rock.'

I grew up in the poor part of Hampstead, and my father was a frustrated businessman, so I saw his frustration at not being successful in business. He was incredibly bright academically, and was top of his year at Trinity Dublin, then got a Fulbright Scholarship to Harvard. He came out of the Air Force at 29, after the war, and went into business, but he wasn't particularly successful. I think he felt he'd started too late.

But there was definitely a retail instinct in the house. My parents met, interestingly, on a management-training scheme at the Kilburn branch of Marks & Spencer. I was born in 1959, and in the sixties, Marks & Spencer was seen as a paternalistic dynasty – much more so than it is now – and the stories at home were all about that amazing family, and how they cared about the staff in the days when no one else did. My mum had always been in retail, and I grew up with that influence. She had a women's boutique, and my dad ran a textiles import business from a tiny little office in Regent Street. But then the business folded. Without much money, he would buy and sell stuff from home through the Exchange and Mart, *although actually he quite enjoyed doing that.*

Then, when he was 46, he took up Law and qualified when he was 50, while my mum supported us out of the shop. He failed his finals first time and tried to commit suicide. We woke him up and got him to hospital. Then he had ten years of being a solicitor, doing bread-and-butter conveyancing, before he died from a heart attack. But he'd been a real character.

For much of that time, we had massive bills and it was all terribly punishing. That alone made me really determined to make money.

We follow Richer into his kitchen where he makes the tea, and we take it into his beautiful drawing room. Sun pours through the windows, drenching the furniture and pastoral-themed oil paintings in warm yellow. It feels a long way from the buzz and beat of urban high street hi-fi shopping. That said, the music world has an unmissable representative in the room, parked in front of the bay windows – a gigantic black concert grand, big enough to make you wonder if it came here first and the house was moved into place around it. Oh, and there's a drum kit, of course.

Richer is friendly and accommodating (he was standing, waiting on his porch, when we drew up in the taxi), but he admits to being a restless creature ('I'd be no good in prison!'), and, after only a few minutes in his company, you see how he always wants to get on; to not waste precious seconds; to do what needs to be done. He is keen to get the narrative up and running, and sits down on one of the sofas, but looks like he has never been in such a sedentary position before. His favourite quote (a line from Pink Floyd's 'Time') warns against missing the starting gun, a metaphor that he uses quite a few times. Being still is not an option;

'never waste a moment' his personal mantra. If there can be such a thing as a *born* entrepreneur – or someone born being in a hurry – here you are.

At 15, Richer visited a careers advice specialist who suggested that he might become an architect; something that interested Richer until he realised that the training period for that profession was seven *years*. Richer would have found the suggestion barely tolerable even if the unit of measurement had been *months:* weeks and it might have been a deal. As it was, he already had five years' experience of entrepreneurial impatience. At the age of ten, no less, he had first plotted schemes to expand his Scalextric through some canny buying and selling among his school classmates – hampered by parents who were already starting to baulk over their son's speed at the retail hustle.

At first, my parents wouldn't let me buy and sell. They thought it wouldn't be a very nice thing to do, and were worried I'd be too rapacious with my school friends. They did allow me to swap stuff without using money, and on that basis, I still ended up with a Scalextric set so large it was too big to fit in the house. But then, later on, when I was 14, my father finally agreed that it would be OK for me to start buying and selling – that is, using real money – and that's when I bought an old B&O turntable for £10. Then I was really off. He'd fired the starting gun.

I wasn't electronically minded, and didn't know how to repair things properly, but I knew how to make things look nice. I put an ad in the Exchange and Mart *– the advert cost £1.50 – and sold it for £22. It doesn't sound much, but in those days, £10.50 profit was like a term's pocket money. And it went from there. All of a sudden, I was taking pressure off my parents for holidays, for pocket money, for uniforms, and I was independent.*

By the time I was 17, I had three people working for me on commission. I had confidence: not only through living by myself, but realising that rich kids are just the same as poor kids; we all wore underpants; we all went to the toilet. And all those kids wanted stereos in their studies, with me their first port of call. Nearly half the school was buying their hi-fi from me, and my study looked like a Laskys stockroom.

Richer had the entrepreneurial bug all right. The downside was that this left no time for any distraction from matters academic. Even before this – before he took the Common Entrance Exam, when he was at UCS as a day pupil – he had been 'doing the wheeling and dealing'.

But I was bottom of the class academically – the dunce – and not doing my homework. That was the main reason for my parents moving me to boarding school. They couldn't afford it, but my grandfather said he'd pay. Then the money ran out, so my parents had to go cap-in-hand, halfway through, and ask for a bursary. That whole experience added to the chip on my shoulder and made me even more determined than ever.

It was at this boarding school in Clifton in Bristol that Richer came into contact with Ernest Polack, his housemaster, who our interviewee names – along with Archie Norman (the businessman and politician, and of whom more later) and his father – as the defining influences on his life.

Ernest Polack was a wonderful man. He only just died recently. Here he was, this socialist housemaster teaching in a British public school. He'd tell us the stories about how he'd been over to South Africa to fight apartheid and had been beaten up by Boer farmers.

Polack would eventually return to Africa to help establish a centre for leprosy. Immediately prior to Clifton, he had been working in a borstal among seriously disadvantaged teenagers. Here, Richer makes the point that everything is relative (a principle that, he says, extends to all walks of life, including issues of personal wealth), and emphasises that Polack, to his credit, took the anxieties of the privileged Clifton boys as seriously as he had done the issues of his previous charges.

Around this time, the relationship between Richer's parents was breaking down, the catalyst for which was his mother's affair with an old flame. Polack knew this was happening and felt that by encouraging Richer's trading passion, the boy would find the break-up less traumatic. In the event, the separation was amicable, and Richer was 'old enough not to be affected in the slightest'. Affected or not, while it was happening, Polack wisely recognised the value of Richer's 'hobby' and sanctioned it, suspecting that it would ameliorate any domestic upheaval.

Richer points out that, at 15, he was driven less by a sense of business in general than by a dash for hard cash. He certainly didn't aspire to be anything as dull as a 'business*man*', which only offered associations of repetitive working days and cheap suits and ties. Instead, he wanted to be wealthy and enjoy the fruits of that wealth, and 'the combination of energy and a chip on the shoulder' gave him the ambition and drive to start doing something about it.

Polack, meanwhile, set some ground rules. He would personally approve each of Richer's deals, and would warn the parents of each of Richer's schoolboy 'customers', prior to visits, that their sons might not have much pocket money left. Richer, meanwhile, was in his element being larger-than-life:

I was independent and making money, and I even ended up having an affair with a French and Spanish languages student teacher, which was great fun. She used to stay at our house in the holidays. Now she'd go to jail! Ernest Polack knew about my affair with the teacher and once he took me aside and said, 'Look, we all know about your affair, but for your sake, just keep your visits to her down to three visits a week, or you'll wear yourself out before your A levels.'

Richer wonders if a lot of his drive came from an early sense of insecurity; possibly even going back to his mother's family being Jewish refugees, some migrating to Palestine before the Second World War, others perishing at the hands of the Nazis. The insecurity was compounded, to some extent, by being a less wealthy pupil among a privileged school population. So much so that when his parents visited him in their old Renault, he would insist on them avoiding the main car park with all its Rolls Royces and Bentleys, and parking round the back.

I was small, not good at sport, not an academic achiever, and with poor parents in a wealthy public school environment – which gave me a chip on my shoulder, which I fully admit. But I also wanted to be caring to people, and that stayed with me when I opened the shops. I've always thought it right to look after anyone you employ. Be firm but fair. We must have done something right because, years later, we became The Sunday Times's *Best British Employer.*

Richer left school at 18, with three (in his description, 'mediocre') A levels. He had a place on an accountancy foundation course, but that was clearly not what he had in mind or where his destiny lay. Indeed, he has often said that higher education is not for everyone, and if that's the case, why should that be an issue? He bemoans the demise of apprenticeships and more practical forms of education, and the burgeoning of spurious university courses that help no one. 'Don't waste three years... if you're wishing you were out there making your mark on the world,' he says in his book. And in his case, Richer was certainly not ready to waste any number of years.

One of the guys I was buying from was opening a place in Moorgate. They'd seen this weird kid in a school uniform, wheeling and dealing, and I'd got chatting with the guys there. So I was offered a job for a year as the manager within this big photographic shop with its own hi-fi department. I went to my parents and told them I wanted to do that, rather than the accountancy course. I thought they'd go mental, after my private education with all the costs. But they just said I could try it for a year. I suppose they'd seen I'd been making money and were quite impressed, and took the view that I could always do the accountancy later if the shop didn't work out.

Within five months I was group retail manager with a little company car and was running the five shops. I was on £5,000 a year plus the car, which for a kid of 18 was pretty good. I definitely didn't want to go to university. I'd lived away from home for all those years at boarding school and felt I'd done all that. I was like a coiled spring. I wanted to get on.

Richer has many talents and strengths; but, if there is a general element that stands out, it is his willingness to confront each personal weakness with the intention of correcting it. He lacked confidence – and so developed self-confidence; he had a hatred of public speaking – so he made himself give speeches; he resented financial struggle – so he went out and made himself wealthy. Showing Richer a challenge is like showing a red rag to a bull; or spraying the bull in the face with red aerosol. Say 'can't' and Richer will say 'can!'

At the back of one of the shops was the office for Vic Odden, who was a photographic retailer trading a few doors along. A lovely older man, a lot older than me. One day, I just said, 'I don't suppose you want to sell me your shop, do you?' and to my surprise he said, 'Well, let's talk about it.' So I took him to dinner to the East India Club in St James's Square – they used to have a very cheap deal, for public schoolboys – with his lawyer, to suss me out. We all got on very well, and agreed that if I put in the money I'd made from school, he'd let me take over his shop and he'd lend me £20,000 – a lot of money in those days.

And within nine months of opening, I'd paid him back the £20,000. We were partners for about ten years, and never had a cross word. Eventually, he sold me his shares back for about £200,000, so he did very well out of it, but I don't begrudge him a penny. I came to feel like one of his sons. He gave me my lucky break.

Richer describes two forms of luck: *passive*, serendipitous luck, over which we have little or no control; and *active* 'make your own' luck, that comes because you are receptive to chance and opportunity. He also believes that one's own luck is infectious: if you get lucky, it pays dividends to share it around a bit.

I've tried to generate goodwill on my way up, because you never know when your luck may change. Certainly, many things have gone my way. Like getting in the Guinness World Records *and a Royal Warrant, for instance. I've been blessed big time: with an able body, able mind, a*

good educational upbringing – no question, I've definitely had plenty of
passive luck. But I've also taken advantage of opportunities... I also feel
I've made my own luck – active luck.

He's not just making a personal statement here. Richer loves to drift into
social commentary about the issues on which he has thought deeply
– and spoken – many a time. He wonders aloud about what would be
the best environment to encourage more people not to wait for passive
luck to arrive at their door (and grumble when it doesn't), but to go running after the rabbits of opportunity, even if many disappear from view
down holes. Surely, he says, this is the way to pull the UK out of its economic doldrums.

When I started, no one wanted to provide the business with credit. A
shop had gone bust in the same place, and there was the matter of me
being 19 years old. They'd come in and say, 'I've got an appointment
with Mr Richer' and I'd say, 'Yeah, that's me'. Then they'd say, 'No, with
your dad. Go and get your dad for us!' I was very, very green. But I
would not take 'no' for an answer.

People so easily look for an excuse not to get off their backsides. A lot
of people didn't like Thatcher, but at least she pushed the entrepreneurial
spirit. Common sense tells us we should encourage people to work
unless there's a good reason why they shouldn't. When you reward
people not to work, it's hugely damaging. The welfare state has gone
bonkers. Don't get me wrong: the elderly and the weak and the disabled
and the sick must be looked after royally by us. But able-bodied people
should work – and if they're really trying to get a job, then they should
have no objection to helping by doing voluntary work...

I didn't get lucky overnight. I had to do hundreds and hundreds and
hundreds of deals, starting off with £10 to make £4,000. Let me tell you,
it was traipsing round town, lugging the boxes around – a lot of bloody
hard work to me.

You've got to eat your greens before you have your pudding. There's
all this get-rich-quick X Factor nonsense on telly, all about being

famous and making millions overnight. Yet we don't have enough apprenticeships in this country. We need plumbers and builders and joiners and scientists and researchers. And programmes like The Apprentice *are not helpful either, because kids just think it's trendy to be rude to people.*

A lot of it is about expectations. Let me give you this example. All our [company staff] holiday homes used to be free on principle. I didn't want to charge people £10 a night because I didn't want them to feel they're paying for it when it was their right. But then I realised that if they pay something towards it, just something modest, then they value it more. As they do with the John Lewis homes.

Richer takes a very personal view of his business. He talks about '*my* shops' and describes how he has 'stuck with them through thick and thin'. Interestingly, when he first started, he didn't automatically think of using his own name. But, then, when it was discussed, it suddenly seemed the only natural thing to do.

Over dinner with Vic [Odden] and Neville Coleman, the lawyer, Vic just said, 'Why don't we call it Richer Sound and Vision?' and I immediately thought it was a fantastic idea. We were going to do tellies and then didn't, so we dropped the 'Vision' and went with 'Richer Sounds'.

Since then, I've thought that if you've got the balls to put your name on the shopfront, it raises your game. You can't hide behind some customer service department. You have to stand up and be counted. So even though I don't want too much media publicity, you can still go into the shops and see a picture of me above the counter. It's not ego; it's accountability. And every receipt says, 'If you're not happy, I want to know about it: freepost Julian Richer.' Anyone not happy gets their complaint investigated and dealt with, along with an individual signed letter from me.

We've been talking for a very short hour, and we're all getting into a panic; it feels like there's too much to discuss, and we're barely out of his teens.

Plus, we keep annoying him by asking questions out of sync. If Richer's life has been a full one, his mind is crammed to match, teeming with views and ruminations on matters low and high. He's written three books (one of them, *Richer on Leadership*, putting down in digestible form his approach to management), sponsored others, and probably has several more of his own inside him, if he can find time to get round to them.

A very significant part of his career has been spent providing management advice on subjects such as employee motivation, service delivery, and retail culture. For some time, Richer was one of the most well-known speakers on the circuit.

But then, when I got into my forties, I stopped. I could talk for an hour and a half without notes, but it stressed me out, and exhausted me. I was getting £10,000 an hour for speaking, but now I'd rather not do it. Well, I'll still do it occasionally for charity, but not the public speaking for money.

I've done my bit with think tanks and committees, but I've come to the conclusion that a lot of them are a waste of time. You never get listened to. But politics is an unattractive environment for people like myself – because of the curse of fame. You're terrified to put your head above the parapet. The moment you try and do anything serious, they'll ruin your life.

They should pay MPs a lot more than £60,000 a year. People who are out of work complain about MPs getting £60,000 a year, but you need the best managers running the country. So it means we've got to pay them, so they don't have to take consultancies and directorships and aren't fiddling their expenses. Good people are often put off and the wrong people take their places. I'd much rather pay more and have transparency and get the best people in there.

He may have stopped much of the public speaking, but his reputation for inspiration and thought-provocation has stuck, not least as a function of his writings, which draw on his many unique experiences helping commercial and political leadership – frustrating or not.

One of those defining experiences was assisting Archie Norman – a man who could not be more different from Richer. Educated at Charterhouse and Cambridge, Norman's career path took him straight into management consultancy with McKinsey, prior to directorships with Railtrack, Kingfisher, and then famously, as CEO and chairman at Asda. Plus, in 1997, he became a Conservative MP.

Before that, in 1992, Asda was, in Richer's words, 'a basket case', and Norman, as CEO, came calling.

He is a brilliant man. We were introduced by a mutual friend and he came for dinner here. He'd just gone in to try and turn Asda around and he asked me if I'd work with him on it. I said, 'What are you talking about? I'm a small retailer. I'm 5 foot 7. [We wondered if Norman thought that was as bad a joke as we did.] How can I possibly advise you with all your supermarkets?' But he said, 'Just go in, lift up the carpet, prod wherever you like, and give me a warts 'n' all report, once a month.' So I did it. And I'd go and see him each month and we'd quite often amicably debate and shout at each other across his open-plan office.

On one occasion, I'd had an argument with a manager at the Pudsey store. They had something labelled for 'managers' and something for 'staff'. Like apartheid. So I said, 'What the heck are you talking about? You're all staff together.' And I went back and told Archie that I thought it wasn't on. And he said, 'What shall we call them?' I said, 'Well you can call them "associates" or John Lewis call them "partners" or we call them just "colleagues".' And he said, 'Right, we'll do it.' And the colleagues are still, 20 years later, being called 'colleagues'.

To be fair to Archie, he took notice of 95% of what I suggested. There were many other people I advised who just ignored what I said.

By this time, only just in his thirties, Richer was mixing in very high circles indeed. He had come a long way in a breathtakingly short time. Less than a decade earlier, he had been trying to get his first Richer Sounds shop off the ground.

My big break was advertising end-of-lines in the Exchange and Mart. *For example, Marantz had some cassette decks and they'd pay for us to run the ad. I took a quarter-page ad and we had people coming to us from all over the country. I figured that, for each person that drove to us from Manchester, there'd be 50 people that weren't bothering because they didn't want the drive – in the days before the internet. So I opened a shop in Stockport – which went crazy. It was the worst property in the street. The freehold was £10,000, and even in those days that wasn't a lot. The only other things in the street were a bookmakers and a public toilet.*

But I'd realised the sense in owning your own property. Where I've been able to afford it, I've gone for it. I own 43 out of 51 freeholds in my chain. That's very unusual. I bet there's not a retailer in the country like us with that. Woolworths used to and M&S, but normally, as soon as chief execs come in, they see how much cash they can give back to shareholders in the short term to get brownie points and just end up in hock to landlords. That's why we're not a public company. I can do what's best and what makes financial sense.

So we're very secure. My rent and rates are less than 2% of turnover, and that means that, even competing with the likes of Amazon, we're still sustainable. Anyone that can't is history. Comet, who have just gone bust, would have had rent and rates that would have been between 10% and 15%. So I have a massive advantage. I'm running Richer Sounds on a gross margin of 13%, which is phenomenally low for a chain of stores, and gives me great sustainability against the internet.

Anyway, to go back. We had a policy of opening shops based on numbers of chimneys. That was the reason I went to Stockport. I looked on the map and I saw that Manchester, where we were aiming for, didn't have a motorway going into it; but Stockport did. So both Liverpool and Leeds would feed into it. I hired a big limo, and took the whole board [of Richer Sounds] round the place – about six or eight of us crammed into this Daimler. The agents had been trying to get us to take certain properties and then I noticed a place they hadn't shown us, which had the freehold for sale. And they said, 'Oh, it's a miserable street – you don't want to go there.' And I just replied, 'Oh, but I do!' and that's what we went for. The freeholds.

Richer knows only too well that, in entrepreneurial terms, he is a prodigy. He is the business equivalent of a double-jointed gymnast or a low-pulse long-distance runner; he does things that shouldn't be possible. Equally, he is refreshingly frank about his weaknesses and anxieties. Perhaps it's the consequence of a settled relationship and a strong spiritual belief system.

I was insecure, but I had loads of energy. I think a lot of entrepreneurs have a lot of sexual energy. There's definitely some correlation there. I was a small kid and not good at sports and not a natural talent with the girls. But I always figured that if I had money, that would make me a lot more attractive... When I got my first jet, it was amazing how many girls suddenly found me attractive. They didn't worry about my waistline or whether I was tall or not. But I was happily married by this point and very settled.

Richer has a lot to say about how we accept and reinforce the stereotypes that people have of us. Rather than being yourself, it can be easier to be what others think you are; and it can be difficult to challenge those preconceptions. And we often think we ought to conform to stereotypical conventions of success. He admits that, for a while he fell foul of this process – albeit doing so with some panache.

At the age of 23, I bought my first Rolls. When I was seven, I'd had a girlfriend whose parents used to bring her to school in a Bentley, and from then on, I had a bee in my bonnet about big cars. As soon as I could, I bought a Silver Shadow 2. Then as soon as they brought out the Silver Spirit, I had to have one of those because it was bigger and even flashier. I gave the Silver Shadow to my dad who'd never been in a Rolls in his life.

I had a Ford Capri Ghia Sports, then a white MGB Roadster, then I went for an XJS, which Rosie [Richer's wife] crashed into a wall at

Regent's Park Zoo – she put her foot on the accelerator instead of the brake. She only destroyed five hundred clay flowerpots in the potting shed on the other side of the wall. Now I'm not into cars at all. Nowadays, we have two 4×4s, but only to cart all the drum stuff around.

In the introduction to one of his books, Richer talks about how he wished he could have read his own collected wisdom when he was 16. Don't we all. 'I thought I knew everything and didn't need advice, but looking back, I can, of course, see very clearly all the things I needed to learn.' Richer and his wife have chosen not to start a family, but he sometimes wonders about what advice he might have given any children of his.

As soon as I started the business, it all went mad. I didn't have a good bookkeeper in the business and my auditors were rubbish. I got turnover confused with profit, and the overheads went mental. And there was theft as well. I made £20,000 in the first nine months, and the same for the second nine months or so, then managed to lose £130,000 from one tiny little shop in London Bridge.

I went to people for help, but no one was interested. So I just had to trade out of it. And let me tell you, that experience was terrifying. Absolutely terrifying. Every week, robbing Peter to pay Paul, keeping creditors at bay, keeping everyone happy, doing what you say you're going to do, learning how to use suppliers' credit to fund the business. I moved auditors to this wonderful guy called Geoff Barnes [now president of Baker Tilly International], who helped me turn it round. At that point, I was about 21.

At one point, I went to my mate's father, who's no longer alive – a great friend, who was very wealthy. I showed him the figures, and he said, 'What are you talking to me for? You do not have a chance. You've completely screwed up. Throw in the towel, son.' But saying that was the challenge to me. And I rose to it.

I worked hard. I would tape all the cashflow sheets together with all my bills each week. What a discipline that was... I sat on the accounts for a whole year, and fobbed the banks off. Boy, did that teach me a lot.

For one thing, it taught him the value of large sheets of paper. It is peculiar that a man at the centre of the electronics industry eschews the apparatus of electronic management. He is evangelical about his paper diaries – idiosyncratic yellow notebooks, which he has custom printed in a certain style that suits his planning. Even more dramatic is his weekly paper grid of everything that he needs to do and wants to achieve. He brings the current page out to show us: a white sheet of A4 (they used to be A3, but he's slowing down) packed with spider-written annotations, and cryptic markings, like the doodles of a Bletchley Park codebreaker: a single-glance map of this week's tasks and ambitions and what he has in mind – on his mind. And, no less importantly, 'my list reminds me that I have achieved some goals, including small personal ones… One of the ways to happiness is… to count your blessings.' Literally.

One of those blessings – the greatest, he says – is his wife of some thirty-odd years, Rosie: Miss Rosie, if we are to use her stage name, because she is the lead singer in his band.

We met on a blind date when I was 21. Although I'd started my business, I was finding it really tough and she gave me stability at a really important time. No one can ever say she married me for my loot, because although I wasn't skint she provided a real ladder to help me get on. I had this flash flat overlooking Regent's Park with suede on the walls. I had to sell that to save money, and move to a cheaper flat in Belsize Park, but we were much happier there.

She's not a business person at all, but she gave me huge emotional support and she must always have credit for that. I absolutely adore her. When we first met, she said I was old beyond my years in business terms, but immature in other ways – the car thing, the jet, the helicopters. It was fun, but eventually you realise what's important in life.

An example being his passion for making music. His band started several years ago, the result of a chance incident. He saw a postcard in the window of the local music shop, put there by a character called Derek, asking for 'ageing rock 'n' rollers'. Obviously, most sane people would give said Derek a wide berth, but Richer saw it as another opportunity. It turned out that Derek was a very normal, and well-adjusted individual – coincidentally a successful fellow businessman – and the pair of them hit it off immediately. The band was formed, and Richer even blagged a recording session at Abbey Road studios, through a director at EMI who happened to have read *The Richer Way*. 'Be open to opportunities,' he says, 'and see where it takes you.'

Now, we're doing 104 gigs this year – three this week. We've got 60 bookings for next year already. It's my new passion. I did do a bit at school and my parents said, 'You drum and we'll kill you – because you'll end up being poor and deaf.' But I took it back up seven years ago, and get huge pleasure from it. Now I've persuaded Rosie to start singing. I'll have to give you an album.

There are numerous paradoxes with Richer. He dislikes ritualistic religion, yet he is an enthusiastic Christian; he hates publicity, but he writes books; he eschews celebrity, yet he loves his music performances. 'I'm a terrible coward,' he says, 'but when I've got my leader's hat on, I'm very brave.' In some people, these would seem like inconsistencies. But with Richer, it all feels like it's part of the excitement of living. The determination to think of something, then do it, before the dream becomes dust. Others ponder and don't; Richer wonders and does.

'If you want to be good at what you do, you can never relax... If it sounds stressful, it is... Keep driving forwards. You've never done enough.' Phew. Not a mantra for faint hearts, that's for sure. So, among all the other claims on his time, Richer is now doing the gigs and loving it. But he is aware of the dangers. Not of getting tired: he's not bothered about that. But of becoming too well known.

I regard celebrity status as a complete curse. Once you're well known, it's for life. You can't put the toothpaste back in the tube. I've been out with famous friends, and we'd go in a bar, and within minutes you're surrounded by people wanting photographs taken, wanting to

shake hands, wanting autographs non-stop. After two minutes of it,
I'm thinking, 'Thank God, it's not me!' And that's when they like you.
Imagine if it goes wrong, like you're a footballer or a businessman
who's had a bad story about you and you start getting attacked and all
the grief.

So I've avoided television. And I'd love the band to be bigger, but at
the moment we're keeping it separate and low-key.

'I want to be rich and unknown' is Richer's aspiration. He says he's
managed the latter more than the former, but we don't believe him.
We ask him what he feels is the most important thing that his wealth
has brought.

If you'd asked me that question when I was 20, I would have said that
it made me more attractive to women – very shallow! Now I couldn't
give a monkey's, because I'm in a happy marriage and I'm so much the
wiser. I regard the wealth as allowing me freedom.

The wealth gives me a great life, but it's all about how you use it.
Like, I've been cycling, going round the country to see my stores. I get
off the trains and I have a little fold-up bike, so I don't have to get
taxis, and I cycle to the shops in a grubby yellow jacket and helmet.
And sometimes, they can't make it out. Here's this guy on the rich list
who's supposed to be worth £100 million, but he turns up on his bike
in the rain. When I go round the country, my fold-up bike goes under
the seat and then I'm free at either end. How good is that? And it's
a wonderful thing, the Brompton [bicycle], and it's British as well: a
fantastic little thing.

I don't need to work anymore. But I really love working. And to enjoy
what you do is a blessing… Some people hate work; they're allergic to
work, or frightened of work. But there are plenty of other people who
actually do want to work.

There are times when Rosie might like me to sell the business, but
I want to keep working. And I have other things as well. I want to be
doing my band and I want to be with my missus and I want to travel,

and I've got the Bible study group. Money gives me the freedom to do what I want to do.

Richer has a respect for the money he has earned, with the attendant dislike of waste and debt, and what the latter can do to a person.

I've never taken a bank for money. I've never taken a supplier for money. I've been absolutely honourable. My reputation's everything and I've tried not to waste money. The Rolls wasn't a new one and I made damn sure I got a good deal on it. I sold my jet back to Gold Air who managed it for me. My helicopter I sold back at a profit.

He spontaneously talks about how Rosie changed his outlook on life. They married with a small ceremony and took a honeymoon in Scotland, and he claims that she was responsible for putting his post-adolescent preoccupation with wealth into better perspective, without losing his entrepreneurial edge.

In *The Richer Way*, he makes the link between business success and just 'getting on with people': something he says is a remarkably uncommon piece of common sense, judging by the number of businesses that do not treat people with sufficient respect. This notion of putting relationships at the heart of a business strategy – be it in terms of employees or customers – may be more familiar practice nowadays, but when Richer was starting off, it was innovative.

I'm very hands-on. I've got nine directors who have been with me 'man and boy', including two female directors. We've got a wonderful workforce, with an amazingly low staff turnover for retail. We've just got, I think, a great strategy. The trick is getting it right with people – especially getting the service right. Anyone can cut prices; but service is all about motivating your staff to give that great service. I had my post for two weeks yesterday and there were two complaints in it: 24,000 customers, and two complaints.

It took me time to grasp this. In the early years, we just expanded too fast and we ended up closing a load of shops. So then we consolidated and then went forwards again. The next difficult patch for the business was the internet. Retail people are only just now saying that it's difficult competing with the internet: you don't say. Well, ten years ago, the writing was on the wall. So I came up with a strategy to make sure we were survivable and sustainable and that's worked fantastically well. We had our best year ever last year and we're possibly the only electrical multiple making money now... There's the odd independent that has got a local monopoly that will survive. But Dixons lost £40 million last year, so there are no chains making money as far as I'm aware of. There are some good reasons for it, not least our property cost.

Richer talks about how, so often, in business and in life generally, we automatically follow routines and protocols; but, sometimes, it pays to think twice about what we do, and if it's flawed, then change it for the better.

Tipping's a good example of this. America's gone too far, because if you don't tip the right amount, they'll get very annoyed. But the British are the other way: they don't get it. For example, I tip when I go into a hotel. Why wait until you're leaving? You want the staff to be nice to you from the start, not when you've gone.

And from a mathematical point of view, the difference in cash between a big tip and small tip is a tiny percentage of what you're spending in the restaurant or hotel. So if you give a bit more and it gets people to be nice, what's the issue? Some people say you're just buying affection. But actually, it's recognition, and when people get recognition, be it in a tip or in some other way, they change for the better, and everyone wins.

In his book, Richer makes the show-stopping comment that 'once you've made your money, you're going to have to give it all away'. Of course, it's another way of saying that you can't take it with you when you die, and that if you don't get rid of it while you're living, HMRC will get it eventually. But developing this theme, he says that material success can be measured by the amount of money you can give away after you've taken out what you feel you want.

Richer's philanthropic pursuits have included the Big Issue Foundation (of which he was the first patron), the RNIB, the RSPCA, Amnesty International, and Whizz-Kidz. He has his own foundation, and is an official 'Ambassador for Youth'. As might be expected, he is a governor of his old college in Bristol. And remarkably, 15% of all the profits made by Richer Sounds are donated to charity: 'the biggest percentage of profits of any company in the country, as far as I'm aware.'

And at that point, he says, you have to ask, 'Where can your money make the most impact?' He approaches that question – that is, his own philanthropy – in the same way he approaches his conventional business dealings: tackling it as a challenge and trying to be as innovative as possible.

Hence, ACTS 435, which he founded and funded, and with which Dr John Sentamu, the Archbishop of York, has helped. This is a web-based scheme that allows people to direct small amounts of money to people who really need it, using the church's existing branch network to avoid overheads.

At first, no one would back it in the church because they were too busy raising money for the bloomin' roofs. So I got the Archbishop of York and his wife Margaret round for tea. And he said, 'Look, I'm so sick of all the bickering about gay people and women bishops. Let's get on with it.' Anyway, we've helped a thousand people so far and it's grown like topsy. We were on Songs of Praise *this year. Any one in the world can just pay via PayPal, and the money goes direct to the church and the applicant, 100%, with no overhead. I think it could be international one day.*

There is no point saying that Richer becomes animated when he talks about helping the poor, and doing this in concert with his own strong Christian beliefs. He's animated about everything he does; so one level of excitement just blends into another. It is clear, however, that religion is central to his view of life and where he wants it to go.

Richer calls his wife Rosie a 'quiet' Christian, in that she is not pushy with it. When they first met, he started accompanying her to church on Sundays, which, he says, he found 'therapeutic and interesting, being surrounded by nice people'. He felt that this was a refreshing change to some alternative systems where the emphasis is, in his view, too much on prohibitions and restrictions and arcane, irrelevant mores.

Through church, I met Roger Simpson, the vicar, a wonderful man, who'd had a tip-off that I had a few bob and that I might help with roof-repairs and that. He came round for coffee and cake and he liked the cake and we got talking.

Thus began Richer's strong commitment to Christianity. He is both a conviction Christian and a liberal: firm of his own beliefs, but accommodating of others'.

Alongside Richer's hangar is a small conferencing facility, where he runs a regular Bible group for his friends and acquaintances in the community. He knows Nicky Gumbel, the man largely responsible for the Alpha course, which Roger Simpson had asked Richer to host. After the first of these, Richer was so taken by the experience and the people that he has continued hosting subsequent courses and Bible classes. However one might define it – and Richer hates anything that tries to put a label on his religious beliefs – he sees his own commitment to Christianity, quite simply, as a commitment to attempt to make society better. At which point in the conversation, he comes right back to his business principles. 'Too often, in business and in life, people think it's clever to be mean and difficult… In my view, it is so much more clever to be nice.' And he feels that Christianity espouses this.

He caveats this by saying that when it comes to his business competitors, it's all-out war – another juxtaposition, but a perfectly understandable one when he explains what he means. He is comfortable holding numerous positions and views, whatever the subject, be it the most trivial issue or the grandest philosophical notion. Being able to think in this way – and act accordingly – is what makes Richer the success he is.

I'm standing with my cricket bat every day, waiting for the next hundred balls to come at me and for me to whack them away. It goes with the job. All day long the buck stops with the entrepreneur and you have to deal with it. Sometimes, you have to change direction and you reinvent yourself. You move with the times. You start there and you end up here, but an entrepreneur will adapt like a chameleon, because that goes with the job.

Two hours were never going to be enough. But it's time to go. Richer is slightly disappointed that we won't be staying for his gig that evening or his Bible group that afternoon or to meet his wife. As if it's his fault, he compensates us with a few CDs and as many sandwiches as we can carry. He greets the taxi driver by name and shakes his hand, wishing him well. He cares. Then he hurries away.

We drive away back up the long drive; back to a smaller world; one that's less 'Richer'. Behind us, someone is playing the drums.

———

'One must always be aware, to notice – even though
the cost of noticing is to become responsible.'

THYLIAS MOSS

———

LORD SAINSBURY OF PRESTON CANDOVER, KG

(Sainsbury's)

INTERVIEWED 29 MARCH 2012

The year 1927 was topped and tailed by crises. One year earlier had been the TUC general strike; one year later and the world would be entering the Great Depression. So it was to be expected that awareness and responsibility were talking points for the intelligentsia, both on the left (Fritz Lang screened *Metropolis*) and on the right (Virginia Woolf published *To the Lighthouse*). The UK witnessed a total eclipse of the sun, which some on Hyde Park Corner saw as a troublesome omen; but on a brighter note, Charles Lindbergh made the first non-stop flight across the Atlantic. This was also the year in which Lord Sainsbury was born, beginning a life in which awareness and responsibility lie at the heart of an extraordinary story.

Yet as we begin, Lord Sainsbury is not altogether sure why we want to interview him, and our opening question about his earliest memories does not go down too well:

Why would you want to know that? Surely you want to talk about my career and not about my life outside of my career?

We are in his understated Linbury Trust office in St James's. The decor bears little testimony to the fact that we are interviewing a member of one of the most famous and enduring British retail and political dynasties, whose surname enters the operational vocabulary of most British infants not long after they have learned to speak; who, with his father and brothers, brought the supermarket to Britain as the Romans had brought the roads. Here is a man whose donations to the British Museum and National Gallery make lottery jackpots look like small change. But a man who is not quite sure why he might be of interest to anyone.

Thus, with a slight judder of the clutch, begins our interview with John Davan Sainsbury, Baron Sainsbury of Preston Candover, KG, Life President of J Sainsbury plc, and a Conservative peer since 1989; for 23 years, the chairman of a company that, when it entered the London Stock Exchange in 1973, recorded the largest floatation ever ('The Sale of the Century' as some newspapers called it), becoming for a time the UK's highest billing supermarket chain, ahead of both Tesco and Marks & Spencer in terms of revenue.

As for answering our very first question, we needn't have worried. Having ruminated for at least half a second, he is quick to access some vivid recollections.

My earlier memories are of living in London when war started, when I was about 12. I can remember my mother saying on the day war had broken out, 'Thank goodness you're as young as you are, otherwise you'd have to fight.' In the event, I was eventually called up in 1945, but it was a few weeks after the war ended. So I was lucky in that way. As a boy, I was protected from knowing what the real dangers were. Not so if you were an adult, and knowing what was going on in the world in 1940, you had every reason to be very depressed. But I don't remember ever being hungry or frightened. I just remember sitting under the stairs in the basement of our London house during one air raid – but they never came too near.

When we meet him, Sainsbury is dressed as you would expect a retired company chairman to dress, with neat tie and a well-cut suit. The jacket stays on through the interview. He is thoughtful, restrained, and punctilious; convivial rather than relaxed; nearer to the proper end of the spectrum, rather than the familiar. When we do stray onto the occasional cheeky question, there is just a hint of a disapproving Prince Philip eyebrow. At moments when we do flatter him, he plays a straight bat in a way not uncommon for his generation.

I've never really thought too deeply about these things. Certainly, I didn't know what I wanted to do after Oxford, but I knew I needed to earn my living somehow, so it would have been foolish not to go into the family business. As a boy, I'd known Sainsbury was a very well-known name, and linked to some shops, and I'd been teased because of it at school. I was quite proud of the shop down the road with our name on it. But at home, it wasn't the thing talked about or thought about really. After university, I thought I'd start and see what it was like. I thought it might be rather boring, but if that happened, I could always pursue interests in other things. I didn't think about it any more than that. So I learned how to pat up the butter, slice the bacon, wire the cheese. And I found rather quickly that I rather enjoyed it – especially the competitive element.

A modern-day youth would, of course, expect their cash inheritance to be handed over promptly along with the tickets for the gap-year flights. But back in those days, millions or no millions, those pre-war generation kids knew that there would be no easy rides in this business. In fact, there is a hint of providence still there with Sainsbury, and his office is comfortably functional, without screaming power – or ego, for that matter; little sign of flashiness or excess. We could be in the boardroom of a mid-ranking civil servant – apart from the presence of a few valuable-looking artworks around the walls from interesting artists like Ivon Hitchens and Anthony Fry.

Sainsbury looks in fine shape for a man of over four score years, and turns out to be a perspicacious interviewee. Yet there is an undercurrent of something else as well; something intangible that never gets said, because it is too elusive a thing to put into words. Subtle and hard to fathom, at first; it feels like there is not so much an elephant in the room as a cautious antelope. Something that separates the quietly sublime world achievers from the loud local mediocrity. It is a sense of *being aware*.

That is: being aware, as he was once, of the sheer scale of his responsibility; and now of what he has done; and perhaps what still might be
ahead of him. Aware of an astonishing company history, that started
long before he was born, and over which – despite being retired – he
still has a sense of guardianship and connection. It is in his blood. Of
course it is.

The greatest influence on me was my family. My parents were divorced
when I was 12 and I saw very little of my father during the war for
that reason. Not for the reason that most people didn't see their father;
because they were away in the war. So I didn't know him that well and
it wasn't until I came into the business much later that I really began to
know him in a fatherly way. But, as I got older, the family was a very
big influence indeed. We were proud of the fact that a founder of the
business – my great-grandfather, who I never knew – had started with
nothing and had ended up a prosperous man.

He'd started with one ambition: to give each of his children a
shop; and once he'd done that, he kept going. So by the time he died
he probably had a hundred small shops spread all over. But built on
the very simple objectives of wanting to have the highest standards
in the quality of the food and highly competitive prices. The founder
recognised the importance of hygiene and cleanliness before others in
the trade did. Someone once made a joke that Sainsbury's made their
fortune out of marble, because all our counters had marble which was
considered a huge extravagance, but important for hygiene. He built a
trade on quality and always trying to be on the customers' side.

In those days, if you were selling a pile of bacon and you had half
a rasher left, you'd slip the half rasher and not let anyone see it. But
that was a capital offence in Sainsbury's. You had to put it on the top
so everyone saw it.

It was 1869 when Britain finally stopped deporting convicts to Australia,
and when, at the age of 24, great-grandfather John James Sainsbury and
his wife, Mary Ann Staples, had set up a small dairy shop, over which

they lived (and shared with no fewer than three other families), in Drury Lane, London.

By the time the founder had died in 1928 (apparently his last words being 'Keep the shops well lit') there were 128 stores in the south and east of England. Indeed, the Drury Lane store actually kept going until 1958. The eldest son, John Benjamin Sainsbury (known as 'Mr John') became chairman, then in his late sixties, handed stewardship to his sons, Alan and Robert Sainsbury, as general managers. Alan became chairman in 1956, followed by Robert in 1967, and then, in 1969, handed the role on to Alan's son, John Davan, our interviewee. There is a distinct pattern here, and it is not just based on there being a lot of Johns involved.

I had luck on my side in so many ways. First of all my two brothers came into the business and that was a terrific strength. My father and uncle had worked out that I should be on the trading side, my brother Simon on the financial and administrative side, and Tim on property, each of us with a major area to look after. Then in the sixties, it all began to really speed up. My father and uncle stepped down when the company was 100 years old. By that time, I'd covered the trading side, taking on more responsibility, but I hadn't had to worry about the things the chairman did. Then by 1969, it became our show. My brothers played a huge part behind the scenes, getting the sites and looking after the admin and so on, which was very difficult. We were the next generation coming in at a time of real opportunity for growth. That was so lucky.

Sainsbury mentions luck a lot. He knows life might have been different. And never more so than when he talks about his wife of nearly half a century, Anya Linden (now Lady Sainsbury), in her time a virtuoso ballerina, and a lifelong inspiration.

I've been very lucky. My wife has always been supportive of everything I've done. If you have a happy and close relationship of that sort, you

'Aye sir, the more they overtech the plumbing,
the easier it is to stop up the drain.'

SCOTTY (*STAR TREK*)

don't worry about what's going to happen when you're at the office. It must be more difficult if your life is uncertain or it is difficult for one reason or other; you can't operate. You can't be as good and as alert, as enterprising, as dedicated to your work, if you're having to solve crisis after crisis at home.

For Sainsbury, the notion of good 'fortune' has more than one meaning, none of which he takes for granted.

I wasn't at all a good officer cadet, just less bad than the others. I was awarded the Belt of Honour at the end of the course, but maybe it was the result of all things being relative. I certainly wasn't as fit or as strong as some of the others, and not a great sportsman. I never thought for one moment I'd be in any way distinguished. But it was all great fun for an irresponsible 19-year-old in 1946. You wore your army uniform all the time, which the ladies found very attractive. I was still an overgrown schoolboy, but I was learning fast – about the army, but also about relating to people in all walks of life.

Then I was sent off to Palestine to join my regiment, stationed near Gaza. We had armoured cars, and had to go round and try and keep the terrorists from blowing things up and killing people. It was either extremely boring because nothing was happening and we just sat round polishing the brass, or it was rather more exciting than you wanted it to be. One fellow officer of mine got shot but he wasn't killed, I'm pleased to say. I wasn't in the thick of it, but if I had been foolish in some way or made a mistake, it could have resulted in awful casualties. When I look back on it, I think I probably had greater responsibility at that time than I ever had after that. Anyway, I remember coming home demobilised and I had to catch a boat from Tel Aviv, and it was the only time I was really alarmed, because I thought it really would be annoying to get blown up on that very last journey.

After that, my father sent me off to Denmark to understand about Danish food exports. It wasn't such a great idea, because to learn what was going on in Denmark you needed to know something about the food industry, but I knew nothing. Denmark supplied a lot of the most important food we sold, with nice friendly people and it was nearby, so there I went. The girls in Denmark were very attractive and they all thought it was absolutely extraordinary to hear that I'd already been in the army. They'd been occupied by the Nazis, but they had all the food in the world, compared to the short rations that we had at home. I was in the land of plenty, in every way, and I was well aware of that.

One might say Sainsbury has always had a sense of history surrounding him. He seems aware of things before they become things to be aware of. In 1948, for example, like a besuited time-traveller from a Wells novel, he happened to be at Wembley.

When I came back, I was lucky again. I was employed by the London Olympic Games in 1948. There can't be many people alive at this moment who worked for the Olympic Games in 1948 and are still here for the 2012 Games in London again. Anyway it was another lovely job. I got £10 a week or so, plus petrol coupons. I was in the communications department with about seven or eight people and I was the junior office boy. I imagine the same department now perhaps has hundreds of people. We looked after all the PR and advertising.

When it was opened by the king and he came on at Wembley, there was a barrage of guns, a salute to the monarch in his honour. The day before this was to happen the organisers suddenly realised that the military were out of sight and wouldn't be able to know the actual moment when he arrived. So they'd need someone to signal when he entered. I got that job, and it was probably the most important thing I had to do. And it meant that I could be at Wembley, as well as many other events, although I didn't get to watch anything. But I was very lucky to be there.

Post-war Britain was broken, filthy, and ugly. Buildings were covered in soot and roads were full of large holes. Most people were having a bath (in a tin one) barely once a week, in front of the fire, and were still peeing at night into a chamber pot under the bed in lieu of an indoor lavatory. False teeth and hairnets were the cosmetic norm for folk in their thirties or above, and there was as much chance of a typical house having a fridge in its kitchen as of it having a particle accelerator in its living room.

In this struggling world, the Sainsbury's company was struggling. It hadn't had the best of wars; some of the Greater London stores had been bombed, and many of the male workers had been called up at the start of the war. People did not want to travel into the middle of towns where the stores were situated. The brand's price-competitiveness had been neutralised during the war years, when prices were controlled and food was rationed. Turnover had dropped to almost half of the pre-war level.

By the time John Davan Sainsbury joined, in 1950, things were picking up somewhat; although life was still lived at austerity level, in a way that makes the current use of the word somewhat risible.

I went into the grocery department because there was less rationing there, and I was put in charge of buying biscuits. I really thought it was rather exciting. It was fascinating how go-ahead some people and companies were – and how stupid some others were. In those days, it was an achievement to get as much stock as you wanted, rather than just getting allocated. The stupid ones didn't realise that Sainsbury's was going to go places, so they kept limiting our allocation. But there was a man called Hector Laing, from United Biscuits – a great character, an absolute leader, bringing in new equipment, new machinery, in the biscuit business. I suppose in me he saw the next generation of entrepreneurs, and he let us have what we wanted. But there were others who took a very different view and limited our allocations.

Before being moved from the biscuit department to the bacon, Sainsbury was sent down to Calne in Wiltshire 'to learn about how they did the bacon'. But the head of that business section was unimpressed by an Oxford arts graduate, asking, 'What good do you think studying history does for your business commercial career? Not much!'

So I said to the man, 'Actually, I think it does me a great deal of good.'
Here was someone who lived on subsidies. All he ever did was go and
talk to the minister and see that he got a better price and then he'd talk
to the Farmers' Union, to get them on side. It was all an appalling way
that the state managed a business. Here was this man living in the
past, running a very profitable business, with no competition. I could
see that the market would change, and my instinct was that we would
be the company to do it.

After bacon, I went to assist my father in the trading side of the
business. He'd been to America in 1949 to investigate this new idea
of frozen foods which we didn't know anything about, and they
found that not only was there this frozen food, but there were these
self-service stores. There were many sceptics at the time, but my
father was confident that it was the future. We set up our first self-
service store – which was our preferred description – in Croydon
in 1950 and as time went by, it did really well. Those days you
couldn't get planning permission to just build stores because there
was a shortage of building resources and so on. But it was possible
to get planning permission for shops in the new towns – Stevenage,
Hitchin, Crawley, etc – if virtually impossible to get planning
permission elsewhere.

The American supermarkets had emerged in response to a real social
and economic need during the Great Depression. Sainsbury's father had
developed a crusading disdain for social injustice, deprivation, and unemployment, so not surprisingly, the new shopping concept gelled with him.
It took a while, however, for the concept to be fully understood by the
public of south London. At the opening, his father had a wire basket flung
at him; and a judge's wife took him to task, swearing at him that she was
not inclined to do the job of a counter-girl.

Opposition didn't last long, though, and twenty years later, by 1970,
half of all Sainsbury's stores were self-service. Yet more revolutionary ideas followed. It was realised that pack designs would take over
from the role of the storekeeper ('the silent salesmen' they were called),

own-brand labels would be introduced, store car parks would be built, and, of course, television advertising would soon grow apace.

The food industry had to adjust enormously – it's always been a very fast-changing industry. Today, it's incredibly different to what it was when I retired 20 years ago and 20 years before that. Back then, I really was proud of what I learned from the Americans. They were incredibly generous with showing people what they did, how they did it, and why. They had the big chains, but very often the regional chains were very strong and had lots of confidential talks about how they did it with people in other regions that weren't competitors. So the tradition of sharing knowledge was there, and they loved having a curious Englishman to educate. Learning all we could from the US meant that, in some respects, we were able to be years ahead of our competitors: for example in scanning, because we were so close to what was going on in the States.

His father was a huge admirer of Marks & Spencer, regarding it as a 'brilliant business', with incredible customer loyalty. The sons, however, always had confidence in their ability to do better than that rival. When John became chairman, M&S were making nine times his own company's profit – by the time he retired, the situation had been transformed, with Sainsbury's generating the higher figure. 'By then, they weren't moving as well or as cleverly as we were and they had failed to recognise the importance of the car and of siting stores where customers can easily get to; that is, not often in the town centres.'

In 1973, the company was floated on the London Stock Exchange, with the family keeping an 85% stake, which was split unevenly. Alan's three sons – John, Simon, and Tim – each received one third of their side of the family's proportion, whereas the one son of Robert – David Sainsbury – (and not the daughters) received the full amount. Perhaps this was to give the more cautious David a greater proportion of votes to balance the more forceful leadership of John. Who knows? But it did not seem to lead to any bad blood.

Finally taking the company public in 1973 was a very important decision and the good thing was, it wasn't controversial. I think we all had somewhat different reasons for thinking it was the right thing to do, but it wasn't a quarrel within the family. Frankly, we felt that such a large company shouldn't stay private, and we wanted to share what we were doing with our customers and staff. In those days, we didn't have unbelievably high bonuses as you can today, but we did have profit-sharing, which went to staff related to their salary, which was really worth having.

Sainsbury tells the story of a bright young graduate trainee, who was asked to explain the company's profit-sharing scheme to a visiting Soviet deputy prime minister. She outlined how she'd been in the company for two years and under the Sainsbury Profit Share Scheme was preferring shares, for the simple reason that she thought Sainsbury's to be 'a very good company', likely to go up in share price. Which all rather bemused the Soviet minister – a communist unfamiliar with capitalism.

A million shares were offered to employees; the offer instantly became fully subscribed, and the shares multiplied in value. Publicity was almost entirely positive, earning the company (and the family) a reputation for business acumen and entrepreneurial foresight, coupled with safe and steady management and shrewd organic growth strategies. During this time, as chairman and chief executive, Sainsbury developed his own reputation as a dynamic and forceful leader, who did not suffer fools gladly. He became known as 'Mr JD', with a reputation for spontaneous, hands-on, quality control. Sainsbury tells how he tried to visit individual stores every week, even occasionally using a helicopter where lengthy distances were involved. 'I tried to go round anonymously, the reason being that you wanted to see it as a customer sees it, not to try and catch anyone out.' But, most of the time, the rumour of his impending arrival would precede him.

Sainsbury is keen to point out the importance of being aware of what other people are doing: competitors, colleagues, anyone who is capable of an interesting idea. He tells, as an aside, how he once sat next to

Warren Buffett at a lunch, and found out how they had both started – or both their families had started – grocery stores in 1869. 'I've learnt from so many people, especially people who were successful, but I always believe the one to learn from most of all is the competition. I used to say that there's always something you can learn, however bad the retailer.'

By the nineties, Sainsbury had decided that he would retire at 65, having transformed the company. He had numerous other projects and interests, and 'didn't want to stay on the board, looking over successors' shoulders'. During his stint as chairman, the company had grown its sales from £1.2 billion (in real terms) to £9.2 billion; profits before tax had risen from £33 million to £628 million; and market share had increased from around 2.5% to 10.5%. The growth had been staggering – and yet was unlikely to continue in that vein forever.

It didn't. After Sainsbury retired, the chairmanship passed to his cousin, David, and it was then that problems developed – over expansion and diversification, loyalty programmes, and whether emphasis would be on value or quality. Margins fell, and store development had to be reigned in. Finally, in 1996 – around four years after John's retirement – Tesco overtook the company as the UK's largest grocer. In due course, David decided that it wasn't right for him, and became a successful and prominent government minister. Today, our interviewee remains president of the firm, 'but it's only a post of honour... Nowadays, there's a brilliant chap in charge, making Sainsbury's a great company again.'

The other interests he wanted to pursue were in the arts (he and his wife being avid theatre, opera, and ballet supporters, as well as collectors of art) and in managing his own vast philanthropic concerns. The Linbury Trust – a composite of his wife's and his names – has donated countless millions of pounds to arts, heritage, education, and other charitable causes.

I gave away more money than I inherited and I was pleased about that. I gave time as well, because I have always enjoyed the visual and performing arts.

At school, I had wanted to be an actor. Then I married a ballerina, so I got to know the Royal Ballet. I was invited to serve on the board of the Opera House, which was from 1969 to 1985, then became chairman from 1987 to 1991. [To be certain, he checks the dates in Who's Who.*] As chairman, I enjoyed it very much, but it was difficult, and so different from Sainsbury's. For a time, I was chairman of Sainsbury's, director of the board of the Opera House, and even on the board of the National Gallery. I got a lot of pleasure working in another world. Artists are impossible in some ways and very loveable in others, but I'd rather talk to some artists than some businessmen... I always liked working with Jeremy Isaacs, when I was chairman of the Opera House and he was chief executive. We got on very well: he understood the arts and was very musical and was a great one for always doing something better and better. And with Neil MacGregor, another man I enormously admire, a very clever man and a scholar, who really embraced the concept of the enlargement of the National Gallery.*

There are many more experiences, marking out a long and, at times, colourful journey. His house was once owned by Peter Cadbury, who was famed in the locality for cutting down trees, to accommodate facilities for his aeroplanes and helicopters. When Sainsbury bought it, he had the landing strip ploughed up and claims to have planted more trees than Cadbury had cut down. There is clearly something mischievous about the man. Perhaps it's a corollary of his love of life, or his attitude to risk and enterprise. Beneath the self-control and properness, there is a hint of the mercurial; so he can switch, without prior warning, between reprising tales of student life at Oxford ('Don't quote any of that') and of the life peer doing his duty for Queen and Country.

Sainsbury wasn't really interested in politics at first, but was aware of it, given that the family were involved. Indeed, he remembers being aware of the post-war Labour Government, and writing letters from Palestine about the bread rationing, which was actually introduced after the war, and the shortage of electricity and power. His father, Alan John Sainsbury, was a Liberal candidate in the thirties before being made a peer by his friend Hugh Gaitskell in 1962, the second year of life peerages, meaning that there was a time when father and son faced each other across opposite benches in the Lords.

There were times when it seemed like they saw as much of each other across those benches as they did in the family home. Indeed, Alan John Sainsbury – gazetted with the rather dapper title of Baron Sainsbury of Drury Lane – could provide us with material for a story in his own right, along with other members of this extraordinary clan. From an early age, when he studied politics, he was on the centre-left, but with different parties. When Gaitskell died in 1963, it prompted him to lose interest in Labour and eventually become a founding member of the SDP. Even up to the time of his death, he would be seen sitting next to Liberal members. Although he liked to indulge himself with a chauffeured Rolls, he was uncomfortable about conspicuous wealth, and it was perhaps his influence in this regard that led the sons to embark on their notable philanthropy. He was reputed to like to say that 'there are two types of people: ones that want to do things, and ones who think of reasons why they can't be done'. Alan served on numerous committees as a peer, and treated it as a career in its own right. It is clear that his son has picked up many of his finest qualities, although he does not have enough time to attend the House of Lords, as his father had done.

Like many things in life, to get the best out of it, you have to put a lot into it, but I was involved in the arts and charitable causes and never had enough time, so I didn't make many speeches. I did get involved when they were reviewing the laws on charity and I thought this was something that I knew more about than most subjects, so I volunteered to go on to an all-party scrutiny committee, chaired by Alan Milburn, who was very good. I was one of the few Tories during a Labour majority on the committee. It was interesting exposure, but there was an enormous amount of paper, an enormous amount of meetings, and an enormous amount of time.

The Sainsbury family is unusual in its connections with all three main political parties. Younger cousin David, as Lord Sainsbury of Turville, was interested in politics from an early age, joining the Labour Party as early as 1960, and later working with David Owen and the SDP. He is, to date, the largest-ever donor to the Labour Party. John Davan Sainsbury has feet firmly in the other camp, which, if nothing else, must make for some interesting conversations over the Sainsbury's own-label cognac.

As he tells it, John Sainsbury first became 'properly involved' in the political world at the time of the Heath government (in the early seventies), when he was summoned to go and discuss the prices and incomes policy. Looking back, it seems a bizarre state of affairs: the prime minister discussing rules to govern retailer profits on tomatoes or turnips, and Sainsbury trying to arrive at a formula within which all retailers could operate.

I remember, I said at one point, 'But Prime Minister, don't you agree with competition? Isn't that the best way to control prices?'

Clearly, however, Heath wasn't having any of it. Sainsbury tells us numerous stories of his dealings with politicians, from Heath to Thatcher to Major; of time spent with them, as much as anything, through the Opera House. Heath was, of course, quite the expert, and possibly felt more at home at the opera than in a crowded room full of people. Thatcher, the scientist, had much less empathy with the arts. Yet Sainsbury recounts – with some nostalgia and fondness – how he introduced her to Joan Sutherland at the soprano's final performance in London and how 'the two great ladies just stood there trying to tell each other how wonderful the other one was'.

When Sainsbury speaks of the business, there is a spark in his eye. When he talks about the arts, there is electricity. He adores the arts. And across many – perhaps all – of its forms. Business and the arts: the same bedfellows? Something dawns on us, and him, at the same moment during the discussion. Is there that much difference?

I feel every company chairman is in a sense a performer, with the shareholders his audience. Sometimes he plays the hero and sometimes he's made a villain, but we all act the part, don't we? Whatever our role, we act it. We have to act it. You've got your lines. You've got to know what you've got to say as a company chairman at your general meeting.

He has just channelled Jaques in *As You Like It,* but we daren't ask if it was deliberate, subconscious, or coincidental. Sainsbury has been talking for close on two hours, and has taken us on a vast journey that started a few miles from where we are sitting, less than a century-and-a-half before we met. During his long life, he has been responsible for turnovers that would make an agreeable GDP for a medium-sized nation-state. It is all some going for a man of 80-odd years who was ambivalent about our project to start off with, and who continually reminds us that he has been fortunate and that he knows that many other people are not. Perhaps that is why he gives so much away.

It has been the story, not just of one man, but of a family and an idea that survives and shines as brightly today as it did in Drury Lane one May evening back in 1869, when John James closed his door after a first day's trading in eggs and bacon out of his drawing room. In the course of our session, John James's great-grandson has spoken a lot about eggs and bacon, and biscuits as well. He knows his products as well as he knows his Gainsboroughs and Verdis. It comes back to where we started, which is that this man's success is the result of an appreciation of detail, and of taking responsibility, and of making difficult decisions.

But above all, it is the result of being aware.

'One should either be a work of art,
or wear a work of art.'

OSCAR WILDE

SIR PAUL SMITH

(Paul Smith)

INTERVIEWED 8 MARCH 2012

The London of 1984 did not turn out to be the brutalist telescreen-surveilled nightmare predicted by Orwell. That wouldn't arrive until twenty-five years later. In the real 1984, life was uniformly upwardly mobile. Virgin Atlantic had made its first flight to the US, Apple had launched its first Mac (with Ridley Scott's ad pastiche of Orwell), and North Sea oil production had hit an all-time high of 85 million barrels. *Newsweek* magazine were calling it 'The Year of the Yuppie'. Covent Garden had transformed from a fruit 'n' veg market into the playground of fresh-faced, freshly loaded urban professionals who drank bottled water at street cafes (how daring it was to actually *pay* for water) and rounded off another perfect day by buying yet more Filofax inserts and designer labels.

To which end, behind the Covent Garden Piazza, along a cobbled street off Long Acre, was a small dark shop named after its owner, Paul Smith. A name with which the style-obsessed new metropolitan class had quite simply fallen in love. Five years after opening, this was, in 1984, the men's fashion shop par excellence. Home of classic British tailoring with a twist. A celebration of tradition and civility, but where each item had the subtle, unexpected coda: perhaps just one extra stripe, one added tweak of colour, one extra button – one final smile.

At Paul Smith, the quality was high, the quantity restrained: delicately striped shirts, a few dark suits, paisley ties, the occasional accessory. Most came for a tie and maybe stretched to a shirt, while those with the serious cash could realise the ultimate achievement of a plain dark Paul

Smith suit, which hopefully might one day fly open to reveal the paisley lining and tiny cotton label, held on by two delicate threads.

To this tenebrous epicurean cavern at 43 Floral Street – Indian rugs on the floor and mahogany shelving on the walls – came anyone who knew anything about what they ought to be wearing, and that included the most famous of music, media, and movie stardom in those excitable times. It was 'The Ivy' of clothing shops.

The world would, of course, change; but in many significant ways, Paul Smith would not. Although the original yuppie is as scarce a species as the northern white rhino, the shop in Floral Street is still going strong. As are hundreds of other Paul Smith outlets dotted around the world in Bahrain, Bangalore, and Beirut, in Manila, Milan, and Moscow, and the rest.

In the London of 2012, the oil tap has been turned off and the City has run dry. And it is in today's uncertain times that we enter the Paul Smith head office. Actually, you don't enter the office as such; you stand there and let it cascade over you, more of which in a minute. Beyond the small door, behind the small reception desk, the place opens up like a TARDIS. Along short, narrow corridors are large, grand, high-ceilinged showrooms, with full coat-rails in between gilded mirrors and cardboard boxes.

Within a famously fickle industry, the Paul Smith brand today remains as talismanic as ever: one of the most admired and valuable fashion names on the planet. While the world has been changing – as have many of the names in that industry – the character, quality, and popularity of this particular brand have remained constant. Although here at the London headquarters, there are surprises.

In reception, every bit of wall space is covered with framed pictures, hung randomly. Framed letters from children worldwide share wall-space with pictures of, or drawn by, or photographed by, famous cultural icons. Here is a picture of the Dalai Lama, with his Paul Smith scarf on. Here is a strange sign in pen that says 'Music off for the princes'. Here is something from Mario Testino. Here is a lady with no clothes on. Here is a picture signed by George Harrison. Here is someone with their Oscar, in between letters from admirers of all ages, near and far: 'Dear Sir Paul

Smith. I really like your clos and want too be a desiner when I leave school. Here is a drawing of my dog...'

We are taken upstairs via a pre-digital-era lift, to wait in an anteroom for our interviewee. Sir Paul Smith is running late. He has a fierce schedule, but famous people pop in anytime, and he doesn't like turfing anyone out. Through the open door we spy animated employees laughing, chatting, cutting, computing... designing.

In our anteroom, several bicycles are propped up against bookcases packed to bursting with an eclectic collection of books and magazines on art, cars, bikes, trains, flowers, chemical elements, US presidents, girl bands, volcanoes... Every surface in the room is covered with piles of magazines, boxes of photographs, oil paintings, trinkets, toys, gadgets, models, rubber chickens, Transformer robots, and other assorted artefacts. In the middle of the room stand a glass coffee table, a sofa, and two chairs that seem to have just arrived from Christie's because the label is still dangling from an arm. They are by the designer Jens Quistgaard, and – a quick bit of research on Google reveals – come with a price tag that would alternatively get you a very nice German coupé. We stay standing.

The door swings open and Paul Smith greets us like we only saw him last night at the pub. 'How are you, boys? How are things? Come in. Sorry I'm late. What can I do for you today?' The accent is pronounced – slight upper-octave, scattered with gravel; his hair is long and silver-grey, and he is dressed in a loose denim shirt, giving rather a good impression of a semi-retired rock legend. We mention the chairs, and he says, 'Where did they come from? Bloody hell. Didn't know we had them...' before showing us through to the boardroom, which is even more full of clutter.

First up, Smith shows us a disco ball, an ET, a wheelbarrow, a giant locust, a sou'wester, a mannequin: they are all stamped and addressed, without any outer packaging, coming (for literally years) from an anonymous admirer in the US. Next, in the corner of the room is a perspex container within which is a pathologically meticulous scale model of this very room made from hair-thin shards of newspaper, a feat of Swiss-watch-calibre engineering that occupied a Japanese fan 24–7 for about a year of his life. In the corner of the model is a scale model of the room, in the corner of which is a scale model of the room – you get the point. Smith hands over the delicate box and it is not a good time to sneeze or trip. Through the course of the chat, he shows us letters, presents, paintings, models, and more. Some big, some small, some ingenious, some banal, from near and far. There are at least five train sets in the room, an awful lot of rabbits, and a quartet of Olympic quality bicycles. In one corner is a bag full of mint-condition Apple kit hand-delivered by Jonathan Ive; in another corner is a Nativity scene made from peanuts by a schoolchild in Belgium. Propped up on the floor is a photograph by Degas that seems to be an original. And so it goes on.

If you're wondering what Smith thinks about this unusual collection, he absolutely treasures it. The British Museum has a smaller inventory. Smith finds inspiration in anything, be it random artefacts or original Impressionist artworks. His mantra is that if you can't find inspiration, look again, because you've not tried hard enough. Interestingly, Smith does not use a computer: it's as if he prefers to collect his own infinity of real objects rather than surf them on Wikipedia.

Smith was born one year after the war ended in Beeston in Nottingham. He says that the great Midlands city was a huge cultural influence on him, not least because of the class mix (from miners to country gentry). Smith left school at 15 to work as errand boy at a clothing warehouse, riding his bike to work every day; his only ambition to become a professional racing cyclist. Then, at 17, came the accident that almost killed him, and definitely killed his cycling ambition. It was a blindingly sunny day, and, looking very stylish in his new Buddy Holly sunglasses, but not looking at the road ahead, Smith smashed his bicycle at full speed into the back of a parked Austin A40. And that was that.

It took three months in the so-called 'Ton-up Ward' of the local hospital (shared with equally badly injured miners and motorcyclists) until his body was pinned back together again. It would prove to be a defining moment for him.

So I literally fell into fashion. I'd had a nothing education; didn't pass any exams; completely uninterested in school. Mum and Dad had been lovely, and taught me so much. Dad was very charismatic; one of those guys: you'd go to your auntie's house on a Sunday and you'd go in the front room and after two minutes everybody's laughing because he'd just got this way with people. I think I got my sense of communication from him. He was an amateur photographer, so there was creative stuff going on at home, but the door hadn't yet been opened for me. I'd kept my bike in my bedroom and worshipped it and liked the way you looked on a bike, so I had a bit of a sense for style. I got out of hospital and arranged to keep in touch with a few guys I'd met there. By chance, we would all meet at a pub where the Nottingham art students went. So suddenly I'm hearing all these things like Warhol, Kandinsky, Mies van der Rohe, Mondrian, none of whom I'd ever heard of, and then it dawned on me that maybe I could actually earn a living connecting with this amazing new world.

It could be a *Marvel* comic story: hit by a radioactive truck carrying paintings and clothing, the penniless young cyclist Paul Smith subsequently finds he has acquired incredible super-powers of creativity. Well, at least enough to be able to help a girl from the pub, whose dad had given her some money to buy her own shop. Smith worked out how to deal with solicitors and estate agents and, before long, he was running the menswear floor in her shop selling turtleneck jumpers and drainpipe jeans. By 1967 – helped in no small part by the frenzied sixties scene going on in the background – Smith was adapting himself to the loss of one possible future, and discovering another. At which point, on cue, Pauline Denyer enters the equation.

Smith mentions his wife almost as soon as we meet. Her role in this story is fundamental, and never does he miss a chance to emphasise the fact.

I'm very privileged now, but you always need to keep your feet on the ground, which I've managed because of Pauline. I met her when I was 21 and I'm still with her and still love her. We have a laugh, and inspire each other in terms of everything – conversation, attraction, the whole thing. She's never been impressed by the falseness of the modern world or by marketing and insincerity and spin and words that mean nothing. She's kept me focused. Pauline and I have always built the business based on the jam-jar on the mantelpiece: if there was money in it, you could spend it, and if there wasn't money in it, you couldn't. We've never borrowed: ever. We're old-fashioned. But I can be myself, not constantly looking over my shoulder worried about shareholders wanting more profit for another yacht or to show off.

He may do a blog for *Vogue* and have the wealth that allows him to buy practically anything he wants, but airs and graces are absent. Sure, it's difficult to get a word in edgeways, but that's because most of what he has to say is interesting or funny. He is unrelentingly upbeat. His enthusiasm is static electricity on nylon.

It sounds so clichéd, but I just love the joy of life. I go to bed quite early, 10pm-ish, then get up in the morning totally positive. I leave home at 5am, swim every morning, then get here around 6-ish for three hours completely on my own, which is fantastic. Then I go for a little bike ride and buy a coffee. Normally Pauline's asleep when I leave, so the first person I speak to most mornings is the road sweeper near where I swim and he's a really nice guy. He's actually a qualified nurse from Poland, but he's sweeping the roads to earn money to send back to his family. One morning, he said, 'You know, you're the only person that speaks to me. It's because I'm a road sweeper.'

There was this time, every morning for eight years or so, when I swam with a guy at the pool. I would say 'hello' and then one morning he just said, 'Are you Mr Paul Smith, fashion designer? Because my daughter brought a book home and I saw your picture.' Later on, I said to him, 'I'm sorry, I don't know your name and may I ask you what you do?' and he tells me that he's a surgeon and he's replaced and repaired about nine thousand children's hearts. But he's just this humble guy who swims every morning. It makes you think that's what it's all about. He pops in to the office here with his daughter sometimes and has a cup of tea. It's the kind of thing that makes life great.

Like my daily postbag. Jonathan [Ive] was really fascinated by this, because we get a lot of the things just sent at random by people who are 8 or 82. I've got these little things here, they're all from a girl who started writing to me when she was 11 and she's 15 now and I only met her for the first time when she came from Belgium with her dad before Christmas. I could show you things all day long like this. I've got twenty or thirty boxes full of nice and mad letters that we keep. I try and reply to them all.

Long before a lot of his fans were born, Smith was taking another early step on the road to fame, by buying his first shop, with all of £600 that he had saved up. Rather splendidly, it was known as Paul Smith Vêtement Pour Homme (although that kind of fancy talk didn't always chime well with the locals). It was down a shady ginnel in Nottingham city centre; the combination of high style and low cobbled alleyway a foretaste of the Covent Garden arrangement to follow. In fact, the formula is recreated in Paul Smith outlets all over the world, with reclaimed mahogany cabinets, oak flooring, and eccentric British curios. Some of the shopfittings in Japan actually came from reclaimed chemist and sweet shops in Sheffield and Newcastle. Back in 1970, that first Nottingham shop at 6 Byard Lane was the only UK stockist of the Margaret Howell and Kenzo labels, but quite soon, Paul Smith's own label started to appear alongside them. And a trip down the M1 would soon beckon.

I knew the danger: the job always changes you and you never change the job. I was very conscious of that at the beginning. I'd seen a lecture by Edward de Bono, and he made me think that if you want to stop this happening and stick by your guns, you've got to work out a way. You've got to somehow keep your purity but still get your income, even when each pulls you in an opposite direction. The little shop in Nottingham was 12 foot square and it was originally full of clothes that were unprofitable because they were very specific, especially for a provincial town.

So I thought, how would Edward [de Bono] work this one out? Should I change to selling clothes that people ask for, but that would mean me watering down the pure malt. If I'd done that, I probably wouldn't be sitting here with you now; I'd probably be fat and just have my shop in Nottingham. So I decided to earn money on five days of the week selling fabrics and suits, and keep the purity of the stuff I wanted to sell for the Friday and Saturday. Then suddenly people started coming from all over the country to Nottingham, because you couldn't get anything like that anywhere else outside of London. We were an oasis, in the middle of the country. That's how I got going. The reason why I've done all right is because I've always worked out a way of having product or income from more commercial things while still being really respectful of image and exclusivity and special things and limited editions.

Smith bought his first London property in 1976 (the same year in which he first showcased his collection in Paris), but, still true to his jam-jar economic model, refused to renovate it until three years later. Back then, Covent Garden was unloved and unfashionable, and the Yuppie movement was several years away. He had time to think about what he wanted, which allowed him to purchase the ancient property next door as well. Taking inspiration from the German Bauhaus and Swiss-French Le Corbusier design schools (more names from the Nottingham art school pub), Smith put together a place where interest and aestheticism met in the cause of fashion. The floors smelled of wood-polish; and the counters contained model racing cars, wooden toothbrushes, army knives, paperweights, pens, and notebooks, including a type of leather loose-leaf ring-binder diary made by two failing businessmen in Notting Hill. Thus did the Filofax become the essential hand-held yuppie accessory, long before mobile smartphones took over that role. 43–44 Floral Street would become iconic. Classic; British; with a twist.

I used the name Paul Smith because when Pauline persuaded me to open my first little shop, we thought that people would want to know who was behind it. They'd got to know me where I was working before in the previous shop, so it was a very practical thing. It was like 'Oh, that's Paul Smith; that's the bloke that used to work there and he's opened up here now'. So it was a very practical reason why I used my own name. Also, at the time, a lot of the shops were called trendy names like 'Birdcage' or 'Doll's House' or 'Guys & Dolls', so using your own name was quite unusual.

He is a man of contrasting characteristics and this is projected, with intent, onto his brand. He says he always aims to imagine himself wearing his clothes and he designs with his own character in mind, rather than an imaginary professional sprite on a catwalk. The success of the brand could be said to be largely because Smith's own liquid self, with all its contrasts, has been poured into his collections. This has required confidence; but it hasn't always been like this. 'In the beginning, I basically did anything that came along to learn my trade. What I wasn't sure about, I made up for in effort and making the best of any situation.'

As with so many of our subjects, the 'luck', if that's how we want to label it, comes to those who are willing to spot the opportunity and grasp it when it appears. And it seems to help too if you meet halfway:

I've tried to make the effort: like helping young designers get things made. It's because I've always been very gung-ho. So I would say things like 'Yeah, I heard there's a trouser-maker in Gloucester', and I'd just drive for hours to try and find somebody who'd make me fifty shirts or so in a certain way that I needed doing. Life is a stepping stone, and as you get older you start to understand how to make the best of things. At one point in my life, one of my friends was working a lot with bands, including Led Zeppelin, especially Jimmy Page. So I got working indirectly with a lot of bands and then eventually directly, and that's kept up, somehow. You know, there was Bowie and Patti Smith and then Travis and Razorlight and then all these young bands that pop in to see me now.

I was never trained, except on the job, therefore the first collections were designed by Pauline and made by Pauline and the actual first

Paul Smith collections weren't done by me at all. It was only in the early eighties that I started to have the confidence to do some things myself. Even then, everything I did was actually quite obvious, quite simple, like a jacket looked like a jacket, whereas a lot of young designers in Britain at the time were doing very extreme things.

Above all, Smith wanted to design clothes that were free of irrelevance and self-indulgence. He didn't want the clothes to dominate the person; they should be a complement to the real business of living; a means not an end, but a very enjoyable means, nonetheless. Of course, he can still do the unexpected – a flash of colour, a novel cut, unusual stitching – not just with his collections themselves, but with what's alongside. In 1995, Rover gave him a Mini to decorate as a limited edition. He has designed suits for football teams (a sport he claims to know nothing about) and was involved with the 2012 London Olympics. As you would expect, he enjoys working on his cycling innovations, such as a limited-edition jersey for the Tour de France during its UK leg and the Rapha partnership. Nor does he ever forget his roots: Nottingham's Broadway Cinema was effectively redesigned by him when it was rebuilt in 2006. Smith is always being inspired, you feel, by almost anything he comes across.

Facebook, tweeting, blogs; I mean I completely get it, and we've a whole department in marketing alone doing this kind of modern company thing. But personally, I'm a real pen and paper guy. I like the idea that when you do something with a pencil, you can make a mistake and from that mistake can come an idea. I still like ripping things up and slashing things. You'll see some of the new textile prints we've got down there, they took an image and just cut through it with scissors and sort of pasted it together.

Inevitably, we only scratch the surface of his achievements. Pauline is known for saying that he can keep a lot of plates spinning at any one time, although Smith does sometimes deliberately let one or two smash. This is the fashion industry after all, and he has been on the receiving end of some of its unscrupulousness, so he knows when to let go. Nice though he may be, he is no pushover.

Things are very tough, especially now. What you hope is that the younger generation will see what's happened and might still be bright enough to readjust and understand about what life on earth is. I said this at the Japanese Society: we all enjoy having some money and we all enjoy the opportunity to buy something that's special, but let's keep it within reason. What's so horrible is that sometimes it's down to just one man sitting in his Porsche with his mobile phone pressing a button that makes shares gain or lose millions. Whereas, take my guy who opens our warehouse and has been with me for 25 years and he opens it at 9 in the morning, every morning, whether it's snowing or not, and he deals with 90 people and when they're not feeling well and one's had a baby or had a bit of a problem with their heart, he deals with it...

I'm not a confrontational person and I don't like to put people in situations which don't feel comfortable. Therefore, I don't like to do clothes that make you look silly or odd or uncomfortable. I just want my clothes to be very wearable, but still have a personality. I remember one of my first freelance jobs designing some white shirts and the guy I was working for said, 'This is just a white shirt.' I said, 'Yeah, but it's got a deep armhole with Sea Island Cotton' and I'd done 22 stitches to the inch, where normally an average shirt was about 14, so it was very beautiful stitching, plus mother-of-pearl buttons, not plastic and then just one little buttonhole in purple and that was enough and it was actually very different.

At the time, one of the big problems of our industry in Britain was the fact that a lot of the fashion designers felt that if you were called a 'fashion designer' then you had to do things that were absurd or strange. Of course, that then became a big problem for the industry because government wouldn't take you seriously, and industry wouldn't take you seriously, because they all thought that, if you were a designer, it was all about bare breasts and red hair and being silly and wearing antlers or something. Whereas my approach was about nice clothes, but giving the old British male a bit of a nudge. And this really kicked in in the early eighties, when just nice guys were really excited to find a Prince of Wales check suit that had got a very thin yellow line through it and it was just so subtle. That sums up what I like doing.

It is an approach that has served him extremely well in the difficult Japanese market. For Smith, entry and expansion here has been one of his greatest business achievements. He is the biggest-selling European designer in Japan, the country now accounting for around half of the business's turnover, with well over two hundred shops. By any yardstick, these are staggering figures.

A Japanese scout was looking for a European designer, following one in Paris, one in Milan and one in London and in the end chose me. They invited Pauline and me out there, economy class, 18 hours to Japan. I spoke at the Japanese Society the other night to raise money for the tsunami, and I was telling them how thrilled I'd been in those days to go to this place called Japan. At that time, masses of designers were being invited, but they were demanding first-class travel and chauffeur-driven cars and the best hotels and just wanted the quick cash. I remember one designer asking me, 'How come you've done so well in Japan and how come that your clothes look so good? They made some handbags for me recently and they were nothing to do with our style at all.' So I said, 'Well how often do you go each year?' The answer was that he had only ever been once, ever. He never even sent them a fax. I was going four times a year. I've been 85 times. I like the people, their heritage, their tradition, their food, and the jet lag doesn't worry me. I've done well in Japan because I just got on with it. I like the Japanese. They embrace me, I embrace them, I work 17-hour days, 14-hour days, and I'm very willing. It's a proper, honest partnership.'

In Japan, Smith has pop-star status, and gets mobbed on the streets by adoring fans. He often has to take escape routes and back doors to evade the hundreds of screaming well-wishers.

I travel around the world alone most of the time. I'm not chased by nutters: I'm nutter-free. People don't recognise me. Except in Japan, where it's slightly different, because I've had a lot of attention, you know on television and stuff... Also, as a race, they do like to have their photograph taken with you or for you to sign, which is nice.

Smith is always keen to keep things in perspective. He regards his industry as one with a job to do and believes it often does that job well. But he also acknowledges that it can be prone to stereotypical hyperbole and pretentiousness. He feels it can be overrated by its protagonists and hangers-on, and that ultimately, there is an important distinction between real art and transient, superficial fashion. Returning back to the story of the surgeon in the swimming pool, he reminds us that, although clothes are fascinating and enjoyable and able to make us feel good, sexy and sporty, at the end of the day, the sewing is of fabric to fabric, not of arms back onto bodies.

Unfortunately a lot of people get drawn in because they're insecure or don't know the dangers. Just don't get involved. Be yourself. In the early days of when you're building a business obviously you have to get more involved to get your name around and introduce people to what you're doing. As a younger couple, we did our bit, but not anything like most people do now. You've only got to look at the media to see how much is about getting drunk and behaving badly and getting noticed. Unfortunately, the last 25 years have been very much about nonsense and falseness. I was lucky.

In the nineties I was offered really large sums of money to sell out and at one point I did go along with it a bit. But in the end, we didn't sell because we had learned that we were as good as anyone else and could do much better in the long run. My approach has always been that, if I can just have a nice day, that'll do. Now, the shops have done OK, and it's all grown, but it was never about anything more than that. It was very tough at the beginning but all our lives we've tried to be a generous couple in terms of meals and inviting people for supper and being generous with time. I've already had somebody here this morning wanting advice. Most weeks, people are coming in, new young designers or the biggest names in the industry.

The thing is, if I've got £100 million today, £50 million, £25 million, it wouldn't make any difference to my day at all. I don't want a private jet or a yacht: I've got love, I've got health, and I've got freedom. I mean obviously, there's the security; the fact that you know where your next meal's coming from, that you can be a little bit indulgent in terms of beautiful things. We own some nice paintings and my wife has a nice art studio where she paints for her own satisfaction, but she doesn't try to sell it and she's quite shy about it. But I can have an office like this which is full of beautiful books and if I see a book I can buy it and if it's £50, I just think that I'll buy it so I can have nice things, but I'm not motivated by the money. I've got a house in Italy but I just drive a Mini.

We are coming to the end of our allotted time, and Smith has a raft of further appointments for the day. In fact, there is probably another conga-line of film stars, media figures, and Belgian fans coming up the stairs to 'just pop in'. But he is too generous to stop chatting. He takes us into more offices, revealing the latest designs, projects, and innovations on which his teams are working. A combination of energy, honesty, and youthful optimism ebbs and flows from floor to ceiling, and it hinges on one simple fact: his team are devoted to him – and the way he goes about his business.

I think I'm just a normal bloke really. I hope I am. Just a normal guy. I know nearly everybody's name in the whole building. There's 180 of us, and I remembered Clare's birthday today downstairs, and I remembered Emma's last week and Nicole's is on Sunday. You just treat people right and remember that everybody goes to the loo and everybody has a bad day and a good day, even the Queen.

It's been such a gentle journey. It's always had to be very much about intuition and about living within your means and understanding it and that's why I think we've had longevity and the thing I'm most proud of is continuity. That's the joy. I tried not to let the industry hype change me. I don't want to be saying, 'Got to keep up, got to keep up.' I want just enough satisfaction in every day to be able to just do our own thing. The accident opened my world to creativity, and Pauline has kept my feet on the ground, because of stability, love, and security, calming me down, keeping me on the straight and narrow.

It is a salutary lesson. One of the most successful and famous figures in one of the most cut-throat and fickle industries on the planet has got to where he is on the back of some down-to-earth, no-nonsense, provincial values – and a good woman behind him. Famous people come here because, for a few moments in their 'limelit' lives, they can take refuge in a sanctuary of sensory mayhem. Honest mayhem.

'Dear Paul, I don't like fashion but I like you.' That's just the way round that Smith wants it. And that's why his is such a timeless, resilient success story. And why everyone keeps sending him stuff they've made for him.

———

'We cannot destroy kindred: our chains stretch a little
sometimes, but they never break.'

MARIE DE RABUTIN-CHANTAL, MARQUISE DE SÉVIGNÉ

———

JONATHAN WARBURTON

(Warburtons)

INTERVIEWED 1 NOVEMBER 2012

And so we come to our final chapter and thirteenth interviewee, and how fitting it is that this baker's dozen of entrepreneurs is completed by the UK's most famous baker-entrepreneur, Jonathan Warburton.

To meet with him, we have journeyed to Bolton on the grimmest of early November days. Most of the physical world is in a kind of slate-textured fug, so from his office, where we're standing, you can't really see the point at which the wet grey rooftops stop and the wet grey sky starts. A contrast is on the wall behind his desk, in the form of a large framed photograph of his children: an Enid Blyton quartet, each in a different coloured top, seated on a bench, backs to camera, looking out onto a sunlit azure sea vista, once upon a time, on a holiday in Cornwall. A family man is Warburton. And a family firm, most definitely, is Warburtons.

The 55-year-old chairman (and latterly chief executive), who has had joint control of the business for over twenty years, makes a particular point about himself and his two cousins, Ross and Brett, with whom he runs this enduring, privately held, family-owned company:

Make sure you stress the ability of the three of us to navigate around 30 years of working together. I'm just one part of a family. That needs to be the most important thing you bring out, because that's been the most important thing for us.

The agreement we've always had is that the good of the business was more important than each individual's ultimate ego. Just think of your *immediate family and ask yourself if* you *could spend your life working with them.* We *have. And built business success by doing it, and that's the strength of our achievement. It's the three of us – plus my sister Jill, who has been very supportive to me. We're now into a fifth generation, which is very unusual: that's a hell of a lot of kids and cousins. You can just see why so few family companies make it, because the skill of keeping everyone happy is important.*

Warburtons: one of the most familiar of household fmcg (fast-moving consumer goods) brands; bread and baking synonymous with waxed-paper packs and bright orange truck trailers. The brand name has no possessive apostrophe, as it refers to the plurality of family members of this close and managerially hands-on dynasty, going back some 137 years.

Britain's second-biggest grocery brand after Coca-Cola, and the UK's biggest baker, had a turnover of £520 million in 2012, and now boasts a current share of around a quarter of the British bakery market. The company sells more than 2 million loaves, buns, and crumpets *every single day*, and family wealth is put at the half-a-billion mark by the 2011 *Sunday Times* Rich List.

Impressive though they may be, those statistics tell only one side of the success story, and not the side that matters most to Warburton. He is stressing the eponymous values even before he sits down. Indeed, where this brand is concerned, the family endorsement has turned into a declaration of intent: 'We care because our name's on it', says the advertising, and the same claim is also on the front page of the website (personally signed, just for good measure).

This is the second dynasty that we have visited, after the Sainsbury family. The latter's first ever shop, 212 miles to the south, had only been going for a few years when Ellen and Thomas Warburton opened their own small shop (only a few hundred yards from where we are now) with financial help from brother George, a cotton-waste merchant...

...which is a posh name for a rag-and-bone man. He had about nine kids, as you did in those days. Bolton had two hundred working cotton

*mills at the turn of the twentieth century, and as in all the industrial
towns, the posh people lived on the west because the prevailing wind
blew all the smoke the other way... June 1876 was when the shop
started, which was the month that General Custer was killed at the
battle of the Little Bighorn. Now, how many businesses were started in
1876 and are still here?*

The Warburton pair were then joined by one of George's nine-or-so kids,
Henry, who would turn out to be the critical player in the drama – a smart
and forward-thinking teenager, who in time would become the skilled
and pioneering baker on site, and the one with the expansive business
acumen too. With loaves in ovens and fingers in pies, before long there
was very little left to stop the man. He became a magistrate, chairman of
the Sewerage Committee (there's status for you), the town's mayor, the
owner and chairman of Bolton Wanderers football club, a Liberal politician, a freemason Lodge Master, and he even holidayed in the Caribbean.
Apropos of the football, his wife had form too. She once had the temerity
to wonder out loud what all the fuss was about when it came to scoring
penalties, and the team's trainer suggested that she didn't know what
she was talking about and should try and get one past him while he took
up position in the Burnden Park goalmouth. In the event, she managed
three from five – which these days would probably get her a place in the
England World Cup squad.

*But in time, the business started to lose direction... and it was the
next generation – my grandfather and his twin brother – who ended
up mortgaging their furniture to get the other shareholders to bring the
shares back in. They took over in the 1930s. And then my parents in
the 1950s. And us now for the last 25 years or so.*

It's fairly obvious that we're in the north-west, given the county-sized
grey raincloud sitting outside at ground level because it can't get over
the Pennines – but there's also the unrelenting amiability of folk. The
nice lady who first meets us in reception is keen to ply us with things to

eat and drink, and is already preparing us a co-ordinating set of doggy bags for when we leave. Total strangers keep saying 'hello', and the three family owners themselves beam at us from a large poster near the reception desk, suggesting not only that they care, but actually 'care *more*' (in big letters). It's probably a little too much ebullience for a serious-faced Thomas Warburton, looking down from his 1876 sepia photograph at the top of the stairs, no doubt thinking it's calmer where he is.

Before long, we're collected by Warburton's PA, who whisks us past old Thomas's uncomprehending eyes to meet with his distant descendant, in whose office we get a hearty welcome, and a reassurance that more food and drink will be on its way soon. We sit with him at a circular table in the corner of a reasonably sized room – uncluttered, tidy, and functional, and without showiness. Warburton himself matches the tone, dressed in a respectably managerial plain shirt and tie combo. They do friendliness here, not flamboyance.

For many years, this company only had bakeries in Lancashire and Yorkshire. The main headquarters, where we are now, are at a place called Back o'th' Bank House – a phrase that is a phonological impossibility for anyone who hasn't been using northern glottal stops since infancy. The closest of the bakeries – one of their two in Bolton, both of which Warburton can see from his office window – was opened in 1915. Then, in the 1990s, with demand increasing from the supermarkets, new baking plants were opened outside of the north, in the Midlands and Scotland. By 2006, the company had built its own £60 million super-bakery near Leeds, which is now the largest bakery in Europe. It is an impressive story of expansion, fuelled by a near-obsessive focus on founding-family principles. Warburton is keen to stress this again:

One of the things about great brands – highlighted even more so when your name's over the door – is that the harder you scratch, the more depth there is. To the consumer, in a world that's so transient, the authenticity of the brand is everything. In our case, we're just 600 yards from where the business started in 1876. We're deeply rooted.

As a northerner, I have a chip on both shoulders, which has driven me to get out of bed every morning to put one over on the south of England. I see it as missionary work. I want people all over the UK to eat Warburtons bread.

Warburton is smiling and there's a glint in his eye, so he looks like he's being playful, but not entirely so. This is a company that values its provenance. Being northern doesn't guarantee the right values, or the right products, but it does give a certain credibility to all the talk of honest-to-goodnessness. He spontaneously alludes to another northern brand, the Morrisons supermarket chain, and their eponymous founder, whom he greatly admires. But he also knows that if the north-south cultural divergence theme is overplayed, you set yourself up for pastiche or being criticised for arrogance. He learned that lesson early.

As a child, I had a higher opinion of my origins and our business than they warranted. So the best thing that happened to me was being sent off to boarding school in Somerset, at Millfield... where absolutely nobody had heard of Warburtons or the bread or who the hell we were. And you suddenly realised that maybe you weren't such a big deal after all. Especially when you're next to the sons of Saudi princes and the like.

When it came to my sons, they all went to Eton; one's still there. It's an excellent if unusual school and not at all like it's portrayed. Yes, it's very academic, but it was also the most rounded and eclectic of any school we looked at. In the event, I think that our boys actually quite enjoyed being northerners in a southern school. You either cave in on the back of it – particularly when you come from the sort of industrial north as opposed to the landed north – or you thrive.

I always said that sending the boys down there would be good for them, because it wouldn't half make them proud of the north or certainly aware of the difference. My youngest revels in being a Manchester City fan... and in the notoriety of being the northern lad. His tutor, funnily enough, is from Leeds, and is a big rugby league fan, so they're mates on the back of being the exiled northerners-down-south.

There's plenty to suggest that, in the case of the Warburtons' brand, the 'missionary' zeal has been balanced perfectly, because the nation has turned a regional success into the UK market leader. Now, there are signs of a different kind of expansion, and there has been a recent move into new product areas such as pitta chips and gluten-free baking. National bread sales have been plateauing, so this is not altogether a surprise. In the past, Warburton has said that he would only diversify in this way if he could be sure that the consumer wouldn't 'think we're bonkers if we do it'. He is not a man to take unnecessary risks with his brand's credibility.

It's all about my reputation – and Brett's and Ross's. That job is an ongoing one and never finishes. Preserving that reputation. Part of our job now, over the next decade, is to attract well-educated, experienced family members to look at coming into the business and keeping it successful.

So many family businesses collapse on the back of ineptitude in the family members, thinking they have a right because their name's on it. I would love it if my children were interested enough to join the company, but no manager will want to work for them if they're not sufficiently experienced and able, irrespective of their surnames. If they're not good enough, then they won't be able to attract the best talent to work with them in that business.

My dad was never a great advice-giver, but one of the things he said was to surround yourself with people who are better than you – just don't necessarily tell them. If you look at a lot of very successful people, behind them or in front of them or by the side of them will usually be some very, very able professional managers. Those kinds of people are attracted to an environment where they see long-term thinking, well-invested. That is what we try to do and need to continue to try and do.

In the past, he has gone on record as saying that he will not give his children an easy, guaranteed, 'inherited life'. He's not going to go soft and make an exception to the prove-yourself-first succession formula now. He recalls his own case, and how, at first, he showed no 'burning desire' to even join the family firm. His view is that if any of the children came into the business prematurely, it would be a disaster for all concerned. It doesn't seem a pressing concern, because, for the moment, his elder daughter is enjoying a successful fashion career in London, and isn't likely to return any time soon. But all the cousins see it as a duty of ownership to make sure that the succession, when it happens, works properly and effectively, with the business coming first.

At the same time, Warburton talks of the sense of inevitability that eventually brought him into the company. He recounts an early memory, involving him 'coming in here on a Sunday morning with my sister and fighting on the flour sacks while my dad went round and looked at the bread'. The business had been in the collective memory of the cousins from a very early age, and even though each of them did other things at various times in their careers, they all returned to the family firm – where you could probably say they belonged.

But Jonathan Warburton was always the more anomalous:

I wasn't an academic and I didn't go to university. Brett and Ross and all my school pals went. But me – I messed about for at least a year, trying to work out what to do. I had sort of half-jobs here and there, going on the vans, and then being a rep for Unilever, selling cooking oil and fruit juices, and I lived for 18 months in hotels around the UK. The truth is that the three of us in the family were always motivated by different things.

Soon enough, of course, Warburton would feel no need to prove anything to anyone. In fact, for a long time, probably the main person to whom he had wanted to prove something had been himself anyway. He hands us his business card, and on its reverse is a picture of a whippet and flat cap, which, he tells us, is there to always remind him of where he came from and never to get above himself.

My father's passion was baking, and he also happened to be half-decent at running a business, but that was coincidental. He was a baker first and a businessman second; rather than being a businessman who baked. I would be the latter: somebody who loves the cut and thrust of business and accepts what makes us good. Brett more than anybody is the true baker, but his background was very much a production guy anyway. But we all care about it.

Brett's 57 and I'm 55 and Ross is 54. As an extended family, we knew each other well. My father and Brett's father were brothers and Ross's father was their cousin, but they lived within a mile of each other. The families even owned a house together in the south of France. I mean, Brett, Ross, and I would never consider buying a house together. They probably did it in those days because that's what they could afford. But they did do that kind of thing. They all went to Harvard as well to do PMDs or that kind of thing.

On cue, Ross enters the office. There's no ceremony, and indeed, not much of a knock, suggesting a kind of ongoing open-door policy among the family board members. These guys are close: you could imagine them sharing a single bowl of soup together if circumstances dictated. In the event, he just has a short question for his cousin, fired from the doorway, and quickly heads off again.

With a PPE (Philosophy, Politics, and Economics) degree from Oxford, Ross became a City investment manager, before taking over as the Warburtons' executive chairman in 1991. He is also director of OnSide, a youth charity working in the north-west. With an MBE for services to the food industry, Ross has recently assumed the role of chairman of the Institute for Family Business, a non-aligned lobby group, which has seen him out and about extolling the virtues of the homespun commercial model. 'In the face of global economic downturn and widespread uncertainty about jobs and prospects, governments and policymakers are struggling to find the elusive elixir of growth,' he wrote in *The Independent*. 'Yet in many cases,' he continued, 'family firms are outperforming other businesses – a testament to their strength and resilience.' He might easily have been talking about his own company. And probably was.

The older cousin, Brett, graduated in Economics and Social History from the University of Kent at Canterbury, which many years later awarded him an honorary doctorate. He started his professional career in the flour business at Rank Hovis McDougall, then worked at the Warburton's Soreen and Bakewell subsidiary bakeries. In 1983, he left for Harvard. Since returning to Bolton, he has become the vice-chairman of Bolton Wanderers and is also chairman of the Lancashire FA. The three men are joined on the Warburtons' board by another family member, Jill Kippax, Jonathan's sister, and the company's corporate affairs director.

Jonathan came into the company at the age of 23, in time becoming national account manager, then sales director, before taking on the marketing director's role. In this latter position, perhaps more than in all the others, he would need to do rather a lot of learning on the job – and do it quickly.

It would have been about 1980. I sat at home one Sunday afternoon on my own and wrote a script for a new ad. I had never, ever set foot in an advertising agency, but I thought, 'This can't be that difficult,' which it wasn't. It was for a product called Health Grains and it did quite well. But some time after that, I thought to myself, 'Actually, what I'm doing is ridiculous. Do ad agencies bake their own bread or do they go to a baker? What on earth are we playing at?' So I contacted the Advertising Agency Register, who gave us a list of about five agencies.

And the staggering thing was that only one returned my phone call: a guy called Chris Still who used to be a part of Still Price Court Twivy D'Souza. He was the only one that bothered to get back to me, and so we went from there.

I was single, and in my mid twenties, so having an excuse to go to London was fantastic. It would've been easier if we'd gone to a Manchester agency, but that was nothing like as glamorous as going to London and spending time in a West End agency.

There had been talk about the Canadian wheat programme as the real essence of the brand, which as a technical point was true, but the creative director turned round to me and said, 'That's probably the most boring story I've ever heard. The only thing that's interesting is that you're a family business.' I could see this, because in fresh food and things like bread, it's just a warm product, so it would make sense that a family would care more about it. And then the agency said, 'So we'd like to use your mother and father in the ads.'

Warburton looks back at himself at that time and says that he was a 'callow youth', far too cheeky for his own good, but now discombobulated by a sharp London ad-man questioning his creative acumen. His parents – Derrick and Joyce – saw this and chose to help him out. They were retired, but agreed to become temporary actors, on the condition that they would be allowed to make fun of themselves. In those days, the two main proprietorial advertising campaigns featured the American president of Remington Inc, Victor Kiam ('I liked the shaver so much, I bought the company'), and Norfolk turkey tycoon, Bernard Matthews ('they're bootiful'), neither of whom was intentionally comic, yet each a source of some ridicule from domestic audiences. The new Warburton commercials – featuring the strapline 'Bakers, born and bred' – set out, from the beginning, to be tongue-firmly-in-cheek, with Mrs Joyce Warburton (*'only* a member of the family by marriage' says the voice-over) shown cremating a loaf.

So that's what drove us into the self-effacing, typically northern, typically British, kind of humour. We made three ads for literally £20,000. They were all done in a white room, and there was nothing glamorous about the sets at all.

Nor was there anything glamorous about the three cousins succeeding to the actual running of the company in 1991, at a time when the operation could not unfairly be described as being in quite a state. As an example, much of the business did not even have the Warburtons brand name on it – including over a hundred high street bakery shops.

My father was 63 and he wanted to retire, and his two brothers sort of said that they wanted to retire as well. And his cousin, Ross's father, who was the most entrepreneurial of them all, felt that there was no way he could've been left on his own. So they all went, leaving in place my father's managing director, Jim Speak, and his team, who then held our hands for about five years, which we needed.

We used to have a very diverse business. We had the large retail bakery shop business, a cake business, we had a meat pie business, but then we also had an engineering business, we had a fish farm, we had a jewellery business, and we had a 50% share in a health spa in Boston, Massachusetts. We made car number plates, because we had a lot of trucks. The fish farm was the most stupid. No, actually it was the jewellery business. Some management consultant or other had come in and said that if we understood High Street baking, we'd understand about High Street retailing, and we needed something with a bit more value.

I think there'd been a real worry over the threat of nationalisation, hence this rush for diversification and looking at the investment in the States. That was driven by a Harvard professor who was a non-exec director for ten years, and he used to come over for every other board meeting, which for a Bolton-based business in the 1980s was pretty radical stuff. But it had left a chaotic range of things we were involved with.

In Warburton's words, 'we were very concerned about the future. We thought about what we were good at and it was bread'. Essentially, the trademark waxed-paper wrapped loaves were the thing that *had* to work well. Anything else was a distraction. A plan to move into crisps was axed (although paradoxically, Warburton now thinks that this might not have been such a bad idea after all), among other areas of product diversification that, it was felt, ought to be abandoned in the interests of a rigorous focus.

As they moved forward, the Warburtons would soon meet different types of problems and resistance – ones that came as a result of growth – and they would have to be increasingly inventive with their solutions. Business on the scale being envisaged can never be easy; success never certain. Recently, there have been major fires at two of the company's sites, which caused huge damage, but from which recovery was thankfully rapid – testimony of the ability of the company and its workforce to deal with the unexpected (including, in the case of the fires, some remarkable heroics from employees). As Warburton is so fond of saying, 'You're never there.'

Inevitably, as the company has expanded, not everyone has been delighted. A case in point came in 2003, when Warburtons opened its eleventh bakery, in Enfield. It was a pioneering, 200,000 square foot, £54 million, state-of-the-art venture. Yet just to show that you can't please everyone:

Tesco had a formidable and extremely able trading director, called John Gildersleeve – in fact, I was with him yesterday, as his guest in the Wolds, so we've become pals over time. John's a very able, if rather intimidating, individual. I'd gone to see him, and he gave me the biggest bollocking of my career. It came down to the fact that we'd built this bakery in Enfield, five miles from Tesco's offices at Cheshunt, without having the decency to ask him if it was all right. That was the gist of the bollocking. And the only thing I said back to him in my defence during that meeting was, 'Well, John, we're clearly not going to agree on this – but it is my money!'

Over the last seven years, the company has invested £300 million, building new bakeries, upgrading others, and improving lines of distribution – and threatening the competition – with the result that external perceptions of the company have changed. Warburtons now commands far more commercial respect; and certainly elicits a lot more competitive attention – perhaps even envy. The brand imagery and values may still be identifiably northern, but there is nothing parochial about UK-wide market leadership.

Around 2007, all of a sudden, we woke up and realised that, in revenue terms, we were truly national: the biggest British grocery brand –

and only Coca-Cola, which of course isn't British, is bigger than us. It was a by-product of the success rather than the motivation behind it. But the consequence was that we'd suddenly come onto everybody's radar. Then, I think you have to accept that people will start to throw a few stones at you, although it's not been too bad, because we're not that flashy.

I'd always been confident in us succeeding: partly borne out of naivety, and partly borne out of the fact that what we do is simply the right thing. As long as we were able to stay sensible on pricing. Which is easier said than done. Gone are the days when you could influence pricing on-shelf; when you would sit down in a room with other bakers and have a conversation about price.

To most people, most of the time, we're worth a premium, because it's fresher when you buy it and it'll stay fresher over time; and because of the quality of the ingredients we use and the baker who produces them. And with baking in Scotland, the north-east, Yorkshire, Lancashire, West Midlands, East Midlands, south-west, south-east, nobody else has got that footprint, with all these bloody wagons that cost us £5 million a year. Now if you want to take a load of cost out of the business, you would rationalise your distribution fleet. But if, like us, your motivation is to get fresher product to the consumer, you accept it is part of the business model.

And then it's my job to convince the consumer it's worth paying a bit more. Not a ridiculous amount. Maybe not 1p a slice, but halfpence a slice. Maybe in recent times we've not got that message across to consumers with the clarity that we needed to.

Hovis and Kingsmill were slow to notice the success of Warburtons – despite the fact that they'd been supplying more and more flour to their northern rival. Now, with around 4,300 people working in the business, the company no longer slips under the radar. When the General Election was called in 2010, David Cameron's first public visit in the UK was to this site. Bolton West and Bolton North East were key marginal seats, and, at the time, the Conservative Party was keen to be seen making its first visit of the campaign to a company operating outside of the south of England. Warburtons was the obvious port of call. Cameron delivered one of his sleeves-rolled-up speeches to the company workers with pallet-loads of Medium Sliced White piled high in the background – providing the kind of peak-hour television exposure for the brand that, as commissioned advertising, would have cost a fortune.

None of us are members of any political faction, but both Brett and Ross know local people politically. But Bolton West is a barometer, like Basildon, so if you win Bolton West you tend to win the election. We got a phone call, asking if David Cameron could come to see us and do a Q&A with our workforce.

Ross and I had half-an-hour in here with Cameron and then he went up to our Variety bakery up the road where he did the Q&A. They put our blue packaging in the background. It was something we advised them against, because we thought it might look contrived, but politicians are politicians, and they wanted to do it their way.

Then there was the Queen's visit. She was brilliant. Her people approached us – we didn't ask for her to come – which was a great honour. She was already planning to be in the area; but even so. The High Sheriff told me that he'd never had a request to go somewhere from the Palace before. She was wonderful. And he [the Duke of Edinburgh] was great as well. He's good fun; really lovely chap; always just being himself.

Warburton certainly places a premium on being *himself*. His belief in family businesses is based on the *personal* responsibility that comes from having the family name over the door or on the advertising (although, perhaps the fact that there are the three cousins makes this less lonely an experience than it might have been had there been just the one, and which might be a significant factor in this firm's success). He is quick to point out that the responsibility – and pressure – has also been felt by his wife, Kim, who he says has been hugely supportive through the good times and the bad.

Personal responsibility is, Warburton argues, different from personal *celebrity*, which doesn't impress him and which, he suggests, may actually diminish responsibility.

One of the criticisms I would have of our taxation system and of Britain in general, is that entrepreneurs that build businesses but then quickly sell them are regarded as heroic. It's the culture in the UK to admire the people who've done little, maybe got a bit lucky, made their quick money, sold the business. Whereas, if you go to Germany, the Mittelstand system encourages entrepreneurs to grow the business over time and rewards longevity. This is something that Britain needs more of.

If what you're really after is the quick money, then your motivation's different. This culture that we're in today where it seems to be all about the fame – the X Factor thing. It's this something-for-nothing thing; it's the celebrity culture that is really undermining what true work and success is really about.

And as part of that, I think society has then assumed that all successful people are greedy and only doing it for the money – not doing it for the fact that it's a really enjoyable way of spending your time and, hopefully, usefully employing people. You have to reward success, but do it properly. The more difficult you make it, the more punitive you are with your tax, the more you create barriers to enterprise. I really struggle with the fact that the state thinks it knows better than me. I don't try and tell the politicians how to run their lives and they should bloody well leave me alone because I'm a decent human being who employs a lot of people, and has spent £400 million in capital in a decade investing in Britain. Let us alone and let us invest and let us go on and make that as easy as possible.

There are ambitious plans in the pipeline, including an aspiration to become one of the world's best family food businesses. Ross has spoken about being both ambitious and prudent, and 'nimble and innovative', and there is a new enthusiasm for diversification into products like snacks and 'free-from' ranges.

Our premise has been to do the opposite of what everybody else does. At one time, we were the only plant-baker in the country who didn't make private label [manufacturing a product for sale under another company's name]. Everybody else did. But why would I want to do private label, because the cost base is higher anyway? So that wasn't some kind of great strategic thinking.

We saw our future in building a great brand that had our family name over the door. To some extent, it's self-fulfilling, because you're far more bothered if it's your name than if it's another name. I couldn't work for anybody else. I've been a non-exec director of a couple of businesses for a long time and I've found them fascinating, interesting, and hopefully I've helped along the way, but I view them so differently than my own business with my own name.

Recently, Warburton has stepped down from a directorship with A. G. Barr, the drinks company that makes Irn-Bru. That move coincided with Warburtons posting a fall in profits (despite the £3 million increase in turnover), so perhaps he felt it was time for him to spend more time where he well and truly belonged.

When I've taken on the day-to-day chief executive role here, there've been many elements of it that I've thoroughly enjoyed. And hopefully, I've added a bit of value to the business. But, in time, I can easily see an orderly transition from a full-time executive to perhaps non-executive chairman for me. In the foreseeable future – but not just yet. I actually think it would be wrong for the business and wrong for me as an individual for the moment. But I would certainly be prepared.

Warburton is, by normal standards, a very wealthy man: 'Not short of cash', he calls it. At the same time, he adds that he is not 'a big collector of stuff'.

What wealth gives you is choice. If Jack and Harry were playing rugby in London, I would arrange a dinner on that night and go down and watch them. That's a privilege you can have – to choose what you do with your own time. I think the only thing that I still sometimes yearn for is private travel. I don't do it now, but I have done it in the past, because travelling is such a stressful experience.

Nowadays, if you ask me what I do, I still say I'm a baker. That never changes. I was talking to somebody last week who had met Sam Vestey, Lord Vestey, at the House of Lords. She was having a cigarette on the balcony and he came out and she said, 'What do you do?' and he said, 'I'm a butcher.' And she replied, 'Funnily enough, I've got a good mate who's a baker...'

The taxi driver is waiting downstairs, half-visible in the ground-level raincloud. It's time to conclude the discussion and leave the bakers and Bolton, with our doggy bags in hand. The town is an acquired taste, that's for sure. But Warburton has a taste for it, and he'll not be moving out to Barbados just yet. Even when that day comes, you sense his departure will be a gradual, rather than sudden, one. 'You can take the lad out of Bolton, but you can't take the Bolton out of the lad,' he is fond of saying.

His other favourite expression is: 'When you get there, there's no *there* there.' It means, ultimately, that there is no stopping place for this memorable family dynasty and their proud, successful company, replete with northern character and determination – predictable, but no less valuable because of that. This has not felt like an interview with one man. It has felt more like an interview with a name and with ghosts of the people who had that name – and a presage of those who one day will shoulder the responsibility that comes with that name and take this company further still.

People who care.

Like family.

———

'This above all: to thine own self be true,
And it must follow as the night the day
Thou canst not then be false to any man.
Farewell, my blessing season this in thee.'

WILLIAM SHAKESPEARE (*HAMLET*)

———

EPILOGUE

What's in a name?

The first decade or so of the twenty-first century has seen more than its fair share of vacuous celebrity. It is sometimes difficult to know which is the greater cruelty: having to put up with talent-show wannabes on their brief ascent; or watching them plunge back into obscurity immediately afterwards, doomed to a life of D-list indignity, with its tawdry paraphernalia of ballroom dancing, kangaroo-testicle eating, cat imitation, and pig masturbation. But it's not just reality TV and talent shows that are responsible for the feculent glut of micro-celebrity. Social media now means you don't even need to appear on TV to attain a modicum of notoriety. One tweet, and any fool can have the Fourth Estate beating a path to his or her door, condemning and publicising in equal measure.

There is, however, one area of public life that seems to have become less celebrity-conscious and more inclined to anonymity. These days you'll find fewer and fewer bankers or chief executives battling for publicity or thrusting themselves too willingly into the limelight. Instead, a more sober, low-key approach prevails: a brief interview on the *Today* programme about the annual results (hopefully without a hectoring cross-examination from John Humphrys or Evan Davis, and before sensible people have woken up), and then back to the relative obscurity of the boardroom.

After the many falls from grace – from Fred the Shred to the unfolding Murdoch saga – it is perhaps understandable that many in big business now prefer a lower profile, away from any potentially awkward glare. What we hadn't expected to find was a similar level of self-effacement and reticence among the new generation of entrepreneurs and brand founders. Yet here too, it seems, publicity isn't what it used to be.

Indeed, one of this book's unintended findings is how the tradition of the eponymous brand seems to be in decline. From the nineties onwards there has been a switch in favour of founders who consciously avoid a brand name that has anything to do with them personally. We may know the identity of the people behind Carphone Warehouse, Pret a Manger, Gü, and Innocent, but there is no clue as to who they may really be from the names under which they have chosen to trade. And the safety of anonymity may not be the only reason why they have kept themselves detached. Since they were formed, so many of these businesses have changed ownership, sold out, or gone public that one is left to wonder whether there was ever quite the same level of personal commitment as in the cases where the founder's name was chiselled over the door. Perhaps they were always more of a commercial exercise than a personal endeavour. Perhaps those businesses are different from the eponymous kind we encountered.

Which brings us to this epilogue and what we can finally say about these very different individuals. What prompted them to put their name, and not just their wallet, on the line? And what motivations, instincts, and idiosyncracies do they share? The temptation could have been to avoid altogether trying to comprehend the incomprehensible. Yet this collection of tales, with their audacity, non-conformity, and innovation, can hardly be left without some kind of unifying comment; even if we must also put up with the continual threat of each individual, by definition, being an exception to a rule.

Uncommon commonalities

Here, then, by way of a final reflection on our Branded Gentry, are six themes that might reasonably be said to run through our collected experiences, to a greater or lesser extent.

1. Defining moments

There are *defined* moments in life – your first day at school, your first kiss, your first girlfriend or boyfriend, your first job, etc. These are the moments we all share. They define us in the same way that they define everyone else. They are universal and predictable.

Then there are *defining* moments – which come out of the blue and which apply only to you personally; arbitrary events, moments of coincidence and timing, of luck or loss, of clarity or danger. At any moment of any day, each and every one of us is surrounded by this Brownian motion of chance. Much of the time, it does not make itself known to us. Sometimes it does.

Without the misfortune of a terrible cycling accident, it is unlikely that Paul Smith would have fallen in with the art school crowd among whom he found his lifelong muse. Had Maurice or Charles been around to take the call, the chances are that Tim Bell would never have become Margaret Thatcher's campaign manager. Had James Dyson not lost his father at such an early age, he may never have felt the drive to refuse the obvious, to question, and thus, to invent. On the positive side of the coin, Lord Sainsbury frequently references his lucky moments, as does Julian Richer, and they do so confident that this in no way diminishes the magnitude of their achievements. But the significance lies not in these moments themselves, rather in the way our people reacted to them.

Everyone has some degree of adversity in their life, and our interviewees had their fair share (or more) of personal illness, family difficulties, financial troubles, and other hardships. But their tendency was to react to resistance by pushing harder; by running faster.

It is easy to see, in these people, evidence of their 'antifragility' (if we can borrow the expression famously coined by Nassim Taleb): the phenomenon of growing stronger from being hurt. It is the business-world version of natural selection. Each time they took a knock, or were faced with an unexpected dilemma, or made a mistake, they seemed to emerge the stronger for it. Johnnie Boden was cleaned out by one of his colleagues; Emma Bridgewater got to the stage where she very nearly broke under the pressure of running business and family together; Tony Laithwaite became embroiled in a struggle for ownership of his own company. There were many instances such as these, and each time, the person gained strength from the challenges thrown at them. Taleb argues that, in contrast, systems designed to avoid risk and insulate from danger only succeed in creating an illusion of safety and will ultimately be the more fragile – whereas those optimised by random blows, such as we have described, will usually be better equipped for survival and success.

One can see this in the way our people dealt with bad luck. Whenever they got a bad throw, they'd simply rolled the dice again – and again, if necessary – until the right number came up. It was telling how some of our subjects eventually learned to harness the very thing that made them different: James Dyson's solitary focus; Jackie Cooper's social attunement, Julian Richer's finding an alternative to school sport... They turned their anomalies to their advantage.

And this reaction was not confined to bad luck either. Our interviewees could sense a raindrop of opportunity when it touched their face, and didn't interrogate it so much that it evaporated back into thin air. They saw chances that others simply might not recognise. Sometimes they did this impetuously; sometimes with the budding entrepreneur's eye. Robert Hiscox ignored the safety-first advice of his consultants. Emma Bridgewater had to visit a supplier in Stoke-on-Trent and, barely off the train, saw a town replete with potential.

Lesser folk move along, fearful of risk, or lazy in effort, and complain about never having been given the chance. Look around: the truth is that, wherever you are at this moment, there may well be chances and opportunities surrounding you, decaying by the second before they slip into the half-life of unfulfilled promise. One day, each of our interviewees defied this protocol and stuck their entrepreneurial neck out, waiting for the consequence.

2. The business of being yourself

So our people took their chances when they came – and this decisiveness is undoubtedly a key ingredient of their success. However, the idea that they all came into the world with a special success-gene could not be further from the truth. Indeed, some of them spent years riddled with insecurity, worrying about whether they were up to the demands of being a schoolteacher or shopkeeper, let alone a successful entrepreneurial

pioneer. In such cases, their self-worth took years of cultivation and con-
solidation – and some, even now, still have those moments in the night
when the doubt-demons come.

Few had anything like an encouragingly normal background, if by
normal we mean being raised by both parents in moderately comfortable, uneventful circumstances. A number recalled not having had much
money, and of pressure put on a (sometimes) single parent. James Dyson
said he had heard the statistic that about 80% of British prime ministers
came, like him, from the 10% of families where the father died before the
children were ten years old. Other interviewees spoke of a dysfunctional
family environment or conflicting temperaments in the family home or
bullying at school.

Racing through childhood, our interviewees had more than enough
to stop them getting complacent or thinking their life-path was going to
be a smooth one – or that they had a special gift for success. Yet, despite
forces that may have tried to undermine or ambush them, from their
early years, our branded gentry often knew instinctively that they were
going *to do their own thing*. Some, like Tim Bell, refused to allow any
early expedient job or half-right business to deflect them from a chosen
course. Others, like Paul Smith, were driven by a singular aim (in his
case, to be a professional cyclist), but when that option was blocked,
quickly replaced it with another, to be pursued with equal determination.
Jonathan Warburton ploughed the thick end of £500 million into taking
his brand from a regional success story into a national one. Our people
were imbued with the sense – whether they would express it in these
terms or not – that their 'job' actually was in *the business of being themselves* (and signing the promise with their name).

That was their purpose in life. They didn't go out into the world to
fit in with it. One way or another, they set out to make the world fit
them. Maybe that's why, more than anything else, their name went over
the door. Life tries to paint each one of us into a corner. And as people
learn things about us, so it is too easy to accept their version of events.
We all suffer from this social and professional typecasting. Friends,
colleagues, parents, the world – they inadvertently condition us in what

we're supposed to be, and especially what we are not supposed to be. Like us, the people in our interviews were told on many an occasion, by word or circumstance, *what they were not* – and sometimes in the harshest of ways. But by way of reply, they chose instead to prove *what they were.*

3. Un-control freaks

They say that powerful personalities exist on a spectrum that goes from enigmatic to charismatic; from implicit to explicit. Many of our interviewees may now seem to be firmly seated at the charismatic end of things, needing little encouragement to give their world view (sometimes in the press), and to explain what they value and admire, as well as what they disapprove of and oppose. They have earned the right, at work at least, to live in a world largely of their own making; in a culture and a value system that is largely an extension of themselves. If you wanted to be pejorative, you might say there is more than a little of the god complex in this state of affairs. But if you were to think that this means that they feel omniscient or omnipotent, or that they are determined to impose themselves on others, you'd be wrong. In fact, the opposite applies.

Strong people like these need to believe in themselves. And back themselves over what they feel is right. Tim Bell and Robert Hiscox, to name two, are not slow to challenge (on record) some of the most powerful figures in the land. But not every determined individual is motivated to project their beliefs on to what they do and, indeed, onto those whom they employ.

You can, no doubt, be a great lawyer or engineer or scholar and never really look beyond yourself or the job you do. Indeed, many successful people make a point of separating their private lives from their commercial lives: when they go home, they can be themselves, in contrast to when they're in the office, where they perform a role that is, largely, defined *for* them. Given the abundance of workplace regulations and Human Resource protocols that have grown up over the years, it is arguably ever more difficult to show your true personality at work – to exhibit flair, take risks, be intuitive or non-conformist. The rising tide of rules, standards, and systems literally require compliance. They were, perhaps, originally intended to prevent the despotism of the boss, but have ironically become a kind of despotism in their own right.

Which may explain the reluctance of a new generation of brand founders to become too prominent in the businesses they start; avoiding putting their name to their enterprise just in case the personal and the public become too blurred – too interlaced to legislate for – in today's on-message business environment. It results in the phenomenon whereby some brand names that appear to represent real people are in fact masquerades – faux personalities designed to evoke the lifestyle of an illusory founder without any *real* person taking the gamble; names like Jack Wills, Ted Baker, Crabtree & Evelyn, Abercrombie & Fitch, et al.

Between these and our eponymous brands, there is more than a semantic difference. When a teacup – or a vacuum cleaner or a loaf of bread – has got your name on it then you'd better be sure you believe in it, because, if it's found wanting, it will be you and not a holding company that's castigated. As the Warburton's tag line would say, 'We care because our name's on it'; and as Freddy Heineken remarked, 'I consider a bad bottle of Heineken a personal insult.' When James Dyson was told by a sales assistant that the gauge of his plastic was inferior to that of a rival, he produced a ball-peen hammer and told her to try and smash his eponymous machine to pieces. Go ahead: make my day.

But the eponymous founder's self-belief is a much bigger deal than mere quality control. In fact, quality control is little more than an output of something more deeply seated, and that is the ethos or culture of the company. This ethos is predominantly a direct expression of the values and beliefs of the founder. In one way or another it is an expression of self. To which end, everyone has his or her own style, inculcated over the years. Some of our individuals command an almost cult-like status, acting as corporate oracles. Some are draconian; some familiar and paternalistic, cultivating the sense of an extended family. One or two are simply eccentric, looking for the same borderline barminess in those around them. But they all have a conviction in what they are doing. Not unquestioned, or necessarily self-righteous, and built more through hard-won experience than from an entrepreneurial training manual. There is no easy or quick way to acquire this self-belief – just *a* way.

Unlike some other captains of industry, most of our interviewees were not interested in control for its own sake or in taking things over. They have remained studiously ungeared (see below) and are not driven by the need for relentless growth or corporate scale. There were a couple of exceptions to this rule, and you may guess who such exceptions were from the texts but, for the most part, our subjects showed surprisingly little impulse to be in control of everything, or indulge in micromanagement. Indeed, more often, they embrace chaos – perhaps at times even courting it, instinctively attracted by risk more than safety.

Except when it comes to debt. Nearly all of our people claimed a fierce and visceral loathing of it, seeing it as a near-fatal enemy. It lives with you, over you, all day long – it even comes to bed with you. It can kill your freedom, make you ill, and affect family and friends. It can cripple countries and companies alike. Debt represents the antithesis of everything these people believe in. And not surprisingly, several remembered the gorgeous moment when they finally had a cleared cheque to give to their creditor, getting back their liberty by getting back into the black. Their advice: if at all possible, stay there.

For most of the time, however, our people have gambled on their instincts and backed themselves personally, and they'd like to see more people doing the same. They relish the idea of a world full of other chaotic particles like them ricocheting around – a world more in their own image, admittedly, but only in the sense of being more individualistic, fallible, and adventurous. They are not scared of failures or flaws. They display vulnerability. They ride their luck. They are instinctive and quixotic. More often, however, many actually seem like *un*-control freaks.

Hence their names over the doors, because eponymity is one more risk to take: one more piece of personal responsibility that did not have to be staked.

4. Parents, partners, and pets

It would be easy to fall into the trap of thinking that our people are such independent, self-sufficient souls, that they always want to go it alone. Perhaps there is a sliver of truth in this, but almost all our interviews included moments where the discussion turned to the importance of support, be it practical, financial, or emotional. In fact, it makes you wonder if the kind of person we have here – shouldering what at times can be a very lonely burden of responsibility – actually requires more support than most.

Parents came into the discussions spontaneously on various occasions – and cathartically too. Mothers and fathers may love you, and you may love them, but they can mess you up as well – as we were sometimes told in no uncertain terms. Some of our people adored their parents and some did not. Some parents had been encouraging about their offspring's entrepreneurial ambitions; others deeply sceptical. Whatever the circumstances and rationale, there was plenty of talk of what late parents might have thought nowadays, if they could have seen their son or daughter in the fullness of their achievements. Sometimes, it felt like a case of the subjects wanting wistfully to raise a head and whisper, 'I did it for you, Daddy'; at other times, it was more like a fist being raised and a cry of, 'Now will you finally be satisfied?' Sometimes, it was a conflicted combination of both.

There was more discussion about the significance of marital support. Several interviewees wanted it on record how their partners had been the difference between make and break. This is anything but the gentle hum of a spouse keeping the home warm or the children fed while the real breadwinner does the hard and important entrepreneurial pedalling. Rather, it was the story of the partner, at one time or another, being the only remaining thing between survival and catastrophe: partners who, in many cases, had a huge influence on the success of the business, especially in the early days: partners who were the first place to go for support and advice, and who still are.

Most of the interviewees had been through periods in their careers when help was not only desired, but absolutely essential, whatever its form, whether coming from family, friends, or even pets. It was interesting the number of our people who added pets to the list of emotional leaning-posts. In Johnnie Boden's case, one decided to attend the interview. Sprout, Shaggie, Smudge, Midge, Otter, Mabel, Dottie... It feels like there's often one snuffling around somewhere at the back of the narrative. A wet nose tends to put the most fiendish of business dilemmas into perspective.

So our interviewees were invariably dependent on others at different times in their careers. It's the cliché of the person behind the person – but no less accurate for being a cliché. It is fashionable to rail against dependency culture, but be careful those who do. Because, it seems, we all depend on someone.

5. Succession

For these entrepreneurs, putting their own name over the door seemed to be the best way to demonstrate commitment. Your name; your responsibility; your head on the promise to the bearer. In fact, in Julian Richer's case, when a customer enters any one of his shops, they will actually see his photograph as well as reading his name; in Emma Bridgewater's case, when the brand was shortened to only her surname, she felt that this wasn't enough and insisted on 'Emma' being reintroduced; David Linley went in the opposite direction, feeling that the surname was the only thing that mattered (partly because a friend reminded him that 'Linley' was literally his maker's mark). But in most cases, by representing themselves through their own name – in whatever form – they were denoting just how much they were their firm and their firm was them: the implication (or maybe it's a post-rationalisation, but we don't believe that) being that success is, in some way, linked to this form of commitment.

But what, then, happens, when they move on? When they sell the company, or simply want – or need – to retire? In the majority of our interviews, the discussion of succession came up spontaneously, and was usually something that they had in varying degrees considered – some more sentimentally than others, it has to be said. However, there was always the realisation that retirement from brand guardianship might be spent either smiling with satisfaction or as a discontented ghost – and no one can know which of those futures will materialise until it is too late to amend it. That, above all, is why passing on your brand – and choosing your successor – can be the most nerve-racking enterprise of all.

Perhaps for that reason, some of our people did not want to think about it too long: James Dyson and Johnnie Boden, just to name two, were too busy and preoccupied to be worrying about a succession strategy.

For others, answering the question had been difficult and sometimes troubling. Laithwaite, Hegarty, and Hiscox, for example, all spoke of the tugged heartstrings when handing over the running of their company to someone else – no matter how necessary this was, or how skilled the new person in charge. In some cases, they solved this conundrum by letting go very slowly: perhaps by gradually reducing their shareholding, such as David Linley; or just changing management roles – although, in Tony Laithwaite's case, all that did was to bring conflict between the newcomer, wanting to try new things, and the founder, wedded to a certain way of doing old things. In the British high street, we have seen how this has led to the odd non sequitur, such as with the Jo Malone brand, owned by Estée Lauder since 1999, and which the eponymous founder left in 2006 to eventually develop her own competitor named Jo Loves.

The obvious answer is to get the kids to take over. In some ways, this seemed to offer the ideal, traditional, and most honest solution, keeping the business in the family as it were. Although actually not so obvious, as it turns out: Julian Richer and Paul Smith don't have any children, for a start. Jonathan Warburton felt that the children might in time maintain their baking dynasty – but he qualified this, by saying that he would not give them an easy ride into the business, and that it would only work if they had both the desire and the requisite skills for the task. He remembered his own somewhat lukewarm attitude to that possibility, as a young man intrigued by hotter subjects than bread-making.

Offspring can be expected to have their own very different plans, or may have seen how hard their parents had worked and decided it was not for them. Then, if the son or daughter does take that step and join the firm, think what it must feel like to be that incoming family member – as were Sainsbury and Hiscox, as well as Warburton, at times in their lives – having to deal with learning the ropes, running the enterprise, and above all, living up to expectations from within the family, from the markets, from members of staff, maybe from the customers. Plus, there is always the danger that the ideal answer will turn into the worst answer if the new generation screw up the legacy.

Perhaps for this reason, some of our entrepreneurs took a more philosophical approach and decided that, once they were gone, nothing really mattered: the business would return to the entrepreneurial ashes from which it had been created in the first place. Johnnie Boden saw his company more as a kind of preoccupying interest, to be enjoyed in the present, rather than an infinitely enduring vocation; Emma Bridgewater was, on the other hand, passionately vocational about what she wanted to achieve for her adopted city rather than keeping the company going for its own sake; Julian Richer and Paul Smith wanted, more than anything, to keep having fun (and they didn't have children anyway), as did John Hegarty, whose company is now a part of the Publicis empire. The Laithwaites, meanwhile, talked proudly of their children continuing the vinous, or, at least, alcoholic tradition with two new winemakers and a brewer in the family.

Another model of longevity is to abstract the founder's values from the founder. In the same way that Virgin or Apple might be said to embody a belief system that transcends Richard Branson or Steve Jobs, so Hiscox or Boden or Bridgewater could come to represent an ethos that lives on long after its originator. Let's hope so.

The point is probably that all our people may ask questions, but some have determined not to ask too many (including 'what next?'); instead they just get on and do things. In some cases, the attitude was that when they're no longer here, whatever happens, their eponymous enterprise will be what will be. And by that time, they will be 'unstill' somewhere else.

6. Perpetual energy

Our interviews took around fourteen months to agree, arrange, conduct, write up, and publish. It has been an extraordinary period, during which the world has changed dramatically and, perhaps, so have our subjects. For one thing is certain: the people in this book barely sit still long enough to be interviewed, let alone have any grassy foundations grow under their feet.

When we met with James Dyson, his office (indeed, most of the building) was scattered with possible inventions and ideas, and he found it difficult to stay seated without showing us stuff. Paul Smith barely sat down at all. Tim Bell spent the whole interview multitasking (and smoking). Emma Bridgewater's desk is as crumby and cluttered as her kitchen table, and why not, given what she specialises in? Here were offices that made 221b Baker Street look well organised.

With many of these people, it seems that only the name over the door stays constant; everything else being in a state of flux that reflects how their brains work. A week barely goes by without something happening in the media that involves their entrepreneurialism: James Dyson chastising the government on its business strategy or defending himself against industrial espionage; Robert Hiscox challenging economic policy; Johnnie Boden adding Helena Christensen to his catalogue. ('Yummy mummy backlash,' screams a tabloid again.) By the time you read this, no doubt many of them will be fighting new battles, or devising further new schemes and innovations with which to preoccupy themselves, thereby condemning some of what we describe right now to historical curiosity.

Maybe they know themselves so well and are so set on a restless course that one of the few constants they have to steer by is their own name. They have signed their door and then rushed through it – and through it again; and again... Never, ever stop is the collective mantra.

Most of our subjects are millionaires many times over, and many would not need to lift another finger in employment terms should they so choose. Yet the idea of stopping what they are doing seems incomprehensible; akin to stopping and laying down dead. They aren't bothered about spending money. They just want to expend energy. Rest is for someone else. The rest of us.

Conclusion – above all: to thine own self be true

Clearly, these people's differences marked them out as much as any commonalities. Some believe in God; some don't. Some are part of the establishment; some aren't. Some belong to dynasties; others are self-made. Some grew up with both their parents; some didn't. Some started rich; some started poor. Some started a family; some didn't; others couldn't. Some avoided bad luck; others seemed to encounter nothing but; some didn't give a monkey's. Some have sold off parts of their company; others would rather trade their kidneys.

For all of us, life is a balancing act between taking part in the team and standing out from the crowd. Get this out of kilter in either direction and we become the sheep or the wolf – neither of which is fulfilling or pretty. In some cases, it seemed that our people had struggled to fit in to the common crowd or with the other kids in the playground. Sometimes the standing apart was not so much forced on them as actively sought out, be it through extroversion or eccentricity. Hence the back stories about esoteric choices of musical instruments, singing, acting and dancing, long-distance running, motorbike riding, and buffalo hunting.

However you look at it, these people are anomalies. Relatively famous ones, now, driven on by a mixture of charisma, eccentricity, resilience, and scar tissue. There is a perceptible difference in their demeanour that makes them extraordinary – and it is difficult to know if this came as a function of the success or they succeeded because they always were extraordinary. But if you did meet them in the street without actually knowing who they were, you may well still look at them twice, without necessarily understanding why you did so. Take them on in a staring competition and the chances are that you'd blink first.

As we were drawing up the idea for this book, one of the world's greatest non-eponymous brand pioneers died. Steve Jobs, the feted and iconic founder of Apple, left behind arguably the world's most popular brand. The death of a pope or president would probably have had less global impact. But it also raised the question as to why one of the most controlling and obsessive of brand pioneers left his name off one of the most pioneering of brands. Steve Jobs insinuated his spirit into every atom of the Apple brand's chemistry, and by the time he died, his name and the brand had become practically interchangeable. A tellingly small number of successful entrepreneurs – notably Jobs and Branson (Virgin) – have achieved celebrity status. And they have done it *without* using their own name.

But for the most part, entrepreneurs do not become celebrities. And eponymous entrepreneurs are arguably even more likely to avoid the limelight. Perhaps that is the point. Maybe putting your name over the door is not a route to celebrity-status, but a check against it because, like it or not, you have to be authentic.

As the connected, always-on, real-time world continues on its headlong rush to leave no stone unturned, no bottom unscrutinised, here among the Branded Gentry is one last place where celebrity-status is neither the main currency nor the endgame – and indeed is, if anything, rejected.

It is a salutary place to finish. By putting their actual names up there for scrutiny – not quite in stone or steel, but up there, nonetheless – these people are declaring responsibility: taking ownership of their reputations, at a time when so many modern celebrities are effectively disowning theirs. The people we met may be famous, but they are such a long way removed from what is oxymoronically known as 'celebrity culture' that this, we feel, is the distinction on which to end.

Our people have earned their prestige. They have turned their names not just into something meaningful, but also something profitable, and they have done so through talent and hard work. Even if they tried, they'd be no good at being celebrities because they'd obstinately insist on being who they already are, rather than a version of what others want them to be. We can be sure of this because they didn't simply invest time and money in their businesses. They invested themselves, unconditionally. And that surely is the greatest investment of all.

If the tradition they represent is faltering, let's hope it revives, because the future needs the Branded Gentry just as much as the past. And then some.

ACKNOWLEDGEMENTS

As our interviewees were quick to tell us, taking an idea and turning it into a reality involves a lot of help and the pulling in of a lot of favours. The list below includes some of those who have contributed – in small ways or large – to our own particular venture, and to whom we extend our unconditional thanks.

Nicole Abbott, Roger de Allesandri, Claire Beale, Christine Beardsell, Cassie Billings, Katherine Bishop, Sophie Boden and Sprout, Elizabeth Buchanan, Dan Burn-Forti, Paddy Byng, Antonia Calnan, Olly Calverley, Lucy Campbell, Caroline Cant, Josie Carol, Janie Carruthers, Glenn Caton, Teresa Chapman, Chris Chaundler, Ben Cole, Alexia Constantinou, Lucy Corbishley, Hazel Cross, Lucy Cross, Amy Dabrowski, Una Doyle, Graham Drew, Adam Edwards, Sue Farr, Ed Faulkner, Tearmh France, Victoria Geoghegan, Marian Geraghty, Annie Gregory, Jade Hallam, Jed Hallam, Adele Hanson, Clare Holley, David Holley, Mike Hopper, Jenn Hunter, Nick Lambert, Angie Lee, Jeremy Lee, Julian Mack, Justin Marshall, Emma McCappin, Paul Mead, Loreta Moras, Lauren Myers-Cavanagh, Michelle Nixon, Keith Ormondroyd, Matthew Paton, Robert Phillips, Laura Porter, Jussi Pylkkanen, David Robinson, Chris Satterthwaite, Patricia Savage, Jan Shawe, Elizabeth Snow, Mark Stone, Rory Sutherland, Maxine Thompson, Amelia Torode, Julian Vallance, Martin Vallance, Phoebe Vela, Kirsty Weatherhead, Adele Williams, Peter York, Colette Youell, Conrad Young.

In particular, we would like to thank these people and their specific contributions:

The transcribers at Language Insight, for all their hard work in turning hours of audio recording into something suitable for print.

Bill Scott-Kerr, who in the early stages of the idea helped us penetrate the workings of the publishing industry.

Emily Cooper, PA at VCCP, for her tireless efforts and organisational prowess, and for remaining calm and cheerful at all times (unlike Charles).

Stephanie Brimacombe, for her outstanding contribution to the marketing of our book, and for remaining tall and stylish throughout (unlike David).

Christie's, for their support in myriad ways, including help with marketing, publicity, and their generous hospitality at launch.

The invaluable assistance of Ben Cole and his team in helping us with numerous photographic and art directional challenges – always with such great results.

Chime, VCCP, and H2 Partners, for supporting this project from the start and allowing us the time and freedom to see it through to fruition. We are truly grateful.

Dan Burn-Forti and his team – professionalism, patient, and fun to work with, in equal measure.

Lorne Forsyth, chairman of Elliott & Thompson, who has thrown the support of his company behind the project. Plus Jennie Condell, Ray Hamilton, Alison Menzies, and Alex Spears as part of that excellent team.

And most importantly – our wonderful editor Olivia Bays, who has had to indulge not one but two sensitive egos. She has provided skill and expertise, but added the all-important elements of sensitivity, common sense, and practicality in getting us to where we are now.

So many people were involved over these many months that it will be a miracle if we have not committed the offence of omission at some point, in which case, our insufficient but sincere apologies are offered.

Finally, of course, special mention must be made of the interviewees who entered the project with interest and good nature, and were our perfect hosts for many an hour. Without their contributions, there would be nothing.

INDEX

A. G. Barr 289
ACTS 435 233
Apex 124–25
Apple 14, 133, 144, 256, 259, 305, 307
Armstrong-Jones, David see Linley, David
Asda 199, 224
Audi 132
Audio Partnership 213
Averys of Bristol 171

Baker Tilly International 227
Barnes, Geoff 227
Bartle, John 13, 132
BBH (Bartle Bogle Hegarty) 8, 13, 131–44
Bell, Tim 8, 19–41, 86, 296, 298, 299, 306
BMP (Boase Massimi Pollitt) 8, 12
Boddington 132
Boden, Johnnie 43–58, 296, 303, 304, 305, 306
Bogle, Nigel 13, 132, 141
Bordeaux Direct 178, 183
Branson, Richard 7, 24, 305, 308

Bridgewater, Emma 61–83, 192, 296, 297, 303, 305, 306
British Museum 239, 259
Brock, Bill 29
Bryan, Felicity 68
Buffett, Warren 153, 249
Burkitt Weinreich Bryant 13

Cameron, David 41, 44, 53, 160, 161, 286–87
Carphone Warehouse 14, 295
Carruthers, Rooney 13
Casals, Pablo 84
Castiglione, Baldassare 190, 195
Cather, Willa 60, 80
Caton, Glenn 186
CDP 8
Charlesworth, Richard 206
Childs, Robert 165
Chime 20
Christie's 192, 194, 197, 203, 205, 207, 258
Chubb 160
Churchill 62
Clifford, Max 97–98
Coca-Cola 275, 286

Coleman, Adrian 13
Colman RSCG 13
Cooper, Jackie 8, 85–108, 297; see also JCPR Edelman
Credit Suisse 206

DDB 8
Dickens, Charles 67, 130, 132
DMB&B 8
Dove 105, 106
Duchy Originals 213
Dudson 62
Dyson, James 12, 13, 111–28, 165, 170, 200, 296, 297, 298, 300, 304, 306

EMI see Thorn EMI
Empire Direct website 213
Equitas Group 152
Estée Lauder 304
Evans, Sir Harold 179

Fry, Jeremy 120–21, 124, 200

Gildersleeve, John 285
Gü 295

Häagen-Dazs 132

INDEX

Hegarty, John 8, 13, 131–44, 304, 305; *see also* BBH
Hiscox, Robert 13, 147–67, 297, 299, 304, 305, 306
Hodder, Greg 182–83
Hovis 286
Hull, Alex 206

Ingham, Bernard 21
Innocent 14, 295
Isaacs, Jeremy 250
Ive, Jonathan 200, 259, 262

JCPR Edelman 85–108
Jobs, Steve 133, 144, 305, 307–8
John Lewis 124, 222, 224
Johnnie Walker 132, 140
Johnson Tiles 62

Kamen, Nick 132, 135
King, Sir Mervyn 150, 153
Kingsmill 286
Kippax, Jill 282

Laing, Hector 245
Laithwaite, Tony 13, 169–88, 296, 304, 305
Laker, Freddie 7
Lawrence, D. H. 168
Levi's 86, 132, 135, 139
Linley, David 72, 191–209, 303, 304
Lloyd's 149, 152–53, 154, 156, 158, 159, 162, 165
Lowe, Frank 31
Lynx 132

MacGregor, Neil 250
Macmillan, Harold 146
Marks & Spencer 45, 185, 214, 225, 239, 247
Masojada, Bronek 165
McKinsey 165, 224
McMurtie, Simon 186

Merlins 8
Microsoft 14, 86, 105
Minton 62
Mitford, Nancy 42
Morrisons 6–7, 278
Moss, Thylias 236

National Gallery 239, 250
Norman, Archie 217, 224

O2 13, 86
Odden, Vic 220, 222
OnSide 281

Padwick, Stuart 202
Phillips, Robert 101–6
Pink Floyd 215
Poe, Edgar Allan 210
Polack, Ernest 217–18
PolyGram 206
Portmeirion 62
Pret a Manger 14, 295
Pretty Polly 101
Priest, Ian 13
Publicis 305
Pylkkänen, Jussi 205, 207, 208

Quistgaard, Jens 258

Rank Hovis McDougall 282
Rapha partnership 265
Reagan, Ronald 18, 29–30, 36
Reece, Gordon 26–27
Remington Inc 283
Rice, Matthew 63, 72, 73, 75, 76, 77, 79–80, 81, 82, 192, 193, 203, 204
Richer, Julian 211–35, 296, 297, 303, 304, 305
Rotork 120–21
Rowley, John 101, 103
Royal Doulton 62
Royal Opera House 250, 252
Royal Worcester 62
Rumbelows 11

Saatchi & Saatchi 8, 12, 22, 23, 26–27, 29, 31, 32, 33, 296
Sainsbury, Lord 237–53, 296, 305
Sévigné, Marquise de 272
Shakespeare, William 292
Smith, Paul 12, 125, 165, 255–70, 298, 304, 306
Speak, Jim 284
Spode 62
Starbucks 105, 107
Steelite International 62
Still, Chris 282

Taleb, Nassim 296–97
TBWA 8, 140
Tesco 186, 239, 249, 285
Thatcher, Margaret 7–8, 21, 26, 27–29, 30, 31, 35, 36, 40, 41, 155, 221, 252, 296
Thorn EMI 11, 229
Trump, Ivanka 2

United Biscuits 245

Vallances 9, 11, 12
VCCP (Vallance, Carruthers, Coleman, Priest) 13
Virgin 7, 14, 256, 305, 308

Warburton, Jonathan 12, 170, 273–90, 298, 304, 305
Warhol, Andy 140–41, 260
WCRS 13
Wedgwood 62
Wilde, Oscar 254
Wonderbra 86, 108

Yellowhammer 96–97
Yeo Valley 132

Zetland Advertising 12